EUTHANASIA, AIDING SUICIDE AND CESSATION OF TREATMENT

Law Reform Commission
of Canada

Working Paper 28

EUTHANASIA,
AIDING SUICIDE
AND CESSATION
OF TREATMENT

1982

Notice

This Working Paper presents the views of the Commission at this time. The Commission's final views will be presented later in its Report to the Minister of Justice and Parliament, when the Commission has taken into account comments received in the meantime from the public.

The Commission would be grateful, therefore, if all comments could be sent in writing to:

Secretary
Law Reform Commission of Canada
130 Albert Street
Ottawa, Canada
K1A 0L6

Commission

Francis C. Muldoon, Q.C., President
Réjean F. Paul, Q.C., Vice-President
Louise D. Lemelin, Commissioner
J. P. Joseph Maingot, Q.C., Commissioner*
Alan D. Reid, Commissioner*

Secretary

Jean Côté

Project Commissioner

Louise D. Lemelin

Project Coordinator

Edward W. Keyserlingk

Special Consultant

Jean-Louis Baudouin

---

*Was not a member of the Commission at the time the text of this paper was approved.

Consultants

Janice Dillon
Gerry Ferguson
Paul-André Meilleur, M.D.
Marcia Rioux
Edward Ryan
Margaret Somerville
R. E. Turner, M.D.
Harvey Yarosky

Table of Contents

Foreword

The problems posed for law and morality by the interruption or cessation of medical treatment are extremely complex. They are of more than merely theoretical or academic interest, for they arise in situations experienced on a daily basis in Canada by the public, doctors and hospital staff.

The Law Reform Commission has already published a number of Working Papers and Study Papers in the *Protection of Life* series.[1] In addition, it has recently submitted to the Parliament of Canada its final recommendations on the criteria for the determination of death.[2]

When the research project was first designed in 1976, it soon became apparent that the question of cessation of treatment and, more generally, that of euthanasia, was a constant and urgent concern among members of the medical profession, a number of lawyers and a large proportion of the Canadian public. In order, then, to respond to what it perceived to be very real interest and need, the Commission has decided to publish a Working Paper on the problem.

Two very important warnings should however be expressed. The first concerns the approach taken by this paper and the second concerns its aims.

First of all, this paper makes no claim to represent a complete and exhaustive examination of the question. There is an impressive number of books, articles and documents on the question, dealing with it from the historical, moral, theological, social, literary, medical or legal viewpoints. The reader will find a short selected bibliography in the appendix. *This paper is thus essentially a synthesis, and a synthesis concerned with*

1

legislative policy in the broad sense of the term. Hence, the reader will not find in our paper an exhaustive analysis of these questions and should not expect a full compilation of all the information available on the subject.

Secondly, because of its particular focus, this paper has only two very specific objectives.

The first is to examine a number of moral and legal problems posed by the cessation of treatment and euthanasia, and to analyse the implications of these problems and acts for the present law and for the law as it might stand after reform.

At the same time, reform implies the acceptance of general social goals, of which legal rules are only one manifestation. Consequently, the second objective of this paper is to examine a number of fundamental questions of social policy and to promote open dialogue of the problem between specialists in the field and members of the Canadian public. Such a dialogue should provide the essential basis for possible law reform.

PART ONE

The Basic Questions

The protection of human life is a fundamental value for all modern legal systems. Law, whatever its specific variations and particular cultural, political or social context recognizes this value to various degrees by forbidding homicide and punishing acts which constitute a danger or serious threat to the lives of other human beings.

The preservation of life is not, however, an absolute value in itself, even for the Canadian legal system. If it were, of course, attempted suicide would not have been decriminalized, nor would self-defence be recognized as legitimate. However, instances in which the law fails to penalize actions intended to terminate human life, are rare and indeed exceptional in nature.

The provisions of the Canadian *Criminal Code* on the subject of homicide (sections 205 to 223), approach human life in an exclusively quantitative, rather than qualitative, sense. Homicide occurs with the death of the victim. Any act which puts an end to an individual's active life, which condemns him for the rest of his days to a very diminished style or quality of life, is punishable under other provisions such as assault. However, a person who, by his actions or inactions renders his victim incapable of leading a life of normal relationships is not considered a murderer.

Law in this respect faithfully reflects one of society's traditional attitudes. For our society recognizes that, morally, religiously, philosophically and socially, human life merits special protection. This recognition of life's fundamental impor-

3

tance has often been expressed through the concept of the sanctity of human life. One expression of this concept is that because life is God-given and we merely hold it in trust, we should not then interfere with it or put an end to it.

Obviously, any detailed analysis of this principle would be beyond the scope of the present paper. A study published by the Commission has already done so.[3] However, it may be useful to indicate briefly its meaning and implications.

Rigid application of the sanctity of life principle has given rise to an approach known as "vitalism". Vitalism has its supporters in literature, philosophy, religion, law and medicine. For those who support this thesis, (though with important nuances and distinctions), human life is an absolute value in itself and every effort must always be made not only to preserve it but to prolong it and hence to combat death with all available means. Considerations as to the quality of life become secondary and even unimportant. Life in the quantitative sense must be saved, maintained and prolonged because it represents a value in itself.

Vitalism has found some support within medical science and the medical profession. The first and traditional role of medicine has always been to save lives, and to try to prolong life by combating disease and death. But success or failure, according to one concept of medicine, is measured by the quality, strength and aggressiveness of the struggle waged. From this point of view, an aggressive struggle represents excellence in the practice of the art of medicine. This approach can hardly be criticized in itself, since it encourages doctors to fight disease and death, not to give up the struggle, and not to admit defeat prematurely. But insofar as some considered the value and prolongation of human life to be an absolute and inflexible policy, the evolution of the practice of medicine has now imposed a modification on that traditional stance.

Thanks to scientific and medical progress, it is now possible to treat conditions or diseases which once were considered incurable. To give a common example, antibiotics now make it

4

possible to cure pneumonia in a person suffering from terminal cancer. Before this discovery, the patient would have died of the pneumonia.

Medical technology too has developed an impressive array of machines and equipment for prolonging lives which once would have been given up for lost. Cardiac and respiratory arrest or kidney failure are no longer fatal. Medical technology in other words has considerably reduced the rate of premature mortality. But at the same time, it has substantially increased the number of individuals who, after receiving such treatment, can only hope to "survive" in a state marked by what is objectively an unsatisfactory quality of life. The classic example, of course, is that of those who have been saved by the last-minute use of a respirator, but have nonetheless suffered an irreversible cessation of certain brain functions and are condemned to a vegetative existence,[4] with no hope of ever regaining cognitive, relational life.

The evolution of medical science and technology obviously represent considerable progress for humanity. Yet this progress has further complicated human and legal problems related to death and dying. It has also imposed a serious reconsideration of the classic "vitalist" or absolute interpretation of the sanctity of life principle.

The number of people who die in hospitals has risen considerably. And, in the hospital context, a wide variety of medical technology is generally available. It is readily made use of, even sometimes where it serves no real therapeutic benefit but merely temporarily delays a death which has become imminent and inevitable. Prolonging the lives of certain terminally ill patients by these means may at a certain point become incompatible with considerations of the quality of the life remaining to them. Such prolongation may, in fact, considerably lessen the quality of the remaining period of life. The decision to make use of medical technology is, unfortunately, sometimes based largely on a technological criterion (whether it is technically possible), rather than on considerations for the patient himself (whether it is humanly desirable). An equation is made between what *can* be done and what *should* be done. It is sometimes simply assumed that, in the struggle against death, the full technical arsenal should be deployed under all circumstances, with few or no "qualitative" considerations being taken into account. This obstinate refusal to admit "defeat" and insistence on using what are termed "heroic measures" has been severely criticized on the grounds that it often works against the patient's best interests, that it is dehumanizing, that it diverts technological progress from its primary aim, which is service to man, and that it tends to prolong the process of dying rather than life itself. The evolution of medical science and technology calls for serious reconsideration of the absolute nature of the classic vitalist option.

In recent years, particularly in the western world, a new approach has developed. This school of thought does not reject the idea that fundamentally human life is of important value and thus that medical and technological resources should be called into play to protect and prolong it. However, it does not subscribe to the vitalist interpretation of the sanctity of life principle. It tempers vitalism with considerations as to the quality of life. The great majority of doctors today appear to subscribe firmly to this approach, and a number of modern codes of medical ethics already reflect this change.[5] This evolution is based on a number of factors. The first is expressed in the phrase, "death with dignity". Patients may wish to eliminate from the process of dying the dehumanizing aspects sometimes imposed on it by the abusive or massive use of medical technology. The second is the greater insistence by patients on direct participation in the decision-making process regarding their medical treatment. Patients are increasingly refusing to consider the doctor as a sort of miracle worker, or to rely simply on what some have described as medical paternalism. Instead, they want to understand and decide freely about the proposed therapy. This should not be interpreted as a sign of lack of confidence in the medical profession, but rather as a healthy attitude by which the patient assumes his own responsibilities and, at the same time, it fosters a more human and professional relationship between himself and his doctor. Since patients increasingly insist that they be the ones who in the final analysis make the choices, obviously they may knowingly refuse the assistance or support of medical technology or a particular treatment and decide in favour of a quantitatively shorter but qualitatively richer life.

The third factor is the relatively recent development of palliative care. The choice for some patients is no longer between continuation of useless treatment and total cessation of all care. It is now possible to discontinue treatment when the patient has reached the terminal stage, but to undertake palliative measures to relieve or eliminate pain, and thus to ease the passage between life and death.

The legal problems associated with the cessation of treatment are extremely complex, because they are also related to, and confused with, the sensitive and controversial question of euthanasia. The particular subject of euthanasia will also be examined in this paper. In addition there are three types of difficulties underlying the problem of cessation of treatment. It is important to identify and discuss these difficulties briefly before attempting to draw conclusions regarding legal rules of conduct.

The first difficulty is that societal views on these matters are currently evolving. This evolution includes attitudes towards life and death, towards science and towards the cessation of treatment. For example, many are still attempting to define more precisely attitudes and policies which not only acknowledge protection for human life, but yet take into consideration other values as well, including the individual's right to decisional autonomy and the individual's quality of life. We have not yet managed to resolve and balance the apparent contradictions between the protection of life itself and the protection and promotion of the quality of life. The question is made all the more difficult by the fact that, as far as the decision to provide or withhold treatment is concerned, no two cases are identical. The individual characteristics of each case make it extremely difficult to establish general norms which might seem more reassuring or provide a greater sense of security.

The second difficulty lies in the relationships between law and medicine. Legal rules, particularly those of criminal law, are designed to sanction conduct considered socially reprehensible. Their role is thus primarily repressive. Yet there is no record in Canadian case-law of a single conviction of a doctor for having shortened the life of one of his terminal patients by administering massive doses of pain-killing drugs. Nor have Canadian courts ever apparently convicted a doctor who has stopped a useless treatment for a dying patient. Finally, Canadian courts have never directly blamed a doctor for refusing to prolong a patient's agony by deciding not to treat him for a secondary complication.

This lack of legal proceedings and precedent does not of course mean that such acts have not and do not take place. Nor does it mean that the courts would necessarily have acquitted or convicted an individual so charged. In other words, the existing legal situation cannot be considered satisfactory solely because it has not given rise to legal proceedings. Because of this situation, a good proportion of the medical profession and of hospital personnel are in the unfortunate position of not knowing the precise content of their legal duties, and of being entirely dependent in this respect on the Crown's discretion not to initiate legal proceedings.

Legal rules, particularly in the area of criminal law, should also have a certain degree of predictability. Both physicians and patients should be able to predict with some degree of certainty the interpretation which the courts will give to the general rules contained in the *Criminal Code* and which govern behaviour in society.

At the present time, however, physicians and lawyers are generally unable to predict with any certainty how the provisions of the present *Criminal Code* would in fact be applied in a case involving cessation of treatment. A comparison with other sorts of cases may, as we shall see, allow some general conclusions as to the theoretical bases for criminal liability. However, the precise nature of this liability remains difficult to determine.

The third and final difficulty is the following. Independently of the inevitable and specific variations of each case, many are concerned that this apparent vacuum may reflect and promote major differences in medical practice and conduct across the country. In the absence of precise rules of conduct or at least of some type of guidance as to what courts would consider acceptable or unacceptable, it is feared that decisions will be based on essentially subjective and personal considerations, determined exclusively by the moral and ethical standards of the individual physician. Whether or not this fear is justified, the uncertainty and unpredictability permit a greater inequality in decisions and conduct, which may well vary from one institution to another, from one province to another, and from one socio-economic group to another.

In conclusion, the current assumption that medical personnel have little to fear in terms of criminal law is probably correct. However, this perception is far from certain and provides no real guarantee as to the meaning and application of the legal rules. It must be borne in mind as well that the present policy of not laying charges could change under the pressure of events. Should this happen, a number of doctors might have to serve as test cases in order to determine just what the current state of the law is. The question is far too important and far too fundamental to be left in such a state of uncertainty. The question of whether to terminate or not to initiate treatment arises particularly in two very specific contexts. Both will be described briefly.

I. The terminally ill patient

The first context is that of the terminally ill patient, namely one who has reached the stage where the administration of therapeutic care has become medically useless to bring about eventual recovery or even effective control of the disease. Beyond this point, the patient's interest lies in the alleviation, as far as possible, of the physical and mental suffering of the terminal phase. As many of the doctors whom we have consulted have confirmed, the patient's needs change once he realizes with certainty that recovery is impossible and that death has become inevitable. Basically, what the patient then requires is effective control of his symptoms and the chance to live what remains of his life as comfortably as possible. For some, it is also important that the passage from life to death take place with dignity and lucidity and that surgical or other forms of intervention which are mutilating or perceived as degrading be avoided. The decision to discontinue a form of treatment perceived as useless and potentially degrading is often made on the suggestion of the patient.

Two particular problems may arise as regards the legal response to the above concerns.

The first is that, traditionally and in theory, once initiated, the cessation of a measure intended to save someone's life may serve as grounds for civil and criminal liability. In the case of an unconscious terminally ill patient, a doctor or a hospital might well delay the decision to cease useless treatment, or decide to continue it, for fear of possible prosecution. The result is quite absurd! To preserve life (in the quantitative sense of the word) and perhaps out of fear of the law, little or no value is assigned to the quality of the time remaining to that patient. These absurdities and fears, understandable given the vagueness of present law, give rise to legislative trends such as that which led to the California *Natural Death Act*. We think that it is both unnecessary and even dangerous to go to such extremes. Our legal system should be able to establish and protect the principle that a terminally ill patient has a right, not a secondary or subordinate right but a primary right, to die with dignity and not to fall victim to heroic measures. To allow practical enforcement of this right, it should be clearly stated that there would be nothing to fear from criminal or civil law when, in a patient's terminal phase, the physician stops or refuses to undertake medically useless treatment which will only prolong the process of dying, unless expressly requested to do so by the patient. Reform, in this case, reflects more a clarification of the true scope of the present law than any fundamental change.

10

The second problem is related to palliative care. Modern medicine has methods and medications capable of eliminating or reducing suffering to an acceptable level in the majority of cases. The experience of various specialized centres in Canada (particularly in Montréal) and in England has shown that this is possible. The only real limits to the wider use of pain control techniques result from a too-limited dissemination among the medical profession of the expertise already acquired and the need for a more systematic development of research in this field.

Control of pain often involves the use of narcotics or drugs to which the patient may eventually develop a tolerance. In addition, with the progression of the disease, it is often necessary to increase the dosage substantially. In time, then, a level of pain may be reached at which a higher dosage may have the secondary effect of shortening the life of the patient. Some doctors hesitate, for the same reasons as those described above out of fear of possible criminal, civil or disciplinary sanctions, should they give the terminal patient care which is effective on the strictly palliative level but which may reduce his life expectancy. Here again, in our opinion, ambiguity as to the scope of the existing legal responses may have the effect of encouraging poor medical practice, medicine which is no longer in the interests of the patient, by restricting the administration of effective palliative care.

In both cases, then, uncertainty can divert medical science from its normal, valid aims and objectives, objectives which should be clearly acknowledged and recognized by the law in order to remove this sword of Damocles.

II. The seriously defective newborn

The rate of infant mortality, a grim problem in Canada barely fifty years ago, has declined significantly since the mid-1950s. Several hospitals have set up intensive care for newborns, thus saving the lives of infants who, because of diseases, deformities or simple prematurity, would not normally have survived. In addition, neonatal surgery has made considerable progress. It is now possible to treat cases which, a number of years ago, would have been considered terminal.

This institutional development, however, together with the progress of neonatological sciences, has also produced a series of new problems. Today, infants are surviving with birth defects which will make it impossible for them to develop normally. Some will have to be placed in institutions. Others may live with their families, but will impose heavy financial, emotional and psychological burdens on them.

The problem of seriously defective newborns is a complex one. The degrees of defectiveness may vary. There are chromosomal anomalies, the effects of which vary widely from one individual to another. For example, the term *spina bifida** covers a wide range, from an extremely serious handicap to one which is relatively mild.

In addition, two other considerations add to the complexity of the situation. First of all, the newborn, unlike the conscious adult patient, is incapable of making a decision for himself. Others (parents, guardian, doctor) are thus called upon to make it for him and on his behalf. Sometimes, this decision means allowing the child to die, assuming perhaps that if he, like the terminal patient, had been capable of making the decision himself, this is what he would have chosen. Secondly, a tragic and additional factor affecting the decision-maker's perception of the problem is that the seriously defective newborn is a human being who has only just achieved independent life and for whom death is nonetheless already a possibility.

Without attempting to generalize about situations which are always highly individual, the problem of seriously defective newborns arises in two different contexts in terms of law and morality.

The first involves the child who, at birth, suffers from defects so severe that, given the current state of medical science, it is certain that he will not survive more than a few

---
* Refer to Appendix II

hours or a few days. This is true, for example, with anence-phaly* or severe cases of *spina bifida**. In this case, despite the seeming paradox, the child is, at birth, already engaged in the process of dying, and medical science is powerless. There is no appropriate treatment, or the treatments which could be applied appear to be medically useless. The problem then is identical to that of the terminally ill adult. The physician's duty is certainly not to abandon the child, any more than he would abandon a dying adult patient, but to provide appropriate palliative care and to avoid useless therapeutic measures.

The second case, which again admits of many variations in degree, involves the defective child who, without treatment, would probably die shortly, but for whom medicine can objec-tively do something. Here again, the great difficulty in analysis lies in the fact that treatment may vary widely in complexity, usualness or duration. As an illustration, consider the familiar example of a newborn suffering from trisomy 21* and atresia* of the digestive tract. If a surgical intervention, relatively minor and simple under normal circumstances, is not performed, the child will be unable to absorb nourishment and will die of starvation.

Generally speaking, two sorts of diagnoses are possible in these cases, each leading to different ethical and legal conclu-sions. A diagnosis in one case may indicate that the trisomic child has no other serious defects, only atresia* of the digestive tract. But a diagnosis in a second case may indicate that the child, in addition to this atresia*, suffers from other serious defects as well (cardiac malformation, etc.), for which there is no appropriate cure or which will necessitate a long series of surgical operations. Both cases clearly raise a problem of value judgment about the quality of the child's life. In practice, the parents, in collaboration with the doctor, will make the deci-sion on whether or not to perform the operation. This decision is a direct reflection of a value judgment on the quality of the child's future life. Some will feel that the quality is not ade-quate and, in all honesty and good conscience, will refuse the operation. Others, on the contrary, will consent to it, knowing

* Refer to Appendix II

that it will restore a certain functional capacity but will do nothing to improve the child's general condition. In terms of both ethics and law (under present legal rules), it is clear that a refusal to provide treatment in the first case may be grounds for civil and criminal liability. The situation has apparently already arisen in Canada. Charges in a number of cases on this factual basis, notably in British Columbia, were eventually dropped.[6]

But the second type of diagnosis is very different. In fact, the question is no longer one of performing a single simple procedure to ensure survival, but of placing the decision in context. The problem would be the same for an adult: is there any purpose in treating pneumonia in a patient whose kidneys are no longer functioning, whose heart has shown signs of extreme weakness, and who would then need a kidney transplant and bypass surgery? Is there any purpose in performing a minor operation on a child who, because of cardiac or other defects, has a very reduced life expectancy, is completely paralyzed from the waist down, suffers from severe convulsions and, in his short life remaining, will require a series of painful operations, with no hope of ever developing in terms of communication with the outside world? It is probable that, in such a case, the law would not blame either a doctor or the parents for a decision not to subject the child to this process and hence to let nature take its course, while still providing all necessary palliative care.

From the physician's standpoint, the problem of the newborn has something in common with that of the terminal patient. Should he decide to undertake treatment, will not the law then require him to continue it, even when it ceases to be truly useful? Can he, without risk to himself, stop aggressive therapy and simply allow nature to take its course? Should he require the parents' consent? Is the decision theirs alone to make? These are all serious problems currently arising in hospital practice and for which the law admittedly fails to offer the precise responses which some would like to see. Here again, it would be socially most unfortunate if medical decisions were to be made solely on the basis of the possible threat of civil or criminal sanctions.

14

PART TWO

The Responses of Present Law

Part VI of the Canadian *Criminal Code*, dealing with offences against the person (sections 196 and following), contains a series of protective provisions for the life and physical security of individuals. It would be beyond the scope of the present document to offer a detailed analysis of the legislation and case-law on the subject. Most provisions are of a general nature and are not restricted simply to medical treatment. In addition, our Working Paper No. 26 on medical treatment and criminal law already contains an analysis of these provisions, which the reader may wish to consult.[7]

However, it is essential that we provide a brief synthesis and explanation of the scope of certain specific provisions directly related to the problems with which we are concerned, and also that we describe how these texts have been applied in practice up to now. Finally, a comparative law study should allow a more critical analysis of the situation.

I. The legislation

Section 197 of the *Criminal Code* imposes a legal duty on certain persons (parents, guardian, spouse, etc.) to provide necessaries of life for those dependent on them. Courts have interpreted this provision as being applicable to a member of the medical profession who neglects or refuses to provide a person with medical care, assuming that all the other conditions of the offence are also met,[8] and, in particular, that the person is incapable of taking care of himself. A doctor who fails to provide treatment for an unconscious person might then, under certain circumstances, be liable to prosecution under section 197 of the *Criminal Code*.

Sections 198 and 199 of the *Criminal Code* deal with two types of duties. The first requires every one who undertakes to administer surgical or medical treatment which may endanger the life of another person to use reasonable knowledge, skill and care in so doing. The second requires every one who undertakes to do an act to continue it if an omission to do so may be dangerous to life.[9]

The use of the word "reasonable" in section 198 obviously leaves a great deal to the evaluation of the particular circumstances of each case. In medical terms, it therefore refers to medical practice and to what can be considered reasonable in the particular circumstances of the case. For instance, a court today would probably consider it reasonable for a doctor not to attempt to resuscitate a person in an irreversible coma. However, it is far less certain that it would absolve a doctor who, after undertaking to treat a defective newborn, subsequently decided not to perform a minor but life-saving surgical operation solely on the basis of a personal judgment as to the quality of life of the patient. Similarly, it can probably be assumed that "treatment" which imposes a disproportionate burden of discomfort or pain on a terminal patient would not be considered "reasonable".

Section 199 of the *Criminal Code* imposes the general duty to continue an act, once undertaken, if an omission to do the act may be dangerous to life. This requirement deserves some explanation. Our criminal law traditionally has not imposed criminal liability on a person who fails to act, to do something, to take positive action, except where this person falls under a specific duty imposed by law. Thus, while action is generally subject to criminalization, mere inaction or omission is not, unless a clear duty to act under specific circumstances has been provided for, and imposed by, law. In terms of medical treatment, then, this section is of great importance, particularly

16

when it is read in conjunction with section 198. In fact, cessation of treatment which may endanger the life of a patient (for example, turning off a respirator) *appears* to come directly under this provision of the criminal law. At least, this is the fear so often expressed by members of the medical profession.

Section 199 of the *Criminal Code*, read in isolation, seems to imply that a physician who has undertaken treatment is not permitted to terminate it if this involves a risk to the life of the patient. If this were the case, the law would require the use of aggressive and useless therapy. It would also have the effect, in many cases, of causing doctors to hesitate seriously before undertaking treatment, for fear of not being permitted to terminate it later, when it no longer appears to be useful. If this were the actual implication of the rule, then the rule would be absurd and would have disastrous effects on medical practice.

Section 199, however, must not be read in isolation, but rather in conjunction with the other provisions of the *Criminal Code*, particularly section 45 and those sections dealing with criminal negligence. Section 45 protects from criminal liability anyone who performs a surgical operation upon any person for the benefit of that person, when it is reasonable to perform the operation, having regard to the state of health of the patient. There again lies the main standard of conduct on which the law is based: the reasonableness of the act under the circumstances. Moreover, the legal provisions dealing with criminal negligence impose a very specific standard of conduct. The law does not criminalize every case of negligence and hence every cessation of treatment which may endanger life, but only those instances which demonstrate wanton or reckless disregard on the part of the agent.

An example may illustrate this distinction: a doctor turns off a respirator, knowing, as he does so, that the patient will no longer be ventilated and thus will probably die. Let us suppose, in one instance, that before doing so he has assured himself, using standard medical procedures and tests, that the patient is already in a state of irreversible coma. Here the act of turning off the respirator, while technically constituting a positive act of cessation of treatment within the meaning of section 199, could not serve as a valid basis for criminal liability, and for two reasons. Firstly, the continuation of treatment is not reasonable in this case given the condition of the patient and, secondly, the cessation of treatment does not reflect wanton or reckless disregard for life on the part of the physician. But on the other hand, let us assume that this same doctor performs the same act without first assuring himself of the patient's condition. There would probably then be grounds for applying these provisions, since by ceasing treatment without taking the precaution of assuring himself that such cessation will not endanger the patient, he would be showing wanton or reckless disregard for the patient's life or safety.

Sections 202 to 223 of the *Criminal Code* deal with criminal negligence and various types of homicide. They are of particular importance within the context of the present discussion. We shall limit ourselves, here again, to a brief analysis of these provisions within our particular context. The forthcoming Commission Working Paper on homicide will contain a more detailed analysis. Every human death caused by another is not necessarily a case of culpable homicide. It is only so if caused by an unlawful act or by criminal negligence. Within the category of culpable homicide, the law further distinguishes between manslaughter and murder. The difference lies in the intent of the agent, which, in the case of murder, is to cause death or bodily harm that he knows is likely to cause death, being reckless whether death ensues or not.

In the case of murder, the legislator does not take into account the motives behind the act. Only the intent to cause death is taken into consideration. It is irrelevant whether a person killed for reasons of vengeance, profit, greed, compassion or charity. In every case, he is guilty of murder, if in fact he intended to cause death. Nor does our law take into account, as section 14 of the *Criminal Code* indicates, the fact that the victim may have consented to his own death. Such consent has no influence upon the criminal liability of the agent. A person who kills a loved one out of compassion, to put him out of his suffering, is therefore still guilty of murder, even if it is shown that the victim wanted to die and in fact asked to be killed. Canadian law, like most other legal systems, thus prohibits active or positive euthanasia, and considers it to be simple murder.

Canadian law has recently decriminalized attempted suicide. However, section 224 of the *Criminal Code* still makes it an offence punishable by imprisonment for fourteen years for anyone to counsel or aid a person to commit suicide. This provision, similar to those found in British law and in most American states, has been strongly attacked recently by groups such as *Exit* or *Hemlock*, which seek the abolition of this type of prohibition in the name of the individual's right to self-determination. A review of Canadian cases shows that this provision is indeed very rarely invoked in practice. However, the difference between aiding suicide and direct participation in homicide is sometimes difficult to determine. Is there a difference, for example, between a person who, at a dying man's request, prepares a poison and leaves it on the bedside table for him to take, and a person who helps the patient to drink it or who administers it directly at the request of a dying person who is unable to take it himself?

Law thus makes a distinction between two types of conduct: the action of killing and the inaction of allowing to die. This distinction, which of course is fundamental, finds a parallel in morality and medical ethics. Wilful, deliberate killing means the direct elimination of all hope, all opportunity, all possibility, however remote, of recovery or a possible prolongation of life. The act is considered immoral, medically unethical and illegal. Allowing to die (in our context, for example, by interrupting a treatment which is no longer useful) does not necessarily deprive the patient of these possibilities. Cessation of treatment may simply restore the situation that existed before treatment was undertaken and allow nature to take its course.

In summary then, cessation of treatment, or its administration, may come under a relatively complex set of provisions of the *Criminal Code*, ranging from assault to homicide and including failure to provide the necessaries of life, failure to use reasonable knowledge, skill and care, and aiding suicide. These various offences should not however be interpreted separately, but within the general context of the law. The sometimes vague terms in which they are formulated makes it difficult, admittedly, to define the exact scope of application in medical matters. It is this fact, far more than the provisions themselves and the values which they represent, which is the source of the present difficulties.

II. The enforcement of legislation

These various sections of the *Criminal Code* (particularly those concerning homicide and criminal negligence) have given rise to a great deal of case-law. However, it is interesting to note that precise instances of enforcement of these provisions, and of those concerning medical treatment, involving physicians or in matters arising directly out of a medical context are extremely rare, if not totally non-existent. The same is true, in Canada, of proceedings based on murder provisions in cases of compassionate murder or voluntary euthanasia.

This almost total lack of criminal proceedings against doctors or hospital personnel would seem to indicate that they have little to fear, in practice, in terms of possible criminal prosecution. This is reinforced by the fact that, as one author has rightly noted, [10] in the rare instances where charges have in fact been laid, the acquittal rate has been very high. Most of these cases involved errors in diagnosis or treatment as a cause of death. However, no case has been found involving the physician's obligation to continue treatment once undertaken. There appears therefore to be a wide gap between the apparent severity of the law and its lack of practical enforcement.

In the area of medical treatment, a number of reasons may explain this situation. The first is that the standard of negligence established by criminal law as a condition of criminal responsibility is not easily applicable in a medical context. Only serious, gross or intentional mistake or fault come under the sanction of criminal law. The quality of medicine in Canada is high enough that such instances are fortunately scarce. In the case of a lesser violation, civil law and civil liability provide an adequate remedy by way of damages and compensation.

A second reason is that the prosecution of these cases encounters certain practical difficulties even when the criminal law standard is violated, particularly in establishing an adequate causal relationship between the act and the result of the act. The *St-Germain* case is a good illustration.[11]

A third reason, one which we sometimes tend to forget, is that our system of criminal justice has a series of built-in filtering processes. The Crown does not automatically prosecute every case actually discovered. There is, in this area, a substantial margin for discretion in the administration of criminal proceedings and only the most apparent abuses come to the attention of the authorities. Of these, only those in which the available evidence offers hope of conviction are actually prosecuted. The number of cases brought to the attention of the authorities is small to begin with. Obviously the number of prosecutions is even smaller.

The situation is practically the same for active euthanasia or compassionate murder. In Canada, prosecution is very rare. A recent Montréal case in which a person was found guilty of having killed a paraplegic friend, out of compassion and at his own request, was one of those rare exceptions.[11a] Yet this rarity is not specific to Canada. In the United States, a country much larger than our own, the legal cases involving active euthanasia can practically be counted on the fingers of one hand.

This absence of legal proceedings may reflect some ambiguity in the thinking and conduct of those responsible for the administration of the criminal justice system (witnesses, police officers, prosecutors, jurors, etc.). It may be that, in the case of a compassionate murder, witnesses aware of the fact will choose not to become involved and will not report the case to the authorities, while they would not hesitate to do so if the act were motivated, for example, by vengeance. It is also possible that the police are not naturally inclined to lay charges in such cases; that the prosecution authorities are not anxious to handle them; that juries are reluctant to bring in a guilty verdict. We may assume, then, that, while the law itself is totally indifferent to motive, all these individuals deliberately or intuitively make an important distinction between ordinary murder and compassionate murder, and that the motives and circumstances involved make the agent in the latter case, in their eyes, not a real murderer who deserves the rigour of the law, but a person who has acted out of compassion or out of charity and whose conduct deserves at the very least tacit approval.

The lack of legal proceedings is, paradoxically, for members of both the legal and the medical professions, a serious handicap. Indeed, case-law and the accumulation of legal precedents make it possible at a certain point in time to determine the degree of social tolerance and, on the practical level, the exact content and intensity of legal duties. While it is probably relatively easy to establish the standard of behaviour that a Canadian driver must meet to avoid being charged with criminal negligence, it is, in contrast, extremely difficult to do so for a doctor or a nurse. Which does not at all mean that we would advocate an increase in the number of prosecutions against such people simply to ascertain the specific content of the legal rules.

III. Comparative law

A brief survey of the solutions offered for these various problems by the legal systems of other countries is instructive.

In a first group, composed primarily of common-law jurisdictions, the solutions are largely the same as those provided by Canadian law. A 1957 case in Great Britain, unfortunately unreported, shed some light on possible limits to the administration of medical treatment. In the *Adams* case, a doctor was accused of murder for having administered a high dose of a pain-killing drug to one of his terminal patients. The Court acquitted the doctor and expressed the following opinion on the state of the law:

> If the first purpose of medicine – the restoration of health – could no longer be achieved, there was still much for the doctor to do, and he was entitled to do all that was proper and necessary to relieve pain and suffering even if the measures he took might incidentally shorten life . . .[11b]

This is however an isolated opinion and not a rule developed by a long line of authority. Moreover it is not certain that it does accurately represent the state of the common law.

In Great Britain as well, several attempts have been made to introduce legislation legalizing active euthanasia under certain conditions and thus decriminalizing the act of aiding suicide and compassionate murder. The first of these attempts appeared in the early 1930s with the founding of the English Euthanasia Society.[12] After a long interruption, the movement became active again during the early 1950s, when Lord Chorley initiated a debate in the House of Lords on the question. In 1958, Glanville Williams published his famous work favouring voluntary and positive euthanasia.[13] Since then, the debate has grown in intensity although, on the medical side, the British Medical Association severely condemned the practice in 1971. A number of attempts to introduce legislation on the subject have been made, notably in 1950, 1969 and 1976, but with no concrete results. It is worth noting, however, that whereas in 1953 the Royal Commission on Capital Punishment concluded that it was dangerous to make compassionate murder an offence distinct from ordinary murder, the Criminal Law Revision Committee in 1976 made a recommendation to the contrary, which however was not adopted.

In the United States, a number of well known cases, including the *Quinlan* and the *Saikewicz* cases, allowed the courts to define somewhat more clearly the exact limitations on the duty to provide treatment, and to determine, with more accuracy, the circumstances under which termination of care can be considered legal. It must be borne in mind, however, that each of these cases involved a number of specific individual characteristics making it difficult to generalize from them a rule of universal application.

In 1970, a new trend began to appear in the United States. This trend materialized in the form of a *Natural Death Act* in California, legislation which was subsequently initiated by other States.[14] However, none of these various Bills, contrary to what is sometimes thought, advocated the recognition of euthanasia. All of them deal with a different problem: the cessation of treatment. As the preamble of the California legislation clearly indicates, the primary goal of the law is to respond to a concrete problem: how to assure to everyone the power of decision-making regarding the continuation or cessation of medical treatment, and how to eliminate existing uncertainty regarding the extent of a physician's obligation to provide care.

The *Natural Death Act* allows a patient to make a written and juridically valid directive (living will), containing instructions to the effect that he does not wish to be provided with artificial means of prolonging life if he has a terminal illness (as defined by the law) and is unable to express his wishes. The law provides that these directives may be revoked. The principal impact of the law as regards doctors and hospital personnel, is to protect them from civil or criminal liability on the basis of refusal to initiate or to continue treatment. Several other American states have introduced similar legislation.[15] Similar efforts in the same direction have been made in Canada,[16] but no legislation has yet been adopted. The *Natural Death Act* and its possible application to Canada will be discussed in another part of this paper (p. 69 and following).

Insofar as compassionate murder and the use of aggressive therapy are concerned, American law has witnessed a number of interesting developments. Until recently, there were approximately sixteen reported cases of active euthanasia in the United States. Without going into the details of each of these cases, the contrast between the apparent severity of the criminal laws (of the same type and tradition as our own) and their practical application is striking. Out of these sixteen cases, ten ended in acquittals, six on the grounds of temporary insanity. Of the six remaining cases, a single life sentence was handed down, one life sentence was completely suspended, and two suspended sentences of five to ten years and three to six years were imposed. In the other two cases, the charges were immediately dismissed.

However, a number of groups in the United States as well have advocated legislative recognition of voluntary euthanasia. Various proposals have recently been submitted in Idaho, Montana and Oregon. All of them are based more or less on the model of the British Bill of 1969. In addition, certain groups, such as *Hemlock*, are currently fighting for decriminalization of acts of aiding the terminally ill to commit suicide.

A second group of countries takes an approach which is very different from that of the common-law tradition. This group consists of those (primarily European) countries which, in one or another, separate ordinary murder from compassionate murder, lessen the gravity of the offence or shorten the sentence attached to it. This group includes Germany, among others. The homicide classification system of the present German Criminal Code makes a distinct category of compassionate murder. The act, however, still remains a criminal offence (murder on request), but the law takes into account the perpetrator's motivation and thus permits a substantial reduction in sentence.

In Switzerland, the Criminal Code provides that the judge may reduce the sentence if the accused had an "honourable" motive for committing the act. Also, a doctor who, out of compassion, assists his patient to commit suicide is apparently not subject to criminal prosecution. He may, for example, give poison to his patient but is not allowed to administer it himself. In 1977, in the Canton of Zurich, a referendum on the possibility of allowing formal legislation permitting a doctor to perform an act of positive euthanasia at the request of a patient suffering from an incurable illness received a strong majority of assenting votes. However, no legislation has yet been introduced.

In such countries as Norway and Uruguay, the problem is dealt with not at the level of classification of the various types of homicide, but rather at the level of sentencing. The judge may either reduce the sentence or set it aside entirely.[17]

Two observations, then, may be made by way of conclusion to this brief study of existing law.

First, there is a definite uncertainty at present with regard to the cessation and interruption of medical treatment. This uncertainty arises fundamentally not primarily from any absence of legislative enactments or dissatisfaction with the way in which they are ordered. It exists essentially because of two factors. The first is that these enactments were not specifically designed to cover the social situation especially in the modern context in which medical and technological progress make possible an often useless, unwanted and painful prolongation of life. The second is that these provisions, for various reasons, have never really been tested before the courts making it impossible to know with any reasonable certainty how the courts would apply them to the medical context. While it is certainly possible to raise hypotheses and possible interpretations, and to note certain tendencies, one must nevertheless admit that uncertainty reigns. Uncertainty is not desirable. It can have a detrimental impact on medical behaviour in that it promotes social tension and anguish, and because it leaves the lawyer in constant uncertainty as to the appropriate legal solutions to this crucial problem.

A second observation is that all legal systems, in one way or another, have refused to allow active and voluntary euthanasia. Some punish compassionate murder as a form of murder; others compromise by taking into account the agent's motives, either through the definition of the offence or at the sentencing level. In all cases, however, case-law in every country reveals an obvious paradox and contradiction between the apparent severity of the law and its application in practice. The offenders are seldom brought before the courts. When they are, they are rarely found guilty, and when found guilty they receive very light sentences.

PART THREE

The Necessity, Objectives
and Imperatives of Reform

In matters as difficult and as complex as the cessation of treatment, euthanasia and suicide, two preliminary questions can be asked. Firstly, why a reform in this area? Secondly, what benefit can the Canadian criminal-law system reasonably hope to draw from a legislative reform?

I. The necessity of reform

Some argue, with some logic on their side, that legislative reform in this area is not necessary. They point out, more particularly, that the sections of the *Criminal Code* which we have analysed, unlike other sections of the *Code*, have not yet raised any serious problems in terms of practical application. Why change provisions which are creating no difficulties in terms of judicial interpretation?

Moreover, as we have seen, these provisions are very rarely applied to the medical and hospital context. It is a fact that there have been practically no prosecutions of doctors, nurses and hospital staff under these provisions. It is also a fact that aiding suicide remains largely a crime with no practical application. Why then waste time settling a purely theoretical problem? Would not a change in the law increase the risk of prosecution?

It is the Commission's opinion, however, that none of these arguments rules out the need for reform, at least the sort of reform envisaged by the Commission. Reform is not necessarily equivalent to eliminating already acquired solutions and starting again from scratch. Proper law reform may consist simply in a reorganization of, or addition to, existing legislation. A number of serious reasons militate for reform.

First, as we have seen, the Canadian medical and social contexts have greatly evolved since the present sections of the *Criminal Code* came into force. These provisions have successfully resisted the inevitable erosion of time because they are drafted in general terms and set standards that are so broad they do not quickly become outdated. However, this generality, while it is a great advantage in terms of the risk of rapid obsolescence, is at the same time a failing when it generates uncertainty, with respect to new situations. These provisions would be adequate if we could be reasonably certain of their ability to settle actual concrete situations without requiring lawyers, judges or juries to twist their meaning or to seek byzantine interpretations, sometimes quite literally deforming the sections in order to force their meaning. All of this without any certainty that the suggested interpretation is correct, given the lack of guidance in case-law.

One author has been particularly critical in this regard, accusing the law of closing its eyes to the realities of medical practice and everyday life, and obliging judges and juries to find technical and sometimes even acrobatic reasons for mitigating the apparent severity of the law.[18] This charge is probably too strong. It overlooks the other functions of the law besides mere repression in the sense that it may play a preventive role as well. The difference between the law as expressed in legislation and the law experienced in judicial reality may be wide; it is not necessarily undesirable or senseless.

However, as the Commission has readily observed, there is, rightly or wrongly, some uneasiness among medical specialists and the public in general. This uneasiness lies particularly in the perception that present legislation casts serious doubt on the legality of certain current medical or hospital practices. Since legal precedents regarding these questions are almost non-existent, the degree of uncertainty is all the greater. This uncertainty is serious, because it may lead to a complete split between legal practice and the legal rule, with practice proceeding as if the legal rule did not exist. It may also give rise to the opposite phenomenon. In an effort to avoid risks, medical practice could remain extremely conservative and conform to the strictest standard which it believes the law establishes.

Medical practice does not generally wait for the legislator. Hospitals, for instance, have not waited for legislation before implementing certain practices with respect to the dying or to seriously defective newborns. Doctors model their conduct on what they believe to be just and ethical under the circumstances, on the basis of their own expertise and the standards established by their codes of ethics. However, it would seem logical and in keeping with our tradition, for the law, at one point or another in its evolution, to take a position and to clearly indicate whether a given medical practice is acceptable. Where human life is concerned, constant temporizing and making do with hypotheses seem unjustified. It is true, of course, that the law can never speak in the singular and give a clear, neat, precise answer to each doctor on each act he performs for each of his patients. Law, however, can speak in the plural and establish certain general parameters, which are still specific enough within the existing context to delineate clearly between what it considers acceptable and what, on the other hand, it considers unacceptable.

For instance, today, many wonder whether it is legal, to use a vernacular expression, to "pull the plug" on an individual. A practice has developed in hospitals, in this connection, based on certain ethical and medical standards. The fact that these practices are found everywhere, have multiplied since the appearance of respirators and are being applied every day without interference from the law, appears to confer on them a certain *a priori* legitimacy and legality. Many believe that there is no longer any problem: the practice is legal because it exists, because it occurs every day and because the law has never seen fit to intervene. The law's silence is thus interpreted as an endorsement or tacit consent on its part.

Current hospital practices involving the turning off of respirators probably do not go against fundamental legal norms. However, other situations do raise the issue. A newborn suffering from trisomy 21,* who has no other serious defects but does have atresia* of the digestive tract, poses a serious problem.

The development of different practices across the country, in the same province or even the same city is probably inevitable. However, when human life is at stake, law should do everything within its power to clarify the situation and to define as precisely as possible the minimal limits which our society considers acceptable.

The Commission believes that it would be burying its head in the sand not to raise the problem of the need for reform, not to examine whether the situation can be improved, and to see whether the veil of uncertainty cannot be raised.

II. The objectives of reform

The identification, within such a controversial field, of the benefits that reform may offer the Canadian community involves, first, identifying the role to be played by law, and, more importantly, learning to recognize its limits.

As the Commission has often stated in the numerous Reports and Working Papers which it has produced over the past ten years, the role of criminal law is not merely to punish the individual. This punitive role does obviously exist. It may even be its most apparent role. However, criminal law is not only punishment oriented.

It also plays an important preventive role when examined within the context of medical practice, cessation of treatment and assisting suicide. The fact that it punishes armed robbery or murder with severity will probably not prevent the perpetration of those crimes. However strict or refined the legislation

---

* Refer to Appendix II

30

may be, society must expect a certain number of cases to continue to occur. However, when the law deals with a specific category of well-informed and educated professionals such as physicians and hospital personnel, likely to understand more readily than others the parameters of the law, and dedicated to an ideal of altruistic service, the probability is much greater that their conduct will conform to legally-established standards if they are sufficiently clear and explicit. For example, if the legislator or the courts were to decide tomorrow that failure to operate on a trisomic newborn suffering merely from atresia* constitutes a criminal act, it is most likely that any physicians currently following this practice would abandon it immediately.

Criminal law is also a powerful educative tool. In theory at least, its rules are the expression of a certain social consensus. Any attempt to change the rule or to clarify it should allow for a good measure of discussion within those groups affected by the change and the public in general, and hence a greater awareness of the dimension of problems created by cessation of treatment, euthanasia and aiding suicide. These discussions and the expression of the various opinions on the subject may then generate a certain number of rules based on a measure of social consensus. Such an approach may appear useless or superfluous to some observers. The Commission, however, considers that it is both useful and necessary. In fact, this was one of the clearly defined objectives of the Protection of Life research project which produced this paper.

At the same time, it is important to remember that, in such a complex and controversial matter, unanimous support for any reform is most unlikely if not impossible. The questions which this paper raises are deeply rooted in individual morality, behaviour, experience and psychology. Thus we cannot hope for either a miracle solution or a solution which will please everyone. However, this is not a sufficient reason for abandoning the task.

Finally, legislative reform is not an end in itself, but rather the beginning of the real reform. Changing the law is one thing,

* Refer to Appendix II

but changing attitudes, conduct, forms of behaviour is another, and one over which the legislator often has very little control. To achieve the desired results, social and institutional policy reforms must accompany specific legislative reforms where necessary.

III. The imperatives of reform

Reforming the criminal law in the areas dealt with in this paper involves asking three very specific questions:

(1) Should the legislator, in one way or another, legalize or at least decriminalize certain forms of active euthanasia, such as compassionate murder?

(2) Should the legislator decriminalize the act of aiding suicide by repealing section 224 of the *Criminal Code*?

(3) Should the legislator intervene within the framework of sections 14, 45, 198 and 199 to define the legal limits of the refusal and cessation of medical treatment?

The answers to these three questions are complex and not clear cut. The issues involved have been examined extensively in the literature on the subject. It is not the Commission's intention once more to deal exhaustively and analytically with them. Rather, it is our intention to discuss the choices and options only in terms of legislative policy applicable to Canadian law, in the light of its basic philosophy.

In order to retain an internal logic essential to reform, we believe that some preliminary reflection is necessary in order to identify the categorical imperatives of this reform. In other words, it is important to ask the following question: what are the principles or fundamental rules on which any reform of the law should be based?

These imperatives are of two types. The first has to do with the nature of the reform, the other with its content.

As regards the nature of the reform, it is essential that any reform be sensitive to the intrinsic limits of criminal law. As the Commission has frequently pointed out elsewhere, criminal law is merely one instrument of social control among others, and a very imperfect one at that. One cannot expect a criminal law reform to serve as a universal panacea; one cannot expect criminal law to provide a miraculous or permanent solution to all problems. Criminal law exists solely to check the most serious and gross abuses. Whatever the reform, it must come to terms with usage and judicial practice, which alone will eventually determine its true scope.

Secondly, the solutions proposed must retain a great deal of flexibility if they are to adapt to the specific circumstances of each case and not to impede the continuing evolution of science, medicine and society. One should therefore be wary of extreme or inflexible solutions incapable of adapting to other realities.

Thirdly, it is best to seek solutions which, wherever possible, fit harmoniously into the existing socio-judicial context and do not represent a radical upheaval of all the basic principles and institutions of our law.

In terms of content, a number of fundamental principles should guide the process of reform. The reform should not be based on a categorization of nebulous, unscientific or discriminatory concepts.

A. *Person and non-person*

First of all, it would be unthinkable to base reform on the recognition of two categories of beings: those recognized as human persons and those not so recognized. History reveals too clearly the dangers of such categorization. Qualifying a human being as "non-person" has frequently been the pretext or justification for considering him an outlaw (in the literal sense of the term), placing him outside the law and thus refusing to apply to him the basic protections which the law grants to all human beings. To give one concrete example, to deny an anencephalic newborn the status of a human person could be used to justify denying him the protection of the law as well, and thus provide grounds for arguments that killing him directly constitutes neither murder nor criminal negligence. History is filled with cases in which witches, the mentally ill, various ethnic groups and entire races have been eliminated after having first been categorized as non-persons. The Commission asserts that the law should continue to be based on the fundamental rule now recognized by our criminal law: everyone born of human parents is equally human. In terms of the exercise of subjective rights, we consider that we must continue to respect at least the basic rule of the *Criminal Code* to the effect that a human being is one who has completely proceeded, in a living state, from the body of his or her mother, and must firmly disagree that any such distinction as that between person and non-person should be applied to living humans. Every human person, whatever his degree of handicap, is entitled to the protection of the law. This is particularly important within the context of medical treatment. This point, moreover, governed the articulation of the reform proposed by the Commission regarding the criteria for the determination of death.[18a]

B. *Ordinary and extraordinary means*

It does not seem useful for the purposes of reform, to adopt the common distinction between ordinary and extraordinary means.

It is customary to trace the origin of this distinction to a response given by Pope Pius XII to a group of anaesthetists in 1957. The Pope, on this occasion, expressed the opinion that a physician was morally obliged to use only ordinary means to preserve life and health, that is, means which do not involve any serious inconvenience for the patient. These terms have received a variety of interpretations. The most commonly known involves a distinction between treatment which is strictly necessary and usual and treatment which is experimental or

---

* Refer to Appendix II

uncommon in the particular circumstances. A doctor is therefore required to use all usual or "ordinary" means, but not those which are unusual or "extraordinary".

This distinction itself was intended to be a clarification. Yet, it still retains a degree of imprecision, making it difficult to use as a criterion for reform. If the word "ordinary" is taken in its most common sense, that of usual, the distinction is meaningless. Medicine is not a stable, fixed science, but a science in constant evolution. What is usual today was not usual a few years ago. Moreover, what may be usual in a given area or well-equipped hospital centre is probably not usual in some other area or poorly-equipped centre. For example, in our times, placing a person in a state of respiratory arrest on a respirator would probably be objectively considered a usual or ordinary procedure. This was certainly not the case in the years immediately following the development of this equipment. Nor is it yet the case in some isolated areas far from any modern hospital facilities. It is therefore difficult to distinguish what is "usual" from what is not, the difference remaining largely arbitrary and fluid. If a doctor owed his patient only usual care, he would be hopelessly condemned to the *status quo* and hence to an extremely conservative practice of medicine. Doctors, of course, have clearly recognized the difficulty, and to them the word "ordinary" always designates what is ordinary according to the particular circumstances of each case.

Others have therefore proposed that one interpret the words "ordinary" and "extraordinary" in a sense other than strictly objective. "Ordinary" treatment would be treatment offering a *reasonable* hope of success and not involving any undue suffering or burden for the patient. "Extraordinary" treatment on the contrary would be treatment offering no reasonable hope of recovery or relief, or that involving unbearable suffering or other burden for the patient. A close scrutiny of this new interpretation reveals that, though it is much more realistic, it does not make the distinction much more useful for purposes of legislative reform. It merely describes true medical treatment in the first case and unwarranted aggressive therapy in the second. In our opinion, while this distinction may be useful for other purposes, it remains too ambiguous to serve as a solid basis for any precise description of the scope of the physician's legal duty to his patient and therefore to serve as a good basis for reform.

C. *The presumption in favour of life*

Preservation of human life is ackowledged to be a fundamental value of our society. Historically, our criminal law has changed very little on this point. Generally speaking, it sanctions the principle of the sanctity of human life. Over the years, however, law has come to temper the apparent absolutism of the principle, to delineate its intrinsic limitations and to define its true dimensions.

The Commission believes that any reform having to do with human life must begin by admitting a firm presumption in favour of life. In other words, the intent of a terminally ill patient to give up life should normally not be assumed without a clear, free and informed expression of the will to do so. This rule is of considerable importance. It may sometimes be impossible to determine whether a person no longer wishes to live or whether, in contrast, he wishes every effort to be made to prolong an already seriously endangered life. This is particularly true of those who have lost the ability to make decisions (for example, the comatose patient). As a general rule then, the only valid legislative policy for respecting life and avoiding abuses is to assume what common sense dictates, that under normal circumstances every human being prefers life to death.

However, and this is where the real problems arise, this presumption in favour of life cannot stand without further qualification. It would be disastrous, for example, if this presumption had the effect of obliging a physician always to use aggressive measures in cases where the patient is incapable of expressing his wishes. Such an application of the principle could lead to intolerable abuses and discrimination against incompetent or handicapped persons.

This presumption in favour of life must therefore be further qualified in the following manner: *if treatment can reasonably be applied to preserve a person's life or health, it should be assumed that this person's choice, if he could express it, would be to receive treatment and not to refuse it.* In practice, of course, this rule is applied every day to emergency cases. When a patient arrives unconscious at a hospital's emergency ward, the physician will normally treat him. He cannot assume, even in the case of an apparent attempted suicide, that the person truly wants to die. Yet, this presumption in favour of life does not oblige that physician to give an unconscious patient a treatment which, under the circumstances, appears unreasonable or useless. The practical effect of such a presumption in favour of life is to place the burden of proof on those proposing a course of action or inaction which will *not* prolong or maintain human life.

D. *Personal autonomy and self-determination*

Law must also recognize, as it now does implicitly, the principle of personal autonomy and self-determination, the right of every human being to have his wishes respected in decisions involving his own body. It is essential to recognize that every human being is, in principle, master of his own destiny. He may, of course, for moral or religious reasons, impose restrictions or limits on his own right of self-determination. However, these limits must not be imposed on him by the law except in cases where the exercise of this right is likely to affect public order or the rights of others.

Our legal system already recognizes that principle. To acknowledge it formally as a basis for reform thus involves no challenge to existing law. In 1972, the criminal offence of attempted suicide was repealed. This was not equivalent to a legislative approval or endorsement of an act which most people regard as profoundly contrary to human nature. It simply meant that our legislators no longer considered the act sufficiently asocial to warrant criminal prosecution. Parliament adopted an essentially pragmatic attitude towards this question. Since in the case of attempted suicide the offender and the victim are the same person, criminal punishment in this case seems somewhat misplaced. Since the person concerned probably needs help and certainly not punishment, prosecution would be inhuman. However, the act continues to be illicit in the broad sense of the term, even though no longer illegal.

The case-law rule that an individual of sound mind is free to refuse treatment takes a similar approach. An adult Jehovah's Witness who refuses a blood transfusion, knowing that it is probably the only means of avoiding death, exercises his right to self-determination. The same is true of the cancer patient who rejects treatment which could prolong his life. In its Working Paper No. 26 on treatment, the Commission recommended the formal legislative recognition of this right to refuse treatment.

Here again, the Commission believes that personal moral choices should be respected by law as long as they do not interfere with public order and morality. It thus believes that the law should not make the preservation of life an absolute principle. Rather, it should continue to respect man's right to self-determination over his own existence, while protecting and promoting the maintenance of life as a fundamental value.

E. *Quality of life criteria*

As already noted, criminal law tends to value human life essentially from the quantitative point of view. It punishes severely those who take or shorten life. A Study Paper prepared in connection with the Protection of Life project has shown the origin of this tendency,[19] the evolution it has undergone and the often artificial nature of the distinction between quantity and quality of life, between the sanctity of life and its quality. We therefore refer the reader to that document for further analysis.

The Commission believes that any reform must recognize something more than a merely quantitative aspect to human life and that considerations of quality of life can be legitimate factors in decision-making and valid criteria in justifying certain acts which may appear to be threats to life seen from an exclusively quantitative perspective.

In medical law, this has already long been recognized in practice. It is for the sake of the quality of their lives that some patients freely refuse treatment and that this choice is respected by doctors. It is also for the sake of the quality of their patient's life that some physicians will decide to stop or not initiate a given form of treatment. The autonomous person has the right to define his own priorities and requirements in terms of the effects of treatment or non-treatment upon the quality of his life. Others should respect these priorities. If the person is not autonomous, others must determine these priorities, taking into account the utility of the act in the light of the benefit to the person involved.

In other words, in formulating a policy for reform, the legislator should not systematically exclude values relating to the quality of life, favouring exclusively the quantitative preservation of life as an absolute value. The law, then, must not interfere with the patient's right to refuse further treatment and with his right to live the time remaining to him with sufficient quality.

F. *Special protection for the incompetent*

The law should protect all citizens equally. Law is also intended to provide additional protection for those who are weaker or whose rights may be more readily violated or ignored. To a certain extent, then, we may say that the law should be prejudiced in their favour. In terms of the protection of life, this prejudice should be maintained, if not reinforced.

A very serious dilemma arises in terms of legislative policy regarding those who are incapable, because of unconsciousness, infancy or a mental handicap, of exercising any effective power of decision. These persons need protection. Federal and provincial laws all recognize this fact and provide legal mechanisms for protection. These provisions normally require some other person (parent, guardian) to give consent on behalf of the incompetent individual. This is of relatively little consequence in the exercise of property or economic interests. However, deciding for another person when this decision affects his health, his physical integrity or his life involves a responsibility of a completely different nature and value. The Commission has recognized the complexity of this question in a Working Paper on the sterilization of the mentally retarded and mentally ill.[20]

It should also be noted that most provincial laws provide some mechanism for resolving possible disputes between parents and doctors over treatment. In Québec, for instance, the law provides that if the parent's consent, when required, is refused or cannot be obtained, a substitute consent may be given by a judge of the Superior Court and that parental consent is not required when the life of the child is in danger.[20a] In the common-law provinces, the law also provides that the child may be placed under the protection of the Court.[20b]

The main difficulty arises from the fact that, since any decision about life or health is essentially of a personal nature, substituted consent could be considered by some to be a totally inappropriate mechanism. If one accepted this principle, one could not allow anyone else (a guardian, for example) to make such decisions. As a result, the incompetent person would be placed in a disadvantaged position compared to that of the competent person, in that decisions may be made against what may appear to be in his best interests. On the other hand, treating an incompetent person on exactly the same footing as one who is fully competent is not a valid solution either, since the incompetent person may not be able to understand the implications and exact consequences of his actions or decisions.

An example may illustrate the problem. A competent person makes a decision not to undergo chemotherapy, because he feels that it is more important not to trade the quality of the life remaining to him for prolonged survival. In this case, the physician should respect that decision. However, when the person is totally incapable of expressing a choice or giving valid consent, the dilemma is that either the doctor aggressively treats the incompetent patient, regardless of the fact that the quality of his life will be radically diminished, or he chooses not to treat him basing his decision largely on his personal value judgment. It is not certain, in other words, that this would or could have been the patient's decision.

The Commission believes that the solution to the dilemma sometimes lies in the development of rules designed to ensure that the substituted decision is in the best interests of the incompetent patient. His "best" interests do not *necessarily* involve the initiation or continuation of treatment. As the Commission pointed out in its document on sterilization, additional protective rules should be established. If adequate rules exist, there should be less hesitation in permitting the cessation of treatment of the incompetent, under the same circumstances in which it would appear legitimate to do so for a person in full possession of his faculties. No rule however is perfect and it is humanly impossible to eliminate all errors. The objective should be to reduce the possibility of their occurrence to an absolute minimum.

PART FOUR

The Proposed Reform

As already indicated earlier, the legislative policy questions regarding possible revisions of the Canadian *Criminal Code* may be reduced to these three:

(1)   Should certain forms of active euthanasia such as compassionate murder be legalized, or at least decriminalized?

(2)   Should aiding suicide be decriminalized by the repeal of section 224 of the *Criminal Code*?

(3)   Should sections 14, 45, 198 and 199 of the *Criminal Code* be revised to define the legal parameters of the refusal and cessation of medical treatment?

I.   Euthanasia

Our first task is to offer some clarification of the terminology used, particularly the meaning of the word "euthanasia" as understood in this paper. This word is often used with very different meanings and acts in mind.

Positive, direct, or active euthanasia is usually contrasted with negative, indirect, or passive euthanasia. The difference between the two concepts is one of action as opposed to omission or inaction. For the purpose of this paper, we shall use the word euthanasia in a very specific sense; it will designate exclusively the positive act of causing a person's death for compassionate motives. The obvious example is the administration of poison to end someone's life.

Voluntary euthanasia is also contrasted with involuntary euthanasia, using as the criterion for distinction the fact that the "victim" did or did not consent to his death, whether caused by some positive act or by an omission. For the purposes of this paper, we shall use the word euthanasia to mean voluntary euthanasia only, that is, the killing of the patient at the patient's explicit request, or when the consent to his killing could be implied from the circumstances of the case on grounds of benefit to the patient.

A. *The legalization of euthanasia*

A number of very eloquent arguments have been advanced to persuade legislators to permit positive euthanasia on the request of the terminally ill patient. A text by Glanville Williams is considered a classic of its kind.[21] Williams attempts to show that law and society are hypocritical and inhuman in refusing to comply with the request of a person dying with excruciating pain that he be killed to put an end to his suffering.

This type of argument is not new. It is found, for example, in the well-known German work published in 1920 by Binding and Hoche.[22] Essentially the same argument is found in all writings advocating the recognition or decriminalization of euthanasia. It would, however, be erroneous and unfair to pretend that all advocates of euthanasia seek the "improvement of the race" or the "elimination of useless or undesirable social elements". Nor should we cloud the issues by focusing only on the euthanasia atrocities of the Nazis. On the other hand, they should not be passed over lightly as they provide important historical lessons.

Many arguments have been advanced in support of legalizing euthanasia. It is not our intention to refer to all of them here. The reader will find additional details in the literature on the subject.[23] Certain points, however, deserve closer examination by us.

One of the points most frequently argued is that the existing rules of law are illogical and cynical. Society recognizes the patient's right to refuse treatment or to request that it be halted, so as not to prolong his agony. The patient, we say, is master of any decisions involving his own body and his own life. Most legal systems even provide penalties against a physician who, disregarding his patient's expressed wishes, administers treatment against the patient's wish. If law now recognizes the patient's decisional autonomy and self-determination as justification for a physician's inaction, would it not be consistent to recognize the same grounds for the positive act of killing as well? What is the essential difference, in fact, between discontinuing aggressive treatment and providing a fatal injection at the patient's request, such that the law should absolve the former but treat the latter as a criminal act?

More importantly, the advocates of euthanasia argue that since the law no longer punishes attempted suicide, it implicitly allows the terminally ill patient to take his own life. Would it not be more compassionate, for those who wish to kill themselves but are physically unable to do so, and for those who wish to have help in doing so under the best possible conditions, to allow death to be administered in some scientific, medically certain and humanly acceptable manner? Would not the legalization of active and voluntary euthanasia be essentially realistic? Would it not represent respect for individual freedom and all its consequences?

A number of legislative proposals for the legalization of euthanasia have been made in Britain and the United States. Without exception, they all propose to limit its availability only to those suffering from an incurable or terminal disease. At the same time, they make every effort to establish some system of determining the person's wishes and obtaining a declaration of his intention. Most provide severe penalties for anyone falsely creating the impression that another person desires euthanasia. Most of the proposals also require that the act of euthanasia be performed by a doctor or be done under medical supervision. They provide that, if all the established conditions are met, a physician acting in good faith does not commit murder and is not liable to criminal or civil prosecution.

The best known examples of this type of legislation are the *British Voluntary Euthanasia Act* of 1936 and 1969, the *Euthanasia Society of America Bill* (Nebraska 1938), and a series of proposals introduced more recently in the legislatures of the states of New York (1947), Oregon (1973), Idaho (1969), Montana (1973) and Florida (1973, 1976).

The Commission recognizes the very laudable intentions behind these recommendations. However, from both the legal and social policy points of view, we believe that legislation legalizing voluntary active euthanasia would be quite unacceptable.

Legalizing euthanasia, given current social conditions, would mean far too great a risk in relation to any possible benefit to our society and its members. First of all, there is the risk of error and accident, since an incorrect diagnosis is always a possibility. In addition, there remains the possibility that a new treatment or the refinement of a known treatment, which will permit either survival or recovery, can never be completely ruled out. This is an important consideration, and one that is too familiar to require further development.

The principal consideration in terms of legislative policy, and the deciding one for the Commission, remains that of possible abuses. There is, first of all, a real danger that the procedure developed to allow the death of those who are a burden to themselves may be gradually diverted from its original purpose and eventually used as well to eliminate those who are a burden to others or to society. There is also the constant danger that the subject's consent to euthanasia may not really be a perfectly free and voluntary act. Medical opposition to euthanasia has often, and with reason, focused on these two considerations.

In fact, there can often be serious doubt as to the psychological and legal value of such a request by a terminally ill patient. The system which the advocates of euthanasia propose would perhaps be arguable if it were possible in each case to be absolutely sure that requests to be killed were free, voluntary and informed. The assumption behind these proposals is always that terminally ill patients are at once lucid, intelligent, informed and courageous. We forget too readily that, while this type of patient does exist, there are others whose faculties have been weakened by disease or drugs, who are suffering anguish and who may see themselves as a burden on their loved ones. This is not at all to imply that a terminally ill patient is never capable of making an informed decision. However, despite all the legal precautions proposed by the proponents of euthanasia, there remain grounds for suspicions that requests to be killed may not reflect the real and stable wishes of those making the request, and may be too easily influenced by circumstances and external pressures.

A further argument against legalizing euthanasia is one made by Kamisar[24] in response to Glanville Williams. A patient seeking active euthanasia clearly does not wish to prolong his agony, but seeks a quick end to his suffering. Yet any proposal for the legalization of euthanasia must necessarily include some process of ensuring that the patient is in fact suffering from an incurable disease and that his decision is free, voluntary and informed. Any such procedures would have to be carefully followed and the results painstakingly confirmed. All this would demand time and by wrapping the decision-making process in red-tape, create the very delays which the euthanasia movement seeks to avoid. Moreover, the medical profession exists to provide important professional services, and does not wish to be nor should be involved in this kind of bureaucratic activity.

In the Commission's view, a final and decisive argument should be made against the legalization of euthanasia. In any law reform, there should be some acceptable proportion established between, on the one hand, the evils to be avoided or the difficulties to be remedied, and on the other hand, the new risks which the reform is likely to produce. In our view, the new risks created by legalizing euthanasia would be greater and more serious than the benefits to be gained.

It would be incorrect to maintain that there is an insistent demand or strong social pressure in Canadian society today for the legalization of euthanasia. As in other countries, the various groups or movements advocating the practice of euthanasia have been very active but have not, on the whole, succeeded in rallying a large proportion of the population to their cause. There appears to be no discernible degree of social unanimity on the question.

Law exists to meet real needs. The Commission has concluded, independently of all other arguments, that in Canada today, there are neither wrongs nor needs sufficiently great to justify overturning a well-established tradition based on time-honoured morality. The extraordinary development of palliative care and pain control in recent years is certainly a safer and far more positive response to the problem of pain and suffering for the terminally or incurably ill.

B. *The decriminalization of compassionate murder*

As we have already noted, Canadian criminal law does not take into account the motive of the person who commits homicide. Only the fact that he did or did not mean to cause death is considered relevant. The motive behind this intention is of little significance from the legal point of view.

In this approach, Canadian law follows the common-law tradition and differs sharply from most of the continental legal systems. These latter distinguish, at least at the point of sentencing if not in terms of the classification of the offence itself, between murder committed for a morally reprehensible motive (for example, the hope of gain) and murder committed for a humanly excusable motive (for example, compassion for suffering).

The choice in terms of legislative policy is clear. Three options are available: to continue with the present stance which ignores motive; to, in one way or another, create a special category of homicide for cases in which the motive can serve as an excuse; or to retain the existing offence but take the motive into account in the sentence.

The creation of a specific offence of compassionate murder is not an acceptable solution, and for two reasons. Firstly, there may be some question as to the practical necessity of such a step. Whether the offence is described as homicide, murder or something else, is, in fact, of little practical importance. What is of interest is only the consequences and legal effects which Parliament assigns to it. In the case of compassionate murder, it is obviously in relation to whether or not to criminalize it, and to the existence or severity of the sentence that the question arises. The problem, then, is not whether the act should be described as murder, homicide, euthanasia or some other name, but whether, in this case, the law should provide for acquittal or acknowledge that extenuating circumstances could justify a lighter sentence than in the case of a truly sordid murder.

Secondly, compassion for the dying is probably not the only valid motive which the law could recognize in connection with homicide. What, for example, of killing in the heat of passion, of killing done out of "necessity", of politically motivated killing, and so forth? The problem thus goes far beyond the simple case of active euthanasia. It is the entire structure of the law on homicide which might require review. Should such a review lead to the conclusion that motive *in general* should be taken into consideration for homicide, it might then be logical to include the motive of mercy, among others, as at least partial justification for violations of the prohibition against killing.

Subject then to the recommendations which the Commission may make in its forthcoming Working Paper on homicide, we think at this time that to create a specific offence for compassionate murder would not represent a practical or valid solution to the problem within the context of Canada's present-day criminal law.

A second solution would retain the present system but allow the court to reduce the minimum sentence by taking into consideration the compassionate motive which inspired the act. One could, for example, make compassionate murder a "third" degree of murder. This solution, as we have seen, has already been adopted by several jurisdictions. Yet the act itself is still considered murder.

The preliminary consultations which the Commission has held on the subject show that this would probably be the most acceptable solution to the public. The public, of course, does not tend to judge these acts by strict legal norms, but rather considers the acts from the moral perspective. It appears to have difficulty granting that a truly compassionate killing, motivated essentially by altruism, should be punished as severely as killing out of vengeance or greed. There is therefore little doubt that legal recognition of this perception would meet with public approval.

The adoption of this solution, however, still leaves a number of complex problems. Firstly, it remains difficult to isolate compassion towards the terminally ill as the one and only case of premeditated homicide in which the law should take motive into account. What of the premeditated murder motivated by passion? What of murder committed in order to escape from mistreatment by another person, the murder committed in the defence of "higher national interests", etc.? Here again it is impossible to isolate compassion for the dying as the only potentially acceptable motive. To be consistent, any such reform would have to recognize that other motives or other reasons may be of equal or greater merit.

Secondly, it is always very difficult to assess the real motives behind homicide. The problem is often discussed in terms of just one type of example: the dying man who begs one of his loved ones to end his suffering for him; the loved one puts aside his reluctance out of love and compassion, and in an act of sublime courage, kills the dying person. The Commission does not deny that there have been real life cases along these lines. But in addition to these clear-cut cases there are others in which the purity and disinterested nature of the motive are far less evident. The infliction of death may be inspired by infinitely more complex and mixed motives. For example, there may be a degree of compassion, but also a desire to put an end to a psychologically and physically difficult and exhausting period for oneself. How can the complexity of human motivation be determined by others with certainty, or even with probability?

Thirdly, the difficulty, again in terms of legislative policy, is the possibility of abuse which may be created by a substantial reduction in the law's traditional protection for human life and integrity. The danger exists at two levels. The first is that true murders may be committed and then disguised as compassionate murders. Since it can be safely assumed that in most cases the act will not be public, one can never be truly certain of either the purity of the motive or of the victim's consent. Would not allowing the motive to reduce the sentence encourage the killing of those who are a burden to the agent, or of those in whose deaths he has some interest? The second danger, which at this point is difficult to evaluate, is that of the imitation effect. Is there not some risk that such a liberalization of the law would promote imitation killings for questionable motives?

It is therefore the Commission's view that, at this time, a legislated reform allowing motive to reduce the sentence would be dangerous. We recognize, however, that such an approach is conceivable and that certain guarantees and measures could be adopted to reduce the risks involved. For example, the act could continue to be treated as murder in terms of sentencing, unless the agent himself demonstrates convincingly that he was guided solely by motives of mercy.

It is essential to consider this question not only within the perspective of the *Criminal Code* and the various offence sections, but also within the perspective of the criminal justice system as a whole. This system has a number of internal mechanisms which generally make it possible to correct inequitable or otherwise unacceptable results of the strict application of the law in individual cases. The experience of certain countries with legal systems similar to ours demonstrates that the actual cases of mercy killing, in which charges are in fact laid, guilty verdicts brought and maximum sentences imposed, are rare, if non-existent. The prosecutor's decision not to prosecute, or the defendant's decision to plead guilty to a lesser offence are two means in actual practice of moderating the apparent severity of the law. Some will claim that the law, as a result, is both hypocritical and illogical in treating mercy killing as pure and simple murder in written law, while refusing to do so in practice in terms of prosecution. In theory there may be some merit to this observation. However, the decision not to prosecute in a case of compassionate killing need not detract from the credibility of the criminal law. Rather, it may show that in the enforcement of the law, the justice system is capable of considering the humanitarian and mitigating aspects of these cases in its exercise of discretion.

Our conclusion is that the existing situation, in which the *Criminal Code* makes no allowance for compassionate murder on the basis of motive, is the least unsatisfactory solution, given the general context of Canadian criminal law. This does not however mean that the Commission finally and irrevocably rules out such a recognition. We continue to welcome the reactions of the Canadian public on this point.

II.   Aiding suicide

Section 224 of the *Criminal Code* states that anyone who aids, abets or counsels a person to commit suicide is liable to imprisonment for fourteen years. The criminal offence of attempted suicide was abolished in 1972.

Decriminalization of the act of aiding suicide has often been proposed as a necessary next step. After all, it is argued, a person who seeks to end his life is legally free to do so, since the law today, no longer punishes attempted suicide. If the person is unable to perform the act himself, is it not illogical to treat the one who assists him as a criminal? Assistance is not murder because there is no positive causal act. Moreover, the person involved is always free to change his mind. Why, then, this severity towards those who help others to commit suicide?

For some years now, in the United States, Britain and other European countries, and now in Canada, various groups have been calling for decriminalization of aiding the terminally ill to commit suicide. These associations do not, as some have claimed, advocate suicide. They are simply demanding what seems to them the necessary corollary to the individual's right to commit suicide: the right to assistance.

At first view, it seems highly incongruous to regard as criminal the participation in an act which itself is no longer criminal. The case is somewhat unique in criminal law. Moreover, what real difference is there on the practical level between watching a terminally ill person swallow poison he has obtained himself and has taken with no assistance, and watching him doing so after having provided him with the poison in question? Some ethicists argue that both of these acts are reprehensible or both are not. Why does the law establish such a fundamental distinction between two such similar types of behaviour?

This distinction is difficult to justify on grounds of logic alone. However, a more convincing response may be made on the basis of legislative policy and the practical consequences entailed in decriminalization of the act of aiding suicide.

First of all, the prohibition in section 224 is not restricted solely to the case of the terminally ill patient, for whom we can only have sympathy, or solely to his physician or a member of his family who helps him to put an end to his suffering. The section is more general and applies to a variety of situations for which it is much more difficult to feel sympathy. Consider, for example, a recent incident, that of inciting to mass suicide. What of the person who takes advantage of another's depressed state to encourage him to commit suicide, for his own financial benefit? What of the person who, knowing an adolescent's suicidal tendencies, provides him with large enough quantities of drugs to kill him? The "accomplice" in these cases cannot be considered morally blameless. Nor can one conclude that the criminal law should not punish such conduct. To decriminalize completely the act of aiding, abetting or counselling suicide would therefore not be a valid legislative policy. But could it be in the case of the terminally ill?

The probable reason why legislation has not made an exception for the terminally ill lies in the fear of the excesses or abuses to which liberalization of the existing law could lead. As in the case of "compassionate murder", decriminalization of aiding suicide would be based on the humanitarian nature of the motive leading the person to provide such aid, counsel or encouragement. As in the case of compassionate murder, moreover, the law may legitimately fear the difficulties involved in determining the true motivation of the person committing the act.

Aiding or counselling a person to commit suicide, on the one hand, and homicide, on the other, are sometimes extremely closely related. Consider, for example, the doctor who holds the glass of poison and pours the contents into the patient's mouth. Is he aiding him to commit suicide? Or is he committing homicide, since the victim's willingness to die is legally immaterial? There is reason to fear that homicide of the terminally ill for ignoble motives may readily be disguised as aiding suicide.

It may be useful to note that there are various legislative reactions to this problem. Some countries, including Britain and the United States, consider aiding suicide a distinct offence, and punish it less severely than homicide. Others do not recognize this offence as such, but may punish this form of behaviour as homicide by extending the concept of causality.

It should also be pointed out that cases involving truly altruistic assistance to a terminally ill patient who wishes to die are very rarely prosecuted.

Assuming that the law continues to discount the motive in homicide, the Commission's view is that no exception should be made in the case of aiding suicide. However, in order to further strengthen the present self-restraint of criminal prosecution in these cases, and their exceptional nature, the

Commission would be prepared to recommend an amendment to section 224 of the *Criminal Code*. This amendment would permit prosecution only on written authorization from the Attorney General. The 1961 amendments to the *British Suicide Act* include this same safety precaution.

III. Cessation and refusal of treatment

As previously noted in this document, there is a considerable gap at present between actual medical practice and what a literal and restrictive interpretation of the *Criminal Code*'s sections relevant to medical treatment might impose. As also observed, the almost total absence of legal precedent in this connection creates a state of uncertainty and ambiguity for patients, members of the medical profession, lawyers and the public. Law cannot speak in ambiguities, particularly on a question of this importance, without the risk of losing credibility and respect.

In a Working Paper published in 1980 entitled *Medical Treatment and Criminal Law*, the Commission already dealt with medical treatment in general. It proposed a number of law reforms touching upon medical treatment. The purpose of the present paper is simply to add to that analysis now in relation to the very specific aspect of cessation and refusal of treatment. Proposals for overall reform will be included in the Commission's Report to Parliament. Solutions to the problem of cessation and refusal of treatment will be examined from two distinct perspectives. Firstly, that of the patient capable of expressing his wishes, and secondly the more exceptional one of the patient who, for one reason or another, is unable to express his wishes.

A. *The competent person*

In its Working Paper No. 26, *Medical Treatment and Criminal Law*, the Commission stated and defended its view that the competent patient should be considered by the law as the absolute master of decisions regarding his own body. In doing so, the Commission was not formulating a new and revolutionary rule, but merely advocating legislative recognition of the common-law rule on this point. The Commission has not changed its opinion that a competent person should have and should retain the right to refuse any form of treatment whatsoever, and to demand that any treatment undertaken be stopped either temporarily or permanently.

However, present law, because of the distinctions which it makes between act and omission and because in theory it requires the continuation of any treatment undertaken if its interruption constitutes a threat to life, clearly promotes certain biases in favour of heroic or aggressive treatment, or at least creates a legal climate likely to encourage this approach.

Medicine's first duty is to fight for life and against death. No one will seriously dispute this fact. Medicine, like law for that matter, must however recognize that at a given point the optimal treatment for a patient is no longer to struggle to maintain a purely vegetative or clinical life but to allow death to occur, while providing the individual with all the palliative care required to relieve his pain. A person who is conscious and capable of expressing his informed wishes should be the sole master of this decision.

This principle is often expressed by the expression "death with dignity". The patient, as master of his own life within certain limits and under certain conditions, should also be master of his death. He should be able to exercise a constant choice over the way in which he intends to die and, in particular, over the way in which he intends to live his final moments. Heroic or aggressive measures, when not requested by the patient, violate this right by imposing on him a constraint which in fact fails to take into consideration his wishes and desires. The law should clearly establish the corollaries which follow: first of all, the physician should not have to risk criminal liability simply because he respects his patient's wish to have medical treatment stopped or not initiated. And secondly, a doctor who proceeds to treat a patient against that patient's clearly expressed wishes should be subject to the provisions of the *Criminal Code* on assault, to say nothing, of course, of any other civil or disciplinary actions. These two rules are consistent with existing law, but have not yet been expressed in the form of legislation.

To recognize these rules is not however equivalent to legalizing euthanasia. There is a fundamental difference, as we have noted, between causing death by a positive, deliberate act and stopping treatment at a patient's request. The first is morally and legally unacceptable and should continue to be subject to criminal penalties. The second, however, is perfectly justified in the name of personal autonomy and the right to self-determination. Respect for this principle demands that present criminal law not be interpreted to impose on the doctor a duty to provide treatment which conflicts with the patient's right to refuse it.

As a result, the Commission therefore proposes that *legislation should clearly and formally recognize the competent patient's absolute right to refuse medical treatment or to demand its cessation.* This refusal or cessation should, in all cases, take precedence over the doctor's duty to undertake or to continue treatment already undertaken.

B. *The incompetent person*

It is regarding the person incapable of expressing his wishes that the truly difficult problems arise. By an incompetent person, we mean here anyone who, because of infancy, temporary or permanent unconsciousness or some other handicap, is unable to express his wishes, make an informed decision, or exercise choice. A number of preliminary observations should be made.

First of all, law should strenuously avoid and forbid any form of discrimination against such persons. Insistence on heroic but useless measures is no more justified for the incompetent patient than it is for the competent. In other words, an individual's incapacity should not serve as a basis or pretext for denying him the fundamental right or opportunity available to the competent patient to exercise choice. It would be regrettable and absurd if, because a person is incompetent, his attending physician were legally obliged to continue or to undertake useless treatment and required to prolong his patient's suffering to no avail. It would be unthinkable that a person should lose his right to die with dignity as soon as one becomes incapable of expressing wishes.

However, the incompetent clearly require additional protection. All modern legal systems, both criminal and civil, have established protective mechanisms such as the appointing of guardians, whose decisions on behalf of the incompetent are carefully controlled by a number of formal requirements. Since we are dealing here with the highest values of life and death, the obvious goal lies in the development of protective measures which leave as little room as possible for error and arbitrary decisions. The solution does not lie in the recognition of some difference in nature between the competent person and the incompetent person. The incompetent must continue to receive protection, but to be in need of protection must not be used to allow the rights of the individual concerned to be weakened or eliminated, nor to make his situation more difficult in the face of death.

Secondly, the law must recognize what is now a medical and scientific reality. It must admit that the cessation or non-initiation of treatment which offers no chance of success is *a good decision and one based on sound medical practice*. Treatment is a measure designed to help the patient recover from his illness, to halt its progress at least temporarily or to relieve its symptoms. It is selected and administered in an effort to protect or to extend life. The competent patient must be free, as we have seen, to refuse the benefit of treatment. With a competent patient, the doctor has the opportunity to explain the prognosis and the likelihood of success of a treatment. With an incompetent patient this dialogue is by definition impossible. The doctor thus cannot count on any communication by the patient of his wishes.

Some will conclude that since there must always be a presumption in favour of life, it is the doctor's solemn duty in the case of the incompetent patient to initiate and to continue treatment in all cases. To do otherwise, they claim, would amount to "negative" euthanasia. In our view, as already indicated, this position is erroneous. Erroneous because it overlooks the fact that the guiding principle for medical decision-making is not life in itself as an absolute value, but the patient's overall welfare. In most instances, this welfare imposes the maintenance of life, but this is not always the case. It is not the case when the prolonging of life has become purely artificial. It is not the case when the maintenance of life can only be achieved by an undue prolongation of the patient's agony. It is not the case when the maintenance of life results only in the infliction of additional suffering. In other words, it is not the case when treatment is diverted from its proper end and merely prolongs the dying process rather than life itself. The competent patient makes a decision on the basis of his own interests. He may, in rare cases, choose to have his life artificially maintained, or to prolong his agony or suffering. In this case, the doctor has little choice. He should respect the terminally ill patient's stated wishes and initiate or continue treatment independently of his own personal views if the circumstances allow, that is, if it is not unreasonable.

However, in the case of the incompetent patient, it is neither legally required nor sound medical practice to transpose the general situation to an exceptional one and to assume that, because the person is incompetent, he would have chosen to have his life artificially maintained, his agony prolonged or his suffering extended. Hence, the law must recognize that even in the case of an incompetent person, the cessation or non-initiation of medical treatment may objectively constitute good medical practice and should not be subject to criminal sanctions.

A third rule merits legal recognition as well. Regarding the incompetent, it is essential to distinguish between two situations which unfortunately are often confused. The first is the one we have just described, involving the stopping or non-initiating of treatment because it offers no reasonable hope of improvement and merely prolongs the dying process rather than life itself. In this case, as we have said, the cessation or non-initiation of treatment is legitimate and should be recognized as legal. The second is the case in which treatment is not undertaken or continued only because the prognosis of the incompetent patient does not measure up to the "accepted norm". These examples will illustrate this difference.

The decision not to undertake treatment in the case of an anencephalic newborn is medically justified since there is no treatment at the present time which can remedy this condition and save that newborn's life. Proceeding with an operation for atresia* of the digestive tract in such a case would be futile and would only prolong the inevitable suffering. It is the physician's duty in this case to ensure that the inevitable death occurs under the best possible conditions. It is not a question of assisting nature, but of allowing nature to take its course, while providing the infant with adequate palliative care.

In contrast, it is just as obviously the physician's duty, in the case of an otherwise normal child suffering from atresia,* to perform the corrective surgery which will enable him to absorb nourishment.

Finally, what is the legal duty in the case of a child born with the characteristics of trisomy 21 (Down's syndrome or mongolism)* and also suffering from atresia* of the digestive tract? In the Commission's view, this child should be treated for the atresia*. To abandon the child and allow him to die of starvation is unacceptable and contrary to the norms of criminal law. A decision not to provide treatment in this case is not based on the absence of any hope of improvement (repairing the atresia* will, in fact, solve that problem). The decision is based rather on the fact that treatment will not change the child's mental handicap. The decision is thus based on a value judgment as to the quality of the infant's present or future life. It is equivalent to a death sentence based on the child's handicap. We are well aware of tragic difficulties created by the birth of a child suffering from serious defects, of the tragic consequences it can have on a couple or family. But in our view the appropriate response lies both in more preventive

* Refer to Appendix II

measures such as better prenatal care and diagnosis, and the assistance and material support which society as a whole should provide for parents after birth.

One important qualification, however, must be made. If the trisomic and atresic child is also suffering from other serious defects for which treatment is useless or inappropriate under the particular circumstances of the case, the decision to withhold treatment should then be considered legitimate. In this case, it is based not on the existence of trisomy,* but on the decision not to prolong a dying process already initiated, as in the first case. The Commission thus proposes that we accept as fundamental the principle of non-discrimination between the competent person and the incompetent, on the one hand, and on the other hand, the rule that when it is impossible to obtain an expression of the patient's wishes, life-saving treatment should be administered, providing it is medically useful.

If these principles are accepted, the problem then becomes one of determining the presumed wishes of the incompetent patient. On what basis and according to what criteria should another person make the decision for him to terminate or not to initiate treatment which is apparently useless? In our opinion, it is often important to apply a distinction between incompetent persons who have previously had the opportunity to express their wishes and those who have never had or never will have that opportunity.

In the first category, we may place the adult who, at some given point, becomes unconscious or incompetent, but who had previously expressed his wishes regarding treatment. This may have occurred in the course of a discussion with his doctor, or a relative or a friend. The refusal of treatment may have been expressed more formally in a letter or document such as a "living will". In this case, these wishes should be respected and the doctor is required to adopt the same position as if his patient were conscious and competent. By treatment, of course, we mean treatment which offers no further reasonable hope of recovery or improvement in the condition of the

_____
* Refer to Appendix II

patient. However, if treatment offers such hope, it is then the physician's duty to initiate or to continue it unless he has been forbidden very clearly to do so by the patient. Any other decision creates a vicious circle and may lead to the absurd situation which in fact has been largely responsible for the development of the living will systems: as soon as the patient becomes unconscious or incompetent, whatever his previous condition or wishes, the doctor may feel himself allowed or obliged to continue or to initiate treatment, even when it is hopeless!

The situation is somewhat different in the case of a patient who, because of infancy or some mental handicap, is totally unable to express his wishes. This is the case with newborns, the severely retarded, and comatose patients who have never previously expressed their wishes. These cases can be described as "neutral", in the sense that we have no indication of what the wishes of the person involved might be or might have been. The only reasonable conclusion possible under these circumstances is that the decision must be made by someone else. The difficulty then lies in determining who this someone else should be, and on what criteria the decision should be based.

Three approaches are conceivable: the first is to leave everything to the physician's judgment, leaving to him the responsibility of judging each case on the basis of the particular circumstances involved and for making the final decision on his own. Naturally, he can and indeed should seek expert advice as required in each case. Obviously, too, he should consult the patient's family and next of kin, if possible, and involve them in the actual decision-making process.

Some are vehemently opposed to this solution and for two reasons. Firstly, it would require giving society a sort of *carte blanche* as a whole to medical science, with no guarantee that the result would be objectively valid. This, it is argued, amounts to allowing doctors to play God. Moreover, it assigns medicine a role which it should not have. This first objection is closely linked to an attitude of trust or mistrust towards medical practice and doctors. The objection also assumes that by giving the power of decision to the physician, we automatically eliminate all forms of societal control. But this need not be so. In giving doctors the final decision-making power, we do not confer on them absolute immunity for the consequences of their decisions. The criminal law, as one of many mechanisms of control, would still punish abuses of professional duty.

Secondly, it is argued that leaving to physicians the decision-making power merely perpetuates the existing situation. Since medical and hospital practices vary considerably from one area to another and from one individual to another, it is feared that decisions will continue to be made on a largely subjective basis and that certain undesirable practices, such as the unjustified use of aggressive measures, will be perpetuated.

There are a number of answers to this second objection. First, one must recognize and accept the fact that it is impossible to eliminate completely all subjectivity or individual judgment. Nor is it desirable to do so. If medicine were to be completely standardized, and medical judgment severely restricted, the quality of practice would suffer. As well, in our view, much of the variation in current practice can be explained by the uncertainty surrounding the state of the law. It is likely that excessive caution and continued use of aggressive measures are due far more to the fear of legal liability and prosecution than to the deliberate and intentional intrusion of the physician's personal attitudes and philosophies. We can reasonably conclude that the removal of these ambiguities and uncertainties will produce correspondingly greater uniformity in medical practice.

A second possible approach would involve the "judicialization" of the decision-making process including within it a wide range of variations. For example, we could have a process in which *any* decision as to the continuation or cessation of treatment for an incompetent person must necessarily be the subject of a judicial or quasi-judicial decision by a court or administrative agency. Or these decisions could be made by hospital committees.

A number of committee processes and purposes are possible. The function of this committee could be to determine and establish, for both competent and incompetent patients, the conditions under which treatment should be either halted or not initiated. Another would be simply to ensure that one or two independent physicians participate in the decision. The committee system has certain advantages, but some practical disadvantages as well. The Commission has not made any firm decision on this matter, preferring to reserve it for its final recommendations. It thus welcomes reactions and comments on this issue from doctors, hospital staff and the general public.

The Commission does not deny the essential role of judicial decision-making in settling disputes. Such decisions offer a guarantee of impartiality and natural justice. At the same time, one would not wish to over-burden the courts by systematically referring to them each and every decision regarding the cessation of treatment for the incompetent. Such a course of action would of course be unrealistic. One would also not wish to judicialize and hence to make adversarial a decision-making process which should be based more on consensus than confrontation. A judicial decision is necessary when there is some real conflict. It may be superfluous when it is used merely to formalize a decision which has already been made and which no one has challenged and which involves no real dispute, controversy or conflict. If, for example, a physician decides, on the basis of his best medical judgment, that under the circumstances further treatment is useless, while the patient's family is adamantly opposed to the cessation of treatment, then and only then the best way of settling the matter would appear to be a judicial decision. Each of the two parties, in fact, interprets the interests of the incompetent patient in a different way. Only an impartial arbitrator can decide. The fact that the decision is a judicial one also implies that it will be based on the best interests of the incompetent patient and that in time the accumulation of such decisions will permit the development of a number of decision-making criteria. At the present time these criteria still seem somewhat vague. In the Commission's views, therefore, the judicial model is valid, but only under the conditions and limitations described above.

The third possibility is to allow the next of kin, family or representative of the incompetent patient (curator, guardian, tutor) to make the decision independently. At first sight, this solution may appear to be the best one. Presumably, these people know the patient and are therefore in a better position to assess the subjective elements involved. It can also be assumed that they will usually have the patient's best interests at heart. All this is true. However, two objections are regularly made to this third approach. The first is that making such a decision normally creates feelings of guilt, no matter what decision is eventually reached. The question then is whether it is really fair to impose the burden for decisions to terminate treatment on people who, unlike doctors, are not prepared by their profession to deal with it. The second is that, in the case of an incompetent person, it may be preferable for the decision to be made by a person other than the next of kin or a family member, less because of the danger of conflicts of interest, than because of the need to surround the decision with as much objectivity as possible, providing the utmost protection for the rights of the incompetent person involved. However, the Commission recognizes, once again, that these people should be involved at some stage in the decision process.

Finally, we are well aware that there is unfortunately no miraculous solution capable of minimizing all the disadvantages, eliminating all the difficulties and achieving universal support. The choice is thus limited. It is a question of finding the solution which, in our particular context, is the least unsatisfactory. The first possibility (i.e. a judgment by the physician) appears to us to meet this criterion.

At this stage, it may be useful to summarize the tentative conclusions which the Commission has reached to date. These conclusions are as follows:

(1)   *the law should recognize the competent patient's wishes and respect them as regards the cessation or non-initiation of treatment;*

(2)   *the law should clearly state that a physician acts legally when he decides to terminate or not to initiate*

*treatment which is useless or which no longer offers
reasonable hope, unless the patient has expressed his
wishes to the contrary;*

(3)　*the law should recognize that the prolonging of life
is not an absolute value in itself and that therefore a
physician does not act illegally when he fails to take
measures to achieve this end, if these measures
are useless or contrary to the patient's wishes or
interests;*

(4)　*the law should recognize that a physician who continues to treat a patient against his wishes is subject
to the provisions of the* Criminal Code;

(5)　*the law should recognize that the incapacity of a
person to express his wishes is not sufficient a reason
to oblige a physician to administer useless treatment
for the purpose of prolonging his life;*

(6)　*the law should recognize that in the case of an
unconscious or incompetent patient, a physician in-
curs no criminal responsibility by terminating treatment which has become useless.*

PART FIVE

The Formulation of the Reform

It may be useful at this point in our analysis, and before presenting the actual formula for reform, to review a number of earlier findings and limitations. No reform, whatever its nature, can solve every problem. The law cannot provide the public or the physician with a complete guide to life and death decision-making based on entirely objective criteria. Reform can only help to dissipate some of the ambiguities involved.

Criminal-law reform cannot realistically judicialize the decision-making process to make it possible to determine *a priori* the validity of every given decision to undertake or to cease treatment. As noted earlier, the purpose of criminal law is only to sanction the most flagrant abuses. Its control over the legality or illegality of a given act must therefore remain largely an *a posteriori* control. In this sense, the law does not and cannot with infallibility reassure the physician or others before they make all treatment decisions. Physicians must make the decision to the best of their ability and their knowledge of their ethical, medical and legal duties. Should the decision taken prove to make one criminally liable for a breach of duty, one must expect to suffer the legal consequences. However, while it is both impossible and undesirable to bypass medical responsibility, judgment and liability, it is possible to clarify in advance the fundamental bases on which the law feels that these decisions should be made.

No reform including that which follows will ever be greeted with universal approval. Moreover, the aim of the present document is not so much to reflect a consensus on this very

67

controversial question as to propose a number of reasonable solutions for discussion and criticism, before submitting final recommendations to the Parliament of Canada in a later Report.

Finally, the proposed reform should not be assessed in a vacuum. Legislation cannot codify the whole of medical and hospital practice. It can only attempt to influence it and help to create a climate which will encourage the protection of certain fundamental human rights and principles. The reader should not therefore expect to find a thorough and comprehensive blueprint for reform in the proposals which follow. These law reform proposals must be complemented by, and placed within, the larger social, cultural and medical contexts.

I. Euthanasia

The Commission does not favour the legalization of active euthanasia in any form. *It therefore recommends that the existing prohibitions of the* Criminal Code *concerning homicide be maintained.* As regards the act of compassionate murder, the Commission believes that it should continue to be a punishable offence under the law. However, if in the Commission's forthcoming proposals for reform with regard to homicide, it concludes that motive should now be taken into account, then and only then may the motive of compassion be taken into consideration as a reason to mitigate sentence.

II. Aiding suicide

The Commission does not favour the *complete decriminalization of the act of aiding or counselling suicide*. In our view, this would be inappropriate and dangerous within the existing context. In so deciding, the Commission does not seek to deny or limit personal autonomy and the right to self-determination. It merely proposes the maintenance of the present prohibition of the Canadian *Criminal Code*, in view of the possibilities for serious abuse which decriminalization might entail.

At the same time, in order to acknowledge more fully the undeniable element of altruism and compassion involved in some cases of assistance provided to a terminally ill loved one, and because we are not convinced that the imposition of a criminal sentence is appropriate in such a case, *the Commission proposes the addition to section 224 of the present* Criminal Code *of a second subsection as follows*:

> *224. (2) No person shall be prosecuted for an offence under the present section without the personal written authorization of the Attorney General.*

III.   Cessation and refusal of treatment

In considering the problem of the cessation of treatment, the Commission has studied at some length the approach taken by certain American states, such as California, and has weighed the possibility of suggesting the adoption in Canada of an equivalent to the *Natural Death Act*.

This option, however, has been rejected for the following reasons. We believe that it would risk the reversal of the already-established rule that there should be no duty to initiate or maintain treatment when it is useless to do so. The living-will approach begins from the opposite principle, since it requires that the patient's wishes be formally expressed in writing in order to authorize the physician not to prolong that patient's agony and death. This approach may be arguable in the context and legal systems of California and other States, but we do not feel it is an arguable reform for Canada.

The decision to terminate or not to initiate useless treatment is sound medical practice and should be legally recognized as such. The law, then, should not begin from the principle that a doctor who fails to prolong life acts illegally, but rather from the principle that a doctor acts legally if he does not prolong death.

It is the Commission's view that this already recognized common-law principle can and should be clearly expressed within the existing *Criminal Code*. Similarly, to repeat in the framework of the present document a suggestion contained in Working Paper No. 26, the Commission also proposes that criminal law should formally recognize in the *Criminal Code* the principle that a competent person has the right to refuse treatment or to demand that it be stopped.

In the case of a person who is incapable of expressing his wishes, the Commission proposes that the decision to halt or not to undertake treatment should be based on two criteria. The first is a criterion of a medical nature and concerns the utility or non-utility of the administration of treatment. The second criterion is based upon the wishes of the person prior to becoming incompetent, or upon his best interests determined by others in the event that that person is not or has never been capable of expressing his wishes. The Commission believes that the "best interests" of the person may in some cases indicate the prolongation of life, but in others the cessation of treatment in order to protect the incompetent person's right to a peaceful death with dignity. In the event of a conflict between, for example, the physician and family, as to the best interests of the patient, the courts should be called upon, as they are today, to settle the dispute. *On this point, then, the Commission proposes the maintenance of existing law and practice.*

Finally, as regards the question of the administration of palliative care, the Commission believes that a doctor must never refuse to administer pain-killing treatment, drugs or similar forms of treatment to a terminally ill patient only because the effective pain-killing dosage may hasten death.

The Commission therefore suggests the addition to the *Criminal Code* of the following texts:

1. *Nothing in sections 14, 45, 198 and 199 of the* Criminal Code *shall be interpreted as requiring a physician*

(a) *to continue to administer or to undertake medical treatment against the clearly expressed wishes of the person for whom such treatment is intended;*

(b) *to continue to administer or to undertake medical treatment, when such treatment is medically useless and is not in the best interests of the person for whom it is intended, except in accordance with the clearly expressed wishes of this person.*

2. *Nothing in sections 14, 45, 198 and 199 of the* Criminal Code *shall be interpreted as preventing a physician from undertaking or ceasing to administer palliative care and measures intended to eliminate or to relieve the suffering of a person for the sole reason that such care or measures are likely to shorten the life expectancy of this person.*

Endnotes

1. The Working Papers are: *Criteria for the Determination of Death*, Working Paper No. 23; *Sterilization*, Working Paper No. 24; *Medical Treatment and Criminal Law*, Working Paper No. 26. The Study Papers are: *Consent to Medical Treatment*; *Sanctity of Life or Quality of Life*.

2. *Criteria for the Determination of Death*, Report No. 15.

3. E. Keyserlingk. *Sanctity of Life or Quality of Life*, Study Paper. Law Reform Commission of Canada, Ottawa: DSS, 1979.

4. See, Law Reform Commission of Canada. *Criteria for the Determination of Death*, Report No. 15. Ottawa: DSS, 1981.

5. See, *inter alia*, the code of ethics of the Canadian Medical Association.

6. *Globe and Mail*, August 16, 1978, "Probe continues in death of baby at B.C. hospital". In this case, however, we have been unable to determine accurately the exact degree of the child's deformity. See also *In re B (A Minor)* (1981) 1 W.L.R. 1421.

7. Law Reform Commission of Canada. *Medical Treatment and Criminal Law*, Working Paper No. 26. Ottawa: DSS, 1980.

8. See *Medical Treatment and Criminal Law*, *op. cit.*, note 7, pp. 25 and 26.

9. For a more detailed analysis of these provisions, see *Medical Treatment and Criminal Law*, *op. cit.*, note 7, pp. 26 and following.

10. H. Picard. *Legal Liability of Doctors and Hospitals in Canada*. Toronto: Carswell, 1978, p. 298.

11. *R. v. St-Germain* (1976) C.A. 185. In this case, it will be recalled, a doctor had been accused of criminal negligence for refusing to treat a patient in serious condition in the emergency ward of a Montréal hospital.

11a. *The Queen* v. *Milliard*, Court of the Sessions of the Peace, Montréal, No. 01-001050-803, March 7, 1980.

11b. H. Palmer. "Dr. Adams' Trial for Murder" (1957) *Criminal Law Review* 365, p. 375.

12. On the history of these movements in Great Britain and the United States, see R. Kaplan. "Euthanasia Legislation: A Survey and a Model Act" (1976) 2 *Am. J. of Law and Med.* 41, p. 52 and following.

13. G. Williams. *The Sanctity of Life and the Criminal Law*. London: Faber and Faber, 1958; also, "Euthanasia" (1973) 41 *Medicolegal Journal* 14.

14. California Health and Safety Code #7185 and following (1976).

15. Oregon, New Mexico, Nevada, Arkansas, North Carolina, Idaho and Texas.

16. Private Member's Bill No. 3, entitled "An Act Respecting the Withholding or Withdrawal of Treatment where Death Is Inevitable", 4th Session, 30th Legislature of Ontario (1973).

17. For details concerning these various forms of legislation, see H. Silving. "Euthanasia: A Study in Comparative Criminal Law" (1954) 103 *U. of Penn. Law Rev.* 350, and D. Maguire. *Death by Choice*. New York: Schocken, 1975.

18. See Maguire, *ibid.*, ch. 2, p. 22.

18a. See Law Reform Commission, Report No. 15.

19. E. Keyserlingk. *Sanctity of Life or Quality of Life*. Law Reform Commission of Canada, Ottawa: DSS, 1979.

20. Law Reform Commission of Canada. *Sterilization*, Working Paper No. 24. Ottawa: DSS, 1979.

20a. *Public Health Protection Act*, R.S.Q. 1977, c. P-35, ss. 42 and 43.

20b. See, for example, the *Child Welfare Act*, R.S.O. 1970, c. 64; the *Child Welfare Act*, R.S.A. 1970, c. 45.

21. See note 13.

22. K. Binding and A. Hoche. *The Release or the Destruction of Life Devoid of Value*. Los Angeles: R. Sassone, 1975 (Original German book published in 1920).

23. See *infra* Appendix I for a selected bibliography.

24. Y. Kamisar. "Some Non-Religious Views against Proposed 'Mercy-Killing' Legislation" (1958) 42 *Min. Law Rev.* 969.

APPENDIX I

Selected Bibliography

BARRIÈRE, I., and LALOU, E. *Le dossier confidentiel de l'euthanasie*. Paris: Stock, 1962.

BEAUCHAMP, T., and DAVIDSON, R. "The Definition of Euthanasia" (1979) 4 *J. of Medicine and Philosophy* 294.

BEHNKE, J. A., and BOK, S., eds. *The Dilemmas of Euthanasia*. New York: Anchor Books, 1975.

BINDING, K., and HOCHE, A. *The Release or the Destruction of Life Devoid of Value*. Los Angeles: R. Sassone, 1975 (Original German book published in 1920).

CHORON, J. *Suicide*. New York: Scribners, 1972.

CRANE, D. "Physicians' Attitudes toward the Treatment of Critically Ill Patients" (1973) 23 *Bio. Sc.* 471.

DELAGLANDE, J., and ARNAUD, R. «Réflexions sur l'euthanasie» (1962) *Études* 305.

DICKENS, B. "The Role of the Family in Surrogate Medical Consent" (1980) 1 *Health Law in Canada* 49.

"The Right to Natural Death" (1981) 26 *Mc Gill Law Journal* 847.

DOWNING, A., ed. *Euthanasia and the Right to Death*. London: Owen, 1977.

FLETCHER, G. "Prolonging Life" (1967) 42 *Wash. L. Rev.* 999.

FLETCHER, John. "Attitudes toward Defective Newborns" (1974) 2 *Hastings Center Studies* 21.

"Abortion, Euthanasia and Case of Defective Newborns" (1975) 292 *New England Journal of Medicine* 75.

FLETCHER, Joseph. "Ethics and Euthanasia" in Robert H. Williams, ed. *To Live and to Die: When, Why and How*. New York: Springer-Verlag, 1973, pp. 113 and following.

"The 'Right' to Live and the 'Right' to Die: A Protestant View of Euthanasia" (1974) 34 *Humanist* 12.

GARLAND, M. "Politics, Legislation and Natural Death" (1976) 6 *Hastings Center Report* 5.

HARRISON, C. "Medicine, Terminal Illness and the Law" (1977) 3 *Can. Med. Ass. J.* 177.

HORAN, D., and MALL, D. *Death, Dying and Euthanasia*. Washington D.C.: University Publications of America, 1977.

HUNTER, R. "Euthanasia" (1980) 25 *Can. J. Psych.* 439.

JARETZKI, A. "Death with Dignity — Passive Euthanasia: Guide to the Physician dealing with Dying Patients" (1976) 76 *N.Y. St. J. of Med.* 539.

JONAS, H. "The Right to Die" (1978) 8 *Hastings Center Report* 35.

KAMISAR, Y. "Some Non-Religious Views against Proposed 'Mercy-Killing' Legislation" (1958) 42 *Min. Law Rev.* 969.

KAPLAN, R. "Euthanasia Legislation: A Survey and a Model Act" (1976) 2 *Am. J. of Law and Med.* 41.

KENNEDY, I. "The Legal Effects of Requests by the Terminally Ill and Aged not to Receive further Treatment from Doctors" (1976) *Crim. L. Rev.* 217.

KEYSERLINGK, E. *Sanctity of Life or Quality of Life*, Study Paper. Law Reform Commission of Canada, Ottawa: DSS, 1979.

«Le testament de vie» (1979) 14 *Méd. du Québec* 63.

KLUGE, E. *The Practice of Death*. New Haven: Yale University Press, 1975.

The Ethics of Deliberate Death. Port Washington N.Y.: National University Publications, 1981.

KOHL, M. *The Morality of Killing*. London: Owen, 1974.

KOZA, P. "Euthanasia: Some Legal Considerations" (1976) 1 *Essence* 79.

KRAUSS, A. "Patients Who Want to Die: A Survey" (1977) *Can. Fam. Physician* 63.

KUBLER-ROSS, E. *On Death and Dying*. New York: MacMillan, 1969.

LAW REFORM COMMISSION OF CANADA. *Medical Treatment and Criminal Law*, Working Paper No. 26. Ottawa: DSS, 1980.

   Criteria for the Determination of Death, Report to Parliament No. 15. Ottawa: DSS, 1981.

   Definition of Death – Euthanasia. A study prepared by the Institute for Research on Contemporary Interpretations of Man, University of Sudbury, 1975.

LEVASSEUR, G. «Suicide et euthanasie en regard du droit pénal» (1957) 32 *Lumière et Vie* 183.

LOUISELL, D. "Euthanasia and Biothanasia: On Dying and Killing" (1973) 22 *Cath. U. L. Rev.* 723.

MAGUIRE, D. *Death by Choice*. New York: Schocken, 1975.

MANTOUT, P. «L'Euthanasie» (1973) 2 *Vie Méd.* 136.

MORRIS, A. "Voluntary Euthanasia" (1970) 45 *Wash. L. Rev.* 247.

NOLAN-HALEY, J. "Defective Children, Their Parents and the Death Decision" (1976) 4 *J. of Leg. Med.* 9.

NOTE. "The Tragic Choice: Termination of Care for Patients in a Permanent Vegetative State" (1976) 51 *N.Y.U. Law Rev.* 285.

PICARD, H. *Legal Liability of Doctors and Hospitals in Canada*. Toronto: Carswell, 1978.

RAMSEY, P. "Prolonged Dying: Not Medically Indicated" (1976) *Hastings Center Report* 14.

REIGH, W. "On the Birth of a Severely Handicapped Infant" (1973) 9 *Hastings Center Report* 10.

ROBERTSON, J. "Involuntary Euthanasia of Defective Newborns: A Legal Analysis" (1975) 27 *Stanford Law Rev.* 213.

SANDERS, J. "Euthanasia: None Dare Call It Murder" (1969) 60 *J. Crim. L. C. and P. S.* 351.

SILVING, H. "Euthanasia: A Study in Comparative Criminal Law" (1954) 103 *U. of Penn. L. Rev.* 350.

SKEGG, P. "Informed Consent to Medical Procedures" (1975) 15 *Med. Sc. and Law* 124.

SPORKEN, P. *Le droit de mourir*. Paris: Dexlée de Brower, 1974.

STARKMAN, B. "The Control of Life: Unexamined Law and the Life Worth Living" (1973) 11 *Osgoode Hall L.J.* 175.

"A Defence to Criminal Responsibility for Performing Surgical Operations: Section 45 of the *Criminal Code*" (1981) 26 *McGill Law Journal* 1048.

STEINBERG, M. "The California Natural Death Act — A Failure to Provide for Adequate Patient Safeguards and Individual Autonomy" (1977) 9 *Conn. Law Rev.* 203.

STEINFELS, P. and VEATCH, R. *Death Inside Out*. New York: Harper and Row, 1974.

TROWELL, H. *The Unfinished Debate on Euthanasia*. London: S.C.M. Press, 1973.

VAUGHAN, N.L. "The Right to Die" (1974) 10 *Cal. West. L. Rev.* 613.

VEATCH, R. "Death and Dying: The Legislative Option" (1977) *Hastings Center Report* 5.

WILLIAMS, G. "Euthanasia" (1973) 41 *Med. Leg. J.* 14.

The Sanctity of Life and the Criminal Law. London: Faber and Faber, 1958.

APPENDIX II

Glossary of Medical Terms

Anencephaly:	Absence of the brain.
Atresia of the digestive tract:	Total or partial obstruction of the digestive tract.
Down's syndrome:	Group of symptoms characteristic of trisomy 21.
Mongolism:	Anomalous condition associated with trisomy 21.
Spina bifida:	Congenital deformity of the vertebral column consisting of a hernial protrusion of a portion of the contents of the rachidian canal.
Trisomy 21:	Congenital anomaly characterized by the appearance of an additional chromosome in one pair. This anomaly produces the condition known as mongolism.

EUTHANASIE,
AIDE AU SUICIDE
ET
INTERRUPTION DE
TRAITEMENT

Disponible gratuitement par la poste

Commission de réforme du
droit du Canada
130, rue Albert, 7ᵉ étage
Ottawa, Canada
K1A 0L6

ou

Suite 2180
Place du Canada
Montréal (Québec)
H3B 2N2

Nᵒ de catalogue J32-1/28-1982
ISBN 0-662-51867-5

Réimpression 1982

Commission de réforme du droit du Canada

Document de travail 28

EUTHANASIE, AIDE AU SUICIDE ET INTERRUPTION DE TRAITEMENT

1982

Avis

Ce document de travail présente l'opinion de la Commission à l'heure actuelle. Son opinion définitive sera exprimée dans le rapport qu'elle présentera au ministre de la Justice et au Parlement, après avoir pris connaissance des commentaires faits dans l'intervalle par le public.

Par conséquent, la Commission serait heureuse de recevoir tout commentaire à l'adresse suivante:

Secrétaire
Commission de réforme du droit du Canada
130, rue Albert
Ottawa, Canada
K1A 0L6

La Commission

Francis C. Muldoon, c.r., président
Réjean F. Paul, c.r., vice-président
Louise D. Lemelin, commissaire
J. P. Joseph Maingot, c.r., commissaire*
Alan D. Reid, commissaire*

Secrétaire

Jean Côté

Commissaire responsable du projet

Louise D. Lemelin

Coordonnateur du projet

Edward W. Keyserlingk

Conseiller de recherche

Jean-Louis Baudouin

---

* N'était pas membre de la Commission lorsque le texte du présent document fut approuvé.

Conseillers

Janice Dillon
Gerry Ferguson
Dr Paul-André Meilleur
Marcia Rioux
Edward Ryan
Margaret Somerville
Dr R. E. Turner
Harvey Yarosky

Table des matières

Avant-propos

Les problèmes que posent au droit et à la morale l'interruption ou la cessation d'un traitement médical sont extrêmement complexes. Loin de revêtir un aspect seulement théorique ou académique, ils s'insèrent dans des situations que vivent chaque jour au Canada le public, les médecins et les membres du personnel hospitalier.

La Commission de réforme du droit a déjà publié plusieurs documents de travail et d'étude dans la série intitulée *Protection de la vie*[1]. Elle a de plus fait récemment part au Parlement canadien de ses recommandations finales sur les critères de détermination de la mort[2].

Lorsqu'en 1976 le projet de recherche a été conçu, il est très vite apparu que la question de la cessation de traitement et, d'une façon plus globale, celle de l'euthanasie, était une préoccupation constante et prioritaire du corps médical, d'un certain nombre de juristes, et d'une proportion importante du public canadien. C'est donc pour répondre à cette attente et à ce besoin qu'elle estime réels, que la Commission a décidé de publier un document de travail sur le problème.

Deux mises en garde extrêmement importantes doivent cependant être faites quant à la perspective de ce document d'une part, et quant aux buts qu'il poursuit d'autre part.

Ce document n'a, tout d'abord, aucunement la prétention de constituer un examen complet et exhaustif de la question. Il existe un nombre impressionnant de livres, d'articles et de documents sur la question, qui en traitent sous l'aspect historique, moral, théologique, social, littéraire, médical ou juridique.

1

Le lecteur trouvera d'ailleurs en annexe une courte bibliographie sommaire. *Ce document se veut donc essentiellement une synthèse, et une synthèse dans une orientation de politique législative au sens large du terme.* Le lecteur ne trouvera donc pas une analyse exhaustive de l'ensemble des questions et ne devra pas s'attendre non plus à une collecte complète de l'information sur le sujet.

Ce document, ensuite, fidèle à une optique particulière, poursuit des objectifs très précis et ceux-là seulement. Ils sont doubles.

D'une part, examiner un certain nombre de problèmes d'ordre moral et juridique que posent la cessation de traitement et l'euthanasie, en analyser les conséquences et en voir les effets sur la règle de droit actuelle et sur celle qui pourrait être la nôtre dans une perspective de réforme.

D'autre part, qui dit réforme dit également acceptation d'une orientation sociale générale dont la règle de droit n'est qu'une manifestation. Ce document a donc pour second objectif d'examiner certaines questions fondamentales de politique sociale et d'amener ainsi les spécialistes de la question et le public canadien lui-même à discuter franchement du problème. Une telle discussion est, en effet, indispensable comme base d'une éventuelle réforme juridique.

PREMIÈRE PARTIE

La définition des problèmes

Pour tous les systèmes de droit modernes, la protection de la vie humaine constitue une valeur fondamentale. Les lois, quelles que soient leurs variations spécifiques et le contexte culturel, politique ou social dans lequel elles s'épanouissent, sanctionnent toutes cette valeur à des degrés divers. Elles interdisent l'homicide; elles punissent les actes constituant un danger ou une menace sérieuse pour la vie d'autrui.

La préservation de la vie n'est toutefois pas une valeur absolue en soi, même pour le système juridique canadien. S'il en était ainsi, en effet, on n'aurait pas décriminalisé la tentative de suicide, ni reconnu la légitime défense. Les cas cependant où le droit ne sanctionne pas un comportement visant à supprimer une vie humaine sont peu nombreux, et sont de nature exceptionnelle.

Les dispositions du *Code criminel* canadien sur l'homicide (articles 205 à 223, *Code criminel*) envisagent la vie humaine dans une conception exclusivement quantitative et non qualitative. Il y a homicide si la victime de l'acte meurt. L'acte qui met fin à la vie active d'une personne, qui la condamne pour le reste de ses jours à un style ou une qualité de vie très diminuée est sanctionné par d'autres infractions (voies de fait, etc.). N'est pas meurtrier cependant celui qui par son acte rend sa victime incapable de mener une vie relationnelle normale.

Le droit reflète d'ailleurs de façon fidèle une attitude traditionnelle de la société qui, elle aussi, reconnaît que sur les plans moral, religieux, philosophique et social, la vie humaine

3

mérite une protection particulière. Cette reconnaissance de l'importance primordiale de la vie a souvent été exprimée par l'idée que la vie humaine avait un caractère sacré. On la dit parfois donnée par Dieu et l'homme n'en est que le dépositaire. Il ne lui appartient donc pas d'intervenir dans son déroulement et de la supprimer.

Il serait évidemment hors de propos, dans le présent document, de reprendre une analyse détaillée de ce principe. Une étude publiée par la Commission l'a déjà fait[3]. Il peut cependant être utile de décrire brièvement certains de ses effets.

Une application rigoriste du principe du caractère sacré de la vie a donné naissance à un courant de pensée connu sous le nom de courant «vitaliste», qui trouve ses adeptes à la fois en littérature, en philosophie, en sciences religieuses, en droit et en médecine. Pour les principaux tenants de cette thèse (il faut cependant tenir compte de nuances et de degrés importants au sein même de ce courant), la vie humaine est une valeur suprême et tout doit être mis en œuvre non seulement pour la préserver, mais aussi pour la prolonger et donc pour combattre la mort. Les considérations de qualité de vie deviennent secondaires et même sans importance. La vie au sens quantitatif du terme doit être sauvée, maintenue et prolongée parce qu'elle représente une valeur en soi.

Le vitalisme a trouvé certains échos au sein de la science et de la profession médicales. Traditionnellement, le principal rôle de la médecine est de tenter de sauver la vie et de la prolonger en luttant contre la maladie et la mort. Le succès ou l'échec se mesure donc, dans une certaine conception de la médecine, par la qualité, la force et l'agressivité du combat qui est mené. Dans cette perspective, l'agressivité de la lutte est un symbole d'excellence de la pratique de l'art médical. Cette optique d'un certain courant médical n'est certes pas blâmable en soi, puisqu'elle pousse le médecin à combattre la maladie et la mort, à ne pas abandonner, à ne pas s'avouer vaincu d'avance. Cette attitude de valorisation extrême de la vie humaine a longtemps été considérée par certains comme une

sorte de ligne de conduite absolue et immuable. L'évolution de la pratique de la médecine a toutefois quelque peu bouleversé cette vision traditionnelle.

Les progrès de la découverte scientifique et de la science médicale font qu'il est désormais possible de traiter des affections ou des maladies qui, antérieurement, étaient considérées comme incurables. Pour en prendre un exemple courant, les antibiotiques permettent facilement, à l'heure actuelle, de guérir des pneumonies chez un individu atteint d'un cancer en phase terminale, alors qu'avant cette découverte, le patient dans un tel cas, mourait de cette pneumonie.

La technologie médicale, pour sa part, a conçu une impressionnante série de machines et d'appareils permettant de prolonger une vie qui, autrefois, eût également été considérée comme perdue. Un arrêt cardiaque, une déficience rénale, un arrêt respiratoire n'entraînent plus nécessairement une issue fatale. L'emploi de cette technologie a contribué à diminuer considérablement le taux de mortalité prématurée. Il a en revanche sensiblement augmenté le nombre de personnes qui, après en avoir bénéficié, doivent se contenter de «survivre» dans un état de qualité de vie objectivement non satisfaisant. L'exemple classique est sans doute celui des personnes qui, ayant été sauvées par l'emploi ponctuel d'un respirateur, mais ayant malgré tout subi une cessation irréversible du fonctionnement de certaines parties de leur cerveau, sont condamnées à mener une vie végétative[4], sans aucun espoir d'en pouvoir sortir un jour pour réémerger dans une vie cognitive et relationnelle.

L'évolution de la science et de la technologie médicales représente pour l'humanité un incontestable progrès. Elle a, par contre, singulièrement compliqué les problèmes humains et les problèmes juridiques touchant la mort. Elle a obligé aussi à reconsidérer sérieusement l'aspect absolutiste de l'interprétation vitaliste classique fondée sur le principe du caractère sacré de la vie.

Le nombre de personnes qui meurent en milieu hospitalier s'est considérablement accru. Or, en milieu hospitalier, la

technologie est, en principe, présente. Il est aisé d'y recourir, même dans les cas où son utilisation n'a pas d'effets thérapeutiques véritables, mais ne fait que retarder de quelque temps une échéance inéluctable. La prolongation, par ces moyens, de la vie de certains patients en phase terminale, peut devenir incompatible avec les impératifs de la qualité de la vie qui reste à vivre au patient. Cette prolongation peut, en effet, se faire aux dépens même de la qualité de cette survie. On peut reprocher parfois à la décision de recourir à la technologie médicale, d'être principalement basée sur un critère technique (la chose est techniquement possible), mais de ne plus être fondée sur des considérations humaines pour le patient lui-même (la chose est humainement souhaitable). Une certaine équation est faite entre ce qui *peut* être fait et ce qui *doit* être fait, et tout se passe donc comme si, dans le combat contre la mort, l'arsenal technique devait en toutes circonstances être déployé complètement, sans qu'aucune considération qualitative n'entre en ligne de compte. On a fort bien qualifié cette attitude «d'acharnement thérapeutique» et on l'a sévèrement critiquée, en montrant qu'elle va souvent à l'encontre du meilleur intérêt du patient, qu'elle est déshumanisante, qu'elle détourne le progrès technologique de sa fin première qui reste le service de l'homme, et qu'au fond elle tend à prolonger bien plus le processus de la mort que la vie elle-même. Cette évolution oblige à reconsidérer sérieusement le caractère absolutiste de l'option vitaliste classique.

Depuis quelques années, surtout dans les pays occidentaux, un nouveau courant a vu le jour. Ce courant de pensée ne rejette pas l'idée que fondamentalement la vie humaine est une valeur importante et donc que les ressources médicales et technologiques doivent être mises en œuvre pour la conserver et la prolonger. Il ne souscrit pas cependant à l'interprétation vitaliste du principe du caractère sacré de la vie. Il tempère le vitalisme par des considérations de qualité de vie. La grande majorité des médecins, de nos jours, souscrivent nettement à cette optique. Les codes d'éthique médicale modernes reflètent d'ailleurs déjà ce changement[5] basé sur plusieurs facteurs. Le premier est souvent exprimé par un vocable devenu courant de nos jours: «la mort dans la dignité». L'individu peut vouloir

éliminer de son processus de mortalité les aspects déshumanisants que lui confère parfois l'utilisation abusive ou massive de la technologie médicale. Le second est la plus grande insistance de la part du patient à une participation directe dans le processus décisionnel concernant l'acte médical. De plus en plus le malade refuse de considérer le médecin comme une sorte de thaumaturge ou de se fier simplement à ce que certains ont qualifié de paternalisme médical. Il veut, au contraire, comprendre et parfois choisir, en toute liberté, la thérapie qui lui est proposée. Il ne faut pas y voir un acte de non-confiance à l'endroit de la profession médicale, mais plutôt une attitude saine de prise de responsabilités de la part du patient, qui permet d'ailleurs un meilleur rapport humain et professionnel entre lui et son médecin. Puisque le patient insiste de plus en plus pour que ce soit lui qui, en dernière analyse, fasse les choix, on doit admettre qu'il puisse refuser consciemment l'aide ou le soutien de la science ou de la technologie médicale et qu'il puisse par choix délibéré préférer une vie quantitativement plus courte mais qualitativement plus riche, à une existence prolongée mais de qualité inacceptable à ses yeux.

Le troisième est le développement relativement récent des soins palliatifs. Le choix de certains malades ne se résume plus maintenant entre la poursuite d'un traitement inutile et la cessation complète de tous soins. Il est désormais possible de cesser un traitement, lorsque le malade a atteint un stade terminal, mais d'entreprendre, par ailleurs, des soins palliatifs destinés à atténuer ou supprimer la douleur et à permettre un passage plus doux entre la vie et la mort.

Les problèmes juridiques touchant l'interruption de traitement sont fort complexes parce qu'ils se rattachent également à une question délicate et controversée, celle de l'euthanasie, et sont souvent mélangés avec elle. Indépendamment de cet aspect particulier qui sera également abordé dans ce document, trois genres de difficultés se trouvent à la base du problème de l'interruption de traitement. Il importe d'en faire état, de les discuter brièvement, pour pouvoir ensuite tenter d'en tirer pour le droit des règles de conduite concrètes.

La première difficulté vient du fait que notre société est, à l'heure actuelle, dans une période de transition. Les attitudes face à la vie et à la mort, face à la science et face à l'interruption de traitement sont en pleine mutation. Le changement n'est pas cependant complet ou complété. Nombre de personnes, par exemple, cherchent encore à définir plus précisément une attitude et une ligne de conduite respectueuses de la protection qui doit être donnée à la vie humaine, mais qui prennent aussi en considération d'autres valeurs comme l'autonomie décisionnelle de la personne et sa qualité de vie. Nous ne sommes pas encore parvenus à un stade où les apparentes contradictions entre la sauvegarde de la vie et les impératifs de qualité de vie sont entièrement dissipées. La chose est d'autant plus difficile que dans la prise de décision de traiter ou de ne pas traiter, il n'existe pas deux cas identiques et donc que l'individualité de chaque espèce rend très difficile l'établissement de normes générales qui pourraient paraître plus rassurantes ou plus sécurisantes.

La seconde difficulté se situe au niveau des rapports du droit et de la médecine. La règle de droit, surtout celle de droit criminel, a pour but de sanctionner une conduite jugée socialement répréhensible. Elle a donc avant tout un rôle répressif. Or, en la matière, on constate que jamais les annales jurisprudentielles des tribunaux canadiens n'ont apparemment condamné un médecin pour avoir abrégé la vie d'un de ses patients en phase terminale en lui administrant des doses massives de médicaments antidouleur. Jamais, semble-t-il, les tribunaux canadiens n'ont condamné un médecin qui, dans le cas d'un patient en phase terminale, a interrompu un traitement devenu inutile. Jamais, enfin, les tribunaux canadiens n'ont directement blâmé un médecin pour refus de prolonger l'agonie d'un patient en omettant de lui procurer des soins pour une affection secondaire.

Cette absence de jurisprudence ne veut cependant pas dire que de tels actes n'ont pas effectivement eu lieu. Elle ne signifie pas, non plus, que les tribunaux auraient nécessairement acquitté ou condamné un éventuel accusé. En d'autres termes, on ne peut pas considérer la situation juridique actuelle

comme satisfaisante uniquement parce qu'elle n'a pas donné naissance à des poursuites. Face à une telle situation, une bonne partie du corps médical et du personnel hospitalier regrettent de ne pas connaître les paramètres précis des obligations que la loi leur impose, et de ne pouvoir se fier en la matière qu'à la discrétion de ne pas initier des poursuites exercées par la Couronne.

La règle de droit, surtout en matière de droit criminel, doit aussi avoir un certain degré de prévisibilité dans son application. Il est normal qu'une personne puisse raisonnablement prédire l'interprétation que donneraient les tribunaux aux règles générales contenues au *Code criminel* et qui règlent sa conduite dans la société.

Or, la chose est certaine, médecins et juristes sont à l'heure actuelle dans la quasi-impossibilité de prédire avec certitude comment les textes du *Code criminel* actuel seraient effectivement appliqués dans une instance portant sur un cas de cessation de traitement. Certes, une étude analogique avec d'autres cas peut permettre, comme nous le verrons, d'établir en gros les bases théoriques d'une éventuelle responsabilité pénale. Celle-ci, cependant, reste difficile à déterminer avec précision.

Enfin, la troisième difficulté est la suivante. Indépendamment des inévitables variations propres à l'individualité de chaque cas, nombreux sont ceux qui s'inquiètent du fait que ce vacuum apparent puisse engendrer des différences importantes dans les pratiques et les conduites médicales à travers le pays. En l'absence de règles de conduite précises ou au moins de guide sur ce que les tribunaux jugeraient acceptable ou non acceptable, on peut craindre en effet que ces décisions soient prises pour des considérations essentiellement subjectives et personnelles, en fonction de la morale et de l'éthique propre à chaque praticien. Que cette crainte soit réelle ou non, il existe dès lors une plus forte possibilité d'inégalité dans l'application de la règle de conduite qui est susceptible de varier d'institution en institution, de province en province, de milieu en milieu.

En conclusion, la perception actuelle que le personnel médical a peu à craindre en matière de droit criminel est probablement juste. Elle est cependant loin d'être basée sur une certitude d'une part et, d'autre part, ne donne aucune véritable garantie quant à l'état de la règle. Il faut songer aussi que la politique actuelle de ne pas poursuivre pourrait venir à changer sous la pression des événements et qu'alors, un certain nombre de médecins pourraient faire les frais de «cas type», de façon à permettre de déterminer l'état actuel du droit sur la question. Il s'agit d'une question beaucoup trop importante et beaucoup trop fondamentale pour être abandonnée à un tel état d'incertitude. La cessation ou la non-initiation d'un traitement se pose en pratique particulièrement dans deux contextes factuels bien précis qu'il importe de décrire brièvement.

I. Le malade en phase terminale

Le premier cas est celui du malade en phase terminale, c'est-à-dire de celui qui a atteint l'étape où l'administration de soins thérapeutiques est devenue médicalement inutile pour assurer une guérison éventuelle ou même un contrôle efficace de la maladie. À partir de ce moment, l'intérêt habituel du patient est de pallier le mieux possible les souffrances physiques et morales qui peuvent accompagner cette phase terminale. Comme nous l'ont confirmé plusieurs des médecins que nous avons consultés, les exigences du patient changent à partir du moment où il réalise avec certitude que la guérison est exclue et que la mort est devenue inévitable. Le patient veut alors fondamentalement un contrôle efficace de ses symptômes et que le temps qui lui reste à vivre puisse être vécu par lui le plus confortablement possible. Pour plusieurs comme lui, il est également important que ce passage se fasse dans la dignité et dans la lucidité et qu'en soient absentes les interventions chirurgicales ou autres ayant un caractère mutilant ou perçues comme dégradantes. C'est d'ailleurs pourquoi la cessation d'un traitement perçu comme inutile et potentiellement dégradant, est souvent prise à la suggestion du patient lui-même.

Deux problèmes concrets se posent alors au niveau d'une éventuelle application de la règle de droit.

Le premier est qu'en théorie et traditionnellement l'interruption d'une mesure destinée à sauver la vie de quelqu'un, lorsque cette mesure a déjà été entreprise, peut servir à fonder une responsabilité civile et pénale. Dans le cas d'un patient inconscient en phase terminale, un médecin ou un hôpital pourraient fort bien, par crainte d'éventuelles poursuites, retarder la décision d'interrompre un traitement devenu inutile, ou décider au contraire de le continuer. Une telle éventualité mène à un résultat totalement absurde! Pour préserver la vie (prise ici au sens quantitatif du terme) de l'individu et peut-être par crainte de la loi, on fait bon marché de la qualité des instants qui lui restent à vivre. Ces exagérations et ces craintes compréhensibles, étant donné le peu de précision de la loi actuelle, donnent naissance à des mouvements comme ceux qui, en Californie par exemple, ont soutenu le *Natural Death Act*. Il nous semble inutile et surtout dangereux d'aboutir à de tels extrêmes. Notre système de droit, quel qu'en soit le moyen, devrait pouvoir consacrer l'idée qu'un patient en phase terminale a un droit non pas secondaire ou subordonné mais principal à mourir avec dignité et à ne pas être victime de mesures d'acharnement thérapeutique. Pour ce faire, il doit être clairement dit qu'un médecin n'a rien à craindre des foudres du droit criminel ou civil, à partir du moment où, en phase terminale, il interrompt ou refuse d'engager un traitement médicalement inutile qui ne ferait que prolonger le processus de mort ou d'agonie, à moins d'en être expressément requis par son patient. C'est donc, à première vue dans ce cas, beaucoup plus une clarification de la portée réelle du droit actuel qu'un changement fondamental des règles de droit qui paraît utile.

Le second problème est relié aux soins palliatifs. La médecine moderne dispose de méthodes et de médicaments aptes à éliminer ou à réduire la souffrance à un seuil acceptable dans la majorité des cas. L'expérience de certains centres spécialisés au Canada (notamment à Montréal) et en Angleterre, a montré que la chose était faisable. Les seules limites véritables à sa

généralisation restent une plus grande dissémination parmi le corps médical de l'expertise déjà acquise et un développement plus systématique de la recherche dans ce domaine.

Le contrôle de la souffrance implique souvent l'utilisation de narcotiques ou de médicaments qui, à long terme, peuvent provoquer un effet d'accoutumance. De plus, au fur et à mesure de la progression de la maladie, il est souvent nécessaire d'accroître sensiblement le dosage. Survient alors un seuil où un dosage supérieur peut avoir comme effet secondaire d'abréger la vie du patient. Cette réalité fait hésiter certains médecins, pour les mêmes raisons que celles que nous avons décrites plus haut. D'aucuns craignent, en effet, de s'exposer à des poursuites pénales, civiles ou disciplinaires, en administrant au patient en phase terminale des soins efficaces sur le plan strictement palliatif, mais qui ont pour effet de diminuer l'expectative de survie du patient. Là encore, à notre avis, l'ambiguïté de la portée des solutions juridiques actuelles peut avoir pour effet de promouvoir une mauvaise pratique médicale, d'encourager une médecine qui n'est plus au service du patient, en restreignant l'administration de soins palliatifs valables.

Dans ces deux cas donc, l'incertitude peut véritablement détourner la science médicale de ses buts et objectifs normaux et valables, objectifs qui devraient être clairement admis et reconnus par le droit, de façon à lever cette véritable épée de Damoclès.

II.   Le nouveau-né souffrant de malformations graves

La mortalité infantile qui, il y a à peine cinquante ans, faisait des ravages au Canada, a vu son taux diminuer de façon très significative depuis le milieu des années cinquante. Plusieurs hôpitaux ont créé des centres de soins intensifs pour nouveau-nés, sauvant ainsi de la mort des enfants qui, en raison de certaines maladies, difformités ou tout simplement de leur naissance prématurée, n'auraient pas normalement

survécu. De plus, la chirurgie néo-natale a fait des progrès considérables et permet de traiter désormais certains cas qui eussent été considérés comme terminaux il y a quelques années.

Ce développement institutionnel, joint au progrès de la science néonatologique, a par contre amené lui aussi une série de nouveaux problèmes. On voit, en effet, survivre de nos jours des enfants qui ont subi à la naissance des dommages tels qu'ils ne pourront se développer normalement. Certains d'entre eux devront être mis en institution. D'autres pourront rejoindre leur famille, mais imposeront à celle-ci d'énormes sacrifices sur les plans financier, affectif et psychologique.

Le problème des nouveau-nés souffrant de difformités graves est complexe. Un nouveau-né peut être atteint à des degrés très divers. Il existe des anomalies chromosomiques dont les effets varient grandement selon chaque individu. Par exemple, un *spina bifida** est susceptible de variations significatives, allant du plus sérieux handicap à une affection qui peut demeurer relativement bénigne.

De plus, deux autres considérations ajoutent à la complexité de la situation. Le nouveau-né tout d'abord, à la différence du patient adulte conscient, est incapable de prendre une décision pour lui-même. D'autres (parents, tuteur, médecin) vont donc être appelés à le faire pour lui et en son nom. Parfois, cette prise de décision implique de laisser mourir l'enfant, en présumant peut-être que si celui-ci, comme le patient en phase terminale, avait pu prendre lui-même la décision, c'est bien celle-là qu'il aurait choisie. Ensuite, il existe un facteur négatif additionnel susceptible d'affecter la perception de celui qui a à prendre les décisions: le nouveau-né souffrant de malformations graves est un être humain qui vient tout juste d'accéder à une vie indépendante et pour lequel, pourtant, la mort est une éventualité déjà présente.

Sans vouloir généraliser des situations qui ont toutes un aspect individuel important, le problème des nouveau-nés souffrant de malformations sérieuses se pose dans deux contextes différents sur le plan de la morale et du droit.

_____
* Voir Annexe II

Le premier cas est celui de l'enfant qui, dès sa naissance, souffre de malformations telles que, dans l'état actuel de la science, il est certain qu'il ne survivra pas au-delà de quelques heures ou de quelques jours. C'est le cas, par exemple, de l'anencéphale* ou de l'enfant affecté d'un *spina bifida** sérieux. Dans ce cas, malgré le paradoxe apparent, l'enfant est dès sa naissance engagé dans un processus de mortalité devant lequel la science est impuissante. Il n'existe pas de traitement approprié ou les traitements qui pourraient être appliqués paraissent médicalement inutiles. Le problème est alors identique à celui de l'adulte en phase terminale. Le devoir du médecin n'est certes pas d'abandonner l'enfant, pas plus qu'il n'abandonnerait son patient adulte mourant, mais de lui donner les soins palliatifs appropriés et d'éviter un acharnement thérapeutique inutile.

Le second cas, qui encore une fois est susceptible d'énormes variations de degrés, est celui de l'enfant malformé qui, sans traitement, est vraisemblablement condamné à mort à court terme, mais pour lequel la médecine peut objectivement faire quelque chose. Là encore, la très grande difficulté d'analyse vient du fait que ce traitement peut être plus ou moins complexe, plus ou moins usité, plus ou moins long. Prenons, pour simples fins d'illustration, un exemple connu, celui du nouveau-né atteint d'une trisomie 21* et souffrant d'une atrésie* du tube digestif. Si une opération chirurgicale, relativement bénigne et simple dans des circonstances normales, n'est pas pratiquée, l'enfant sera incapable de se nourrir et mourra donc d'inanition.

D'une façon générale, deux hypothèses sont possibles. Elles conduisent à des effets différents sur le plan moral et juridique. Dans la première, le diagnostic révèle que l'enfant trisomique n'a pas d'autres malformations sérieuses. Dans la seconde, le diagnostic révèle que l'enfant, en plus de cette atrésie*, souffre aussi d'autres malformations importantes (malformations cardiaques, etc.), pour lesquelles il n'existe pas de remède approprié ou qui vont nécessiter une longue série d'interventions chirurgicales. Ces deux cas présentent clairement un problème de jugement de valeur sur la qualité de la

---

* Voir Annexe II

14

vie de l'enfant. En pratique, ce sont les parents, en collaboration avec le médecin, qui vont prendre la décision d'effectuer l'opération ou de ne pas l'effectuer. Cette décision est directement fonction d'un jugement de valeur sur la qualité de la vie future de l'enfant. Certains estimeront que celle-ci est trop faible et, en toute honnêteté et conscience, refuseront l'opération. D'autres, au contraire, l'autoriseront, conscients du fait que celle-ci restaurera une certaine capacité fonctionnelle, mais ne fera rien pour améliorer l'état général. Sur le plan de l'éthique et du droit, il n'y a pas de doute qu'un refus de traitement dans cette première hypothèse, et dans l'état actuel de la règle de droit, peut être générateur de responsabilité civile et criminelle. La situation s'est apparemment déjà posée au Canada. Certaines poursuites qui éventuellement devaient être prises sur cette base factuelle, notamment en Colombie-Britannique, ne l'ont finalement pas été ou ont été abandonnées[6].

La seconde hypothèse est très différente. En effet, il ne s'agit plus d'administrer un seul traitement bénin pour assurer la survie, mais de replacer cette décision dans un ensemble. Le problème serait d'ailleurs le même pour un adulte: vaut-il la peine de soigner une pneumonie chez un patient dont les reins ne fonctionnent plus, dont le cœur a déjà donné des signes de grande faiblesse, et qui nécessiterait donc une greffe rénale et un pontage? Vaut-il la peine de procéder à une opération bénigne sur un enfant qui, en raison de malformations cardiaques ou autres, a une expectative de vie très réduite, est paralysé complètement à partir de la taille, souffre de convulsions sévères et aura besoin dans le court temps qui lui reste à vivre d'une série d'opérations douloureuses sans pouvoir jamais se développer sur le plan de la communication avec le monde extérieur? Il est probable que devant une telle situation, le droit ne porterait aucun blâme à l'endroit du médecin ou des parents qui décideraient de ne pas soumettre l'enfant à ce processus et donc de laisser la nature suivre son cours, tout en prodiguant les soins palliatifs nécessaires.

Vu du côté du médecin, le problème du nouveau-né présente des analogies certaines avec celui du patient en phase

terminale. S'il décide d'entreprendre un traitement, la loi ou le droit ne va-t-il pas l'obliger ensuite à le poursuivre, alors même qu'à un moment donné la chose n'est plus véritablement utile? Peut-il, sans risques, interrompre une thérapie agressive et simplement laisser la nature suivre son cours? Doit-il le faire avec l'accord des parents? Ceux-ci ont-ils seuls le droit de prendre la décision? Autant de problèmes qui se posent à l'heure actuelle avec acuité dans la pratique hospitalière courante et auxquels, il faut bien l'avouer, le droit n'apporte pas les réponses précises que certains souhaiteraient. Là encore, il serait socialement fort regrettable que les décisions médicales ne soient conditionnées que par l'éventuelle menace de sanctions civiles ou criminelles.

DEUXIÈME PARTIE

Les réponses du droit actuel

Le *Code criminel* canadien, dans sa Partie VI portant sur les infractions contre la personne (articles 196 et suivants), contient une série de dispositions visant à protéger la vie et la sécurité physique des individus. Il serait hors de propos dans le présent document d'en présenter une analyse législative et jurisprudentielle détaillée. La plupart ont une portée générale et ne sont pas restreintes simplement au traitement médical. De plus, notre Document de travail n° 26 sur le traitement médical et le droit criminel contient déjà une analyse de ces textes à laquelle le lecteur pourra donc se référer[7].

Par contre, il est indispensable d'expliquer brièvement et de façon synthétique la portée de certaines dispositions spécifiques touchant les problèmes qui nous concernent et de décrire aussi la façon dont ces textes ont été appliqués dans la pratique courante jusqu'ici. Enfin, pour permettre une analyse plus critique de la situation, il est utile de donner quelques éléments de droit comparé.

I. Les textes

L'article 197 du *Code criminel*, en premier lieu, impose à un certain nombre de personnes (parents, tuteur, époux, etc.) l'obligation de fournir à ceux qui dépendent d'eux les choses nécessaires à la vie. La jurisprudence a interprété ce texte comme susceptible de s'appliquer à la situation où un membre du personnel médical néglige ou refuse de fournir des soins

médicaux à une personne, à condition que toutes les autres conditions de l'infraction soient également remplies[8], notamment que cette personne soit inapte à prendre soin d'elle-même. Le médecin qui négligerait d'administrer un traitement à une personne inconsciente pourrait donc, dans certaines circonstances, être passible de poursuites en vertu de l'article 197 du *Code criminel*.

Les articles 198 et 199 du *Code criminel* en second lieu, contiennent deux sortes d'obligations. Le premier article oblige celui qui entreprend un traitement médical ou chirurgical susceptible de mettre la vie en danger, d'employer une connaissance, une habileté et des soins raisonnables. Le second oblige celui qui entreprend un acte à le continuer si l'omission de le faire comporte un danger pour la vie[9].

L'emploi par l'article 198 du mot «raisonnable» laisse évidemment une large part à l'évaluation des circonstances particulières de chaque cause. En matière médicale, il fait donc référence à la pratique médicale et à ce qui peut être considéré comme raisonnable dans les circonstances de chaque cas. Ainsi, il est probable qu'à l'heure actuelle, un tribunal estimerait raisonnable de la part d'un médecin de ne pas tenter de «ressusciter» une personne en état de coma dépassé. Par contre, il est beaucoup moins certain qu'il absoudrait de toute responsabilité celui qui, ayant entrepris de traiter un nouveau-né atteint de malformation, déciderait ensuite de ne pas procéder à une opération chirurgicale bénigne pour lui sauver la vie, sur la seule base d'un jugement personnel sur l'éventuelle qualité de vie de celui-ci. De même, on peut probablement prétendre que ne seraient pas «raisonnables» des «traitements» ayant pour effet d'imposer à un patient en phase terminale un fardeau disproportionné d'inconvénients ou de souffrances.

L'article 199 du *Code criminel* de son côté impose l'obligation générale de continuer un acte entrepris, si l'omission de le faire peut être dangereuse pour la vie. Il mérite quelques commentaires particuliers. Notre droit criminel, à la suite d'une longue tradition, refuse en général d'imposer une responsabilité

pénale à celui qui omet d'agir, de poser un geste, de faire un acte positif, sauf lorsque la loi lui impose spécifiquement une obligation d'agir. Si donc l'action est en général susceptible de criminalisation, la simple inaction ou omission ne l'est pas, à moins qu'un devoir d'agir dans des circonstances précises n'ait été prévu et imposé par la loi. En matière de traitement médical, cet article a donc une grande importance, surtout lorsqu'il est lu en conjonction avec l'article 198. En effet, la cessation d'un traitement qui risque de mettre en danger la vie d'un patient (par exemple l'arrêt d'un respirateur), *semble* tomber directement sous le coup de cette disposition de la loi criminelle. C'est du moins la crainte maintes fois exprimée par les membres du corps médical.

La règle de l'article 199 du *Code criminel* lue seule donne à penser que le médecin qui a entrepris un traitement, n'a pas le droit de l'interrompre si cette interruption comporte un risque pour la vie du patient. Si tel était le cas, la loi imposerait l'acharnement thérapeutique. Elle aurait aussi pour effet, dans bien des cas, de faire sérieusement hésiter les médecins à entreprendre un traitement, par crainte précisément de ne pouvoir l'interrompre par la suite, lorsqu'ils ne l'estiment plus utile. Cette règle, si telle était sa portée, toucherait à l'absurde et aurait des conséquences funestes sur la pratique de la médecine.

L'article 199 ne doit cependant pas être lu de façon isolée, mais plutôt en conjonction avec les autres dispositions du *Code criminel*, notamment avec l'article 45 et les textes sur la négligence criminelle. L'article 45 protège de la responsabilité criminelle celui qui exécute sur un autre une opération chirurgicale pour le bénéfice de ce dernier, lorsqu'il était raisonnable de la pratiquer eu égard à l'état de santé du patient. On voit ici réapparaître le standard de conduite principal auquel se fie la loi: celui du caractère raisonnable de l'acte dans les circonstances. Les textes touchant la négligence criminelle imposent eux un standard particulier de conduite. La loi ne pénalise pas n'importe quelle négligence et donc n'importe quelle interruption de traitement qui met la vie en danger, mais seulement celle qui démontre de la part de son auteur une insouciance déréglée ou téméraire.

19

Un exemple permettra d'illustrer cette nuance: le fait pour un médecin d'arrêter un respirateur en sachant qu'en ce faisant, le patient va cesser d'être ventilé et donc probablement mourir. Supposons, dans un premier cas, qu'avant de poser ce geste, il se soit assuré selon les procédures et tests utilisés couramment par la pratique médicale, que le patient est déjà en état de coma dépassé. L'interruption du respirateur, même si elle peut constituer techniquement un acte positif d'interruption de traitement susceptible de tomber dans le champ de l'article 199, ne pourrait servir alors à fonder une responsabilité pénale. La continuation du traitement dans ce cas n'est pas raisonnable eu égard à l'état du patient d'une part et d'autre part son interruption ne manifeste pas une insouciance déréglée ou téméraire de la part de l'homme de science. Supposons, par contre, que ce même médecin, sans prendre la précaution de s'assurer de l'état du patient, pose le même geste. Il y aurait alors probablement lieu de lui appliquer les dispositions de ces textes, puisqu'il manifeste une insouciance déréglée ou téméraire pour la vie ou la sécurité de son patient, en interrompant un traitement sans prendre la précaution de s'assurer qu'une telle interruption ne se fera pas aux dépens de celui-ci.

En troisième lieu, les articles 202 à 223 du *Code criminel* traitent de la négligence criminelle et des différentes sortes d'homicide. Ils revêtent une importance particulière dans le contexte de notre discussion. Nous nous limiterons, là encore, à une brève analyse dans ce contexte particulier, renvoyant le lecteur pour de plus amples détails au document de travail sur l'homicide que la Commission publiera dans un avenir rapproché. Toute mort d'homme causée par un autre ne constitue pas nécessairement un homicide coupable. Pour être coupable, il faut, en résumé, que la mort d'un individu ait été causée par un acte illégal ou par une négligence criminelle. À l'intérieur de la catégorie de l'homicide coupable, la loi distingue en outre l'homicide involontaire et le meurtre. La différence se situe au niveau de l'intention de l'agent, laquelle, dans le cas du meurtre, est de tuer ou de causer des blessures en sachant qu'elles sont susceptibles de causer la mort, tout en étant indifférent au fait que la mort survienne ou non.

Pour le meurtre, notre législateur ne fait aucunement entrer en ligne de compte la motivation de son auteur. Seule compte l'intention de supprimer la vie. Qu'une personne donc en tue une autre par vengeance, par lucre, par cupidité, par compassion ou par charité, peu importe. Elle est, dans tous les cas, coupable de meurtre si elle avait vraiment l'intention de causer la mort. Notre droit ne tient pas compte non plus, comme l'énonce l'article 14 du *Code criminel*, du consentement de la victime à sa mort. Ce consentement n'a aucune influence sur la responsabilité pénale de l'auteur. La personne qui, par compassion et pour mettre fin aux souffrances d'un proche, le tue, reste donc coupable de meurtre, même s'il est démontré que la victime voulait la mort et l'avait même priée de la lui donner. Le droit canadien, comme d'ailleurs la plupart des autres systèmes juridiques, prohibe donc l'euthanasie active ou positive, la considérant comme un meurtre pur et simple.

Le droit canadien a récemment décriminalisé la tentative de suicide. Par contre, il a maintenu à l'article 224 du *Code criminel* une infraction punissable de quatorze ans de prison pour quiconque conseille une personne de se suicider ou l'aide à le faire. Cette législation, dont on retrouve le modèle dans le droit anglais et la plupart des droits des États américains, a fait l'objet récemment de vives attaques de la part de certains groupes comme *Exit* ou *Hemlock* qui revendiquent l'abolition de ce type de prohibition au nom du droit à l'autodétermination de la personne. Une revue rapide de la jurisprudence canadienne montre que ce texte est très rarement invoqué en pratique. Cependant, la différence qui sépare l'assistance au suicide et la participation directe à un homicide est parfois difficile à cerner. Qu'en est-il, par exemple, de celui qui, à la demande d'un autre, prépare un poison et le laisse sur la table de chevet du mourant pour que ce dernier se l'administre lui-même, par rapport à celui qui aide le malade à l'ingurgiter ou qui l'administre directement à la demande du mourant incapable de le prendre lui-même?

Le droit consacre donc une certaine différence entre deux types de conduite: l'action de tuer et l'inaction de laisser

mourir. Cette différence qui est d'ailleurs très importante, trouve une résonance au niveau des règles de morale et de déontologie médicale. Tuer de façon voulue et délibérée, c'est éliminer directement toute chance, tout espoir, toute possibilité, aussi lointaine soit-elle, d'une guérison ou d'une prolongation éventuelle de la vie. Le geste est considéré comme immoral, contraire à l'éthique médicale et illégal. Laisser mourir (dans notre contexte, par exemple en interrompant un traitement qui n'est plus nécessaire) ne prive pas nécessairement l'individu de cette chance. L'interruption peut simplement replacer les choses dans l'état où elles étaient avant que le traitement ne soit entrepris et permettre à la nature de reprendre son cours.

En résumé donc, l'interruption de traitement, comme d'ailleurs son administration, peut tomber sous le coup d'un ensemble relativement complexe de dispositions du *Code criminel* allant des voies de fait à l'homicide, en passant par le défaut de fournir les choses essentielles à la vie, le défaut de faire preuve de connaissance, d'habileté et de soins raisonnables et l'aide au suicide. Toutefois, ces infractions ne doivent pas être interprétées de façon isolée, mais dans un contexte général. Le caractère parfois vague de leur formulation rend, il est vrai, difficile de tracer le périmètre exact de leur champ d'application en matière médicale. C'est beaucoup plus de ce fait que des dispositions en elles-mêmes et des valeurs qu'elles représentent, que proviennent les difficultés actuelles.

II. L'application des textes

Ces différents textes du *Code criminel* (notamment ceux concernant l'homicide et la négligence criminelle) ont naturellement donné naissance à une abondante jurisprudence. Par contre, il est frappant de constater que l'application de ces textes et de ceux concernant le traitement médical à des médecins ou à des affaires relevant directement d'un contexte médical est rarissime, sinon inexistante. Il en est de même, au Canada, pour les poursuites intentées sur la base des dispositions sur le meurtre dans des cas de meurtre par compassion ou d'euthanasie volontaire.

22

On peut penser que cette absence quasi-totale de poursuites criminelles dirigées contre des médecins ou des membres du personnel hospitalier démontrerait que ceux-ci ont, au fond, bien peu à craindre en pratique d'éventuels procès criminels. Ceci d'autant plus, comme l'a très justement noté un auteur[10], que dans les rares cas où des poursuites ont été effectivement prises, le taux d'acquittement a été sensiblement élevé. La plupart de ces instances portaient d'ailleurs sur une erreur de diagnostic ou de traitement ayant entraîné la mort. On ne retrouve, par contre, aucune cause portant sur l'obligation du médecin de continuer un traitement déjà entrepris. Il est donc permis de s'interroger sur le fossé qui semble séparer l'apparente rigueur des textes et leur manque d'application pratique.

En matière de traitement médical tout d'abord, plusieurs raisons peuvent être invoquées pour expliquer cet état de choses. La première est que le standard de négligence que fixe le droit criminel comme condition à la responsabilité pénale est élevé. Seuls les cas d'erreur et de fautes lourdes, grossières ou intentionnelles font l'objet des préoccupations du droit criminel. La qualité de la médecine au Canada est telle que ces hypothèses sont heureusement relativement rares. S'il y a violation d'un standard moins élevé, la faute et la responsabilité civiles sont là pour apporter un remède adéquat à la situation, sous la forme d'une compensation en dommages et intérêts.

La seconde est que, même en cas d'entorse à la norme du droit criminel, la poursuite se heurte en pratique à certaines difficultés, notamment quant à l'établissement d'un lien de causalité suffisant entre l'acte et le résultat de l'acte. L'affaire St-Germain en est une bonne illustration[11].

La troisième que l'on tend parfois à oublier, est que notre système de justice pénale comporte une série de processus de filtrage des poursuites faisant que tous les cas effectivement découverts ne font pas automatiquement l'objet d'une poursuite par le bureau du procureur général. Il existe, en la matière, une marge respectable de discrétion dans l'administration de la poursuite pénale. Seuls les cas d'abus les

plus flagrants attirent l'attention des autorités. Parmi ceux-ci, seuls ceux où la preuve amassée donne une espérance de réussite sont effectivement poursuivis. Le nombre des cas portés à l'attention des autorités étant au départ peu élevé, il est normal que le chiffre des poursuites soit lui-même encore plus faible.

La situation est pratiquement la même pour ce qui est des cas d'euthanasie active ou de meurtre par compassion. Au Canada, les poursuites sont très rares. On peut cependant rappeler une affaire récente qui s'est passée à Montréal, où une personne fut trouvée coupable pour avoir tué par compassion un de ses amis paraplégique, à la demande de ce dernier[11a]. Ce phénomène n'est toutefois pas particulier au Canada. Dans un pays beaucoup plus populeux que le nôtre, les États-Unis, les instances judiciaires portant sur l'euthanasie active se comptent, en effet, pratiquement sur les doigts de la main.

Cette relative absence de poursuites reflète peut-être une certaine ambiguïté dans la pensée et la conduite de ceux qui sont responsables de l'administration du système de justice criminelle (témoins, officiers de police, procureurs, jurés, etc.). On peut penser que, dans le cas d'un meurtre par compassion, certains témoins qui ont connaissance du fait préfèrent rester dans l'ombre et ne pas le porter à la connaissance des autorités, alors qu'ils ne se gêneraient pas pour le faire si l'acte, par exemple, était motivé par la vengeance. On peut aussi soupçonner que la police n'est pas naturellement encline à porter des accusations dans ce cas; que le bureau des poursuites n'est pas pressé d'entreprendre celles-ci; que les jurés sont réticents à prononcer un verdict de culpabilité. On peut donc croire, même si le motif n'intervient aucunement au niveau de la loi elle-même, que toutes ces personnes font, elles, délibérément ou intuitivement, une distinction importante entre le meurtre ordinaire et le meurtre par compassion et que les motifs de l'agent et les circonstances de l'espèce font à leurs yeux, de son auteur, non un meurtrier véritable qui mérite les foudres de la loi, mais une personne ayant agi par compassion ou par charité et dont la conduite mérite donc plutôt une approbation, au moins tacite.

24

Pour le juriste cependant, de même que pour le personnel médical, l'absence de poursuites est paradoxalement un handicap sérieux. En effet, c'est par la jurisprudence et par l'accumulation des précédents judiciaires qu'il est possible, à un moment précis de l'évolution du droit, de déterminer le seuil de tolérance sociale et, sur le plan pratique, le contenu exact de l'intensité des obligations imposées par la loi. S'il est probablement relativement facile d'établir au Canada le standard de comportement que doit avoir un automobiliste pour ne pas être accusé de négligence criminelle, il est au contraire fort malaisé de le faire pour un médecin, un infirmier ou une infirmière. Loin de nous cependant la pensée de souhaiter un accroissement des poursuites contre ces personnes aux seules fins de découvrir le contenu exact des règles de droit.

III. Le droit comparé

Un bref examen des solutions offertes à ces divers problèmes par les systèmes juridiques de certains autres pays est instructif.

Dans un premier groupe, qui comprend surtout les pays de tradition britannique, les solutions sont, à peu de choses près, les mêmes que celles du droit canadien. En Grande-Bretagne, une cause de jurisprudence malheureusement non rapportée a, en 1957, jeté une certaine lumière sur les limites de l'administration du traitement médical. Dans l'affaire *Adams*, un médecin fut accusé de meurtre pour avoir administré à l'un de ses patients en phase terminale une forte dose de drogue antidouleur. La Cour, qui acquitta le médecin, émit l'opinion suivante sur l'état du droit anglais:

[TRADUCTION]
Si le but premier de la médecine — le recouvrement de la santé — ne pouvait plus être atteint, il restait encore beaucoup à faire pour le médecin. Il était de son devoir de faire tout ce qui était utile et nécessaire pour soulager la douleur et la souffrance, même si les mesures qu'il prenait pouvaient, par incidence, raccourcir la vie ...[11b]

Il ne s'agit là cependant que d'une opinion isolée et non d'une règle mise au point par une tradition jurisprudentielle véritable. Il n'est pas certain non plus qu'elle représente fidèlement l'état du common law.

En Grande-Bretagne toujours, de nombreuses tentatives ont été faites pour essayer d'introduire une législation qui aurait pour effet de légaliser l'euthanasie active à certaines conditions et donc de décriminaliser l'aide au suicide et le meurtre par compassion. Le premier de ces mouvements eut lieu au début des années trente avec la formation de l'*English Euthanasia Society*[12]. Après une longue interruption, le mouvement reprit de l'ampleur vers le début des années cinquante, lorsque Lord Chorley provoqua un débat à la Chambre des Lords sur la question. En 1958, Glanville Williams publiait ses pages célèbres dans lesquelles il se déclarait favorable à l'euthanasie volontaire et positive[13]. Depuis cette époque, le débat s'est ravivé même si, du côté médical, la *British Medical Association* en 1971 prononçait une condamnation sévère de cette pratique. Plusieurs tentatives pour introduire une législation sur le sujet ont été faites, notamment en 1950, 1969 et 1976, mais sans résultats concrets. Fait significatif cependant, alors qu'en 1953 la *Royal Commission on Capital Punishment* concluait qu'il était dangereux de faire du meurtre par compassion une infraction distincte du meurtre ordinaire, le *Criminal Law Revision Committee*, en 1976, recommandait le contraire. Cette dernière recommandation n'a cependant pas été adoptée.

Aux États-Unis, quelques affaires célèbres, comme l'affaire *Quinlan* et l'affaire *Saikewicz*, ont permis aux tribunaux de cerner un peu mieux les pourtours exacts de l'obligation de traiter et de déterminer, avec plus de précision, les circonstances dans lesquelles il devenait légitime d'interrompre les soins. Il faut cependant tenir compte du fait que chacune de ces instances présentait des caractéristiques individuelles particulières et qu'il est difficile, par extrapolation, d'en tirer une norme d'application générale et universelle.

À partir de 1970, un nouveau courant est apparu aux États-Unis. Ce courant s'est matérialisé dans la législation californienne intitulée le *Natural Death Act* imité par d'autres États[14]. Aucun des différents projets de loi de ce genre ne préconise toutefois la reconnaissance de l'euthanasie comme on l'a parfois laissé croire. Ils traitent tous d'un problème différent: l'acharnement thérapeutique et la cessation de traitement.

Comme l'indique clairement le préambule de la législation californienne, le but premier de la loi est de répondre à un problème concret: comment assurer à chaque individu le contrôle du pouvoir décisionnel sur la continuation ou la cessation d'un traitement médical et comment éliminer l'incertitude qui existe sur l'étendue de l'obligation du médecin de pourvoir aux soins.

Le *Natural Death Act* permet au patient de donner une directive écrite (*living will*) valable sur le plan juridique, contenant des instructions à l'effet qu'il n'entend pas bénéficier de mesures de prolongement artificiel de la vie, s'il est atteint d'une maladie incurable (telle que définie par la loi), et est alors dans l'impossibilité de manifester sa volonté. La loi prévoit que ces directives peuvent être révoquées. L'impact principal de la loi quant aux médecins et au personnel hospitalier, est de les mettre à l'abri de poursuites civiles ou criminelles qui pourraient être intentées sur la base du refus d'entreprendre ou de continuer un traitement. Plusieurs autres États américains ont d'ailleurs introduit des lois semblables[15]. Des tentatives dans le même sens ont été faites au Canada[16], où cependant aucune législation n'a été adoptée. Nous réservons la critique du *Natural Death Act* et de son application possible à la situation canadienne, pour une autre partie du présent document (p. 79 et suivantes).

En matière de meurtre par compassion et d'acharnement thérapeutique, le droit américain a connu certains développements intéressants. Jusqu'à récemment, on connaissait environ seize instances portant sur des actes d'euthanasie active aux États-Unis. Sans vouloir rentrer dans les détails de chacune de ces causes, le contraste existant entre l'apparente sévérité des lois criminelles (du même type et de la même tradition que les nôtres) et la pratique est frappant. Sur ces seize instances, il y eut en effet dix acquittements, dont six pour raison d'insanité temporaire. Dans les six causes restantes, une seule sentence à vie fut prononcée. Une sentence à vie fut complètement suspendue, et deux sentences suspendues de cinq à dix ans et de trois à six ans furent données. Dans les deux autres cas enfin, la poursuite fut rejetée dès le début du procès.

Comme en Angleterre cependant, plusieurs mouvements aux États-Unis ont préconisé la reconnaissance législative de l'euthanasie volontaire. Certains projets de loi ont même vu le jour récemment en Idaho, au Montana et en Oregon. Tous se basent d'ailleurs plus ou moins sur le projet anglais de 1969. De plus, certains groupes, notamment le groupe *Hemlock*, se battent à l'heure actuelle pour obtenir la décriminalisation de l'aide au suicide pour les personnes en phase terminale.

Un second groupe de pays se démarque nettement par rapport à la tradition de common law. Il est constitué de ceux (surtout les pays européens) qui, d'une façon ou d'une autre, séparent le meurtre ordinaire du meurtre par compassion, en diminuent la gravité ou allègent la sentence qui peut l'accompagner. Dans ce groupe on retrouve, entre autres, l'Allemagne. Le système de classification de l'homicide dans le Code pénal allemand actuel fait que le meurtre par compassion est placé dans une catégorie à part. L'acte constitue quand même une infraction criminelle (meurtre sur demande), mais la loi fait entrer en ligne de compte la motivation de l'auteur, ce qui permet une réduction importante des normes sentencielles.

En Suisse, le Code pénal prévoit que le juge peut mitiger la sentence lorsque l'auteur avait un motif «honorable» de commettre l'acte. De plus, il semble dans ce pays que le médecin qui, par compassion, aide son patient à se suicider n'est pas sujet à une incrimination de la part de la loi. Le médecin pourrait, par exemple, donner un poison à son patient mais non lui administrer lui-même. En 1977, dans le Canton de Zurich, un référendum sur la possibilité d'admettre d'une façon législative et formelle qu'un médecin puisse poser un acte d'euthanasie positive à la demande d'un patient souffrant d'une maladie incurable, récolta une forte majorité de oui. Aucune suite législative n'a cependant été donnée.

Dans d'autres pays enfin, comme la Norvège ou l'Uruguay, le problème ne se résout pas au niveau d'une différence dans la classification des différentes espèces d'homicide, mais plutôt au niveau de la sentence elle-même, le juge pouvant soit réduire celle-ci, soit même n'en imposer aucune[17].

En conclusion donc de cette brève étude du droit actuel, deux observations sont possibles.

Premièrement, au niveau de la cessation et de l'interruption d'un traitement médical, on sent une nette incertitude face à la situation actuelle. Ce malaise ne vient pas d'une absence de textes législatifs ou d'une mauvaise rédaction de ceux-ci. Il vient essentiellement de deux facteurs. Le premier est que ces textes n'ont pas été conçus spécifiquement en fonction de la situation médicale, et surtout pensés en rapport avec le contexte moderne actuel, où les progrès médicaux et technologiques permettent des prolongations de la vie humaine, prolongations parfois pénibles parce que non souhaitées par le patient ou parce que l'exposant à des souffrances et à une extension inutile de son agonie. Le second est que ces textes, pour des raisons fort diverses, n'ont jamais vraiment connu le «baptême du feu» devant les tribunaux. On ne sait donc pas avec certitude raisonnable comment les tribunaux les appliqueraient en pratique dans le contexte médical. Il est certes possible d'élaborer des hypothèses et des schèmes d'interprétation, de noter certaines tendances. Malgré tout, l'incertitude règne. Cette incertitude n'est pas souhaitable, puisqu'elle peut avoir une influence directe sur le comportement médical, puisqu'elle crée dans la société certaines tensions et même certaines angoisses et enfin, puisqu'elle laisse le juriste dans une constante interrogation quant aux solutions juridiques appropriées sur un problème aussi important.

Deuxièmement, tous les systèmes juridiques, d'une façon ou d'une autre, se sont refusés à admettre l'euthanasie active et volontaire. Alors que certains punissent l'homicide par compassion comme un meurtre véritable, d'autres cherchent des accommodements en tenant compte des motifs de l'auteur, soit au niveau de la définition même de l'infraction, soit au niveau de l'imposition de la sentence. Dans tous les cas cependant, l'étude de l'expérience judiciaire de tous les pays révèle un paradoxe ou une contradiction évidente entre l'apparente sévérité de la loi et la réalité judiciaire où les auteurs sont rarement traînés devant les tribunaux, et où, quand ils le sont, sont rarement trouvés coupables ou sont alors condamnés à des sentences ou des peines légères.

TROISIÈME PARTIE

La nécessité, les objectifs et les impératifs de la réforme

Dans des matières aussi difficiles et aussi complexes que la cessation de traitement, l'euthanasie et le suicide, il n'est certainement pas superflu de poser deux questions préliminaires: tout d'abord le pourquoi d'une réforme en ce domaine, ensuite ce que le système de droit pénal canadien peut raisonnablement espérer tirer comme profit d'une éventuelle réforme de la règle de droit sur ces questions.

I. La nécessité de la réforme

Certains argumenteront avec logique qu'une réforme du droit dans ce domaine n'est pas nécessaire. Ils invoqueront notamment que les dispositions du *Code criminel* que nous avons analysées n'ont pas jusqu'ici posé de problèmes d'application pratique sérieux comme ont pu le faire d'autres articles du *Code*. Pourquoi donc changer des textes qui ne créent pas de difficultés d'interprétation judiciaire?

De plus, comme nous l'avons vu, ces textes sont très rarement appliqués dans le contexte médical et hospitalier. C'est un fait que médecins, infirmiers, infirmières et personnel hospitalier ne sont pratiquement jamais poursuivis devant les cours criminelles pour des infractions à ces textes. C'est un fait aussi que l'aide au suicide reste largement un crime sans application pratique. Pourquoi donc perdre du temps à régler un problème théorique? En changeant la loi enfin, ne court-on pas le risque de voir précisément ces poursuites augmenter?

31

De l'avis de la Commission toutefois, tous ces arguments n'ont pas pour effet d'exclure une réforme, du moins du genre de celle que la Commission envisage. Il faut bien comprendre que réformer ne signifie pas faire table rase de tout ce qui existe et repartir de zéro. Une réforme bien comprise peut consister en un réaménagement ou en un complément des textes actuels. Plusieurs raisons militent impérieusement en faveur d'une réforme.

En premier lieu, comme on a pu le constater dans les pages qui précèdent, le contexte médical et le contexte social canadiens ont grandement évolué depuis que les textes actuels du *Code criminel* sont entrés en vigueur. Ces textes ont su résister à l'érosion inévitable du temps parce qu'ils ont été conçus en termes généraux et parce qu'ils imposent des normes tellement larges qu'elles ne perdent pas rapidement de leur actualité. Toutefois, cette généralité qui est, sur le plan du risque d'obsolescence rapide, une grande qualité, constitue en même temps un défaut lorsqu'elle engendre, comme c'est le cas ici, une incertitude face aux situations nouvelles. Ces textes seraient adéquats si l'on pouvait être raisonnablement certain qu'ils puissent régler les situations concrètes actuelles, sans que le juriste ne soit obligé de les torturer ou d'en rechercher une interprétation byzantine et parfois de les déformer littéralement pour les forcer à s'adapter, sans pour autant être sûr que l'interprétation suggérée est correcte, vu l'absence de directions jurisprudentielles.

Un auteur s'est montré particulièrement dur en la matière en accusant le droit de fermer les yeux sur les réalités de la pratique médicale et de la vie de tous les jours, et d'obliger juges et jurys à trouver des raisons techniques et parfois acrobatiques pour adoucir les apparentes rigueurs de la loi[18]. Cette condamnation est probablement trop sévère. Elle ignore en effet que la loi a d'autres fonctions que la simple répression et qu'elle peut avoir aussi un rôle préventif. La différence entre le droit écrit dans les lois et le droit vécu dans la réalité judiciaire peut paraître grande; elle n'est pas nécessairement mauvaise ou dépourvue de sens.

Toutefois, comme la Commission a pu aisément le constater, il existe, à tort ou à raison, un malaise certain chez les spécialistes médicaux et dans le public. À la base de ce malaise, on retrouve notamment l'idée que la rédaction actuelle des textes permet de jeter un doute sérieux sur la légalité de certaines pratiques médicales ou hospitalières courantes. Comme la jurisprudence sur ces questions est presque inexistante, le degré d'incertitude est d'autant plus élevé. Cette incertitude est sérieuse, parce qu'elle risque d'entraîner une coupure complète entre la pratique et la norme de droit, la pratique faisant comme si la règle de droit n'existait pas. Elle peut aussi provoquer le phénomène contraire. Pour éviter tout risque, la pratique médicale pourrait demeurer très conservatrice et se conformer au standard le plus strict qu'elle pense que la loi établit.

Or, les pratiques médicales n'attendent pas en général le législateur. Les hôpitaux n'ont pas, en effet, attendu un texte législatif pour mettre en œuvre certaines pratiques à l'égard des mourants ou des nouveau-nés souffrant de malformations sérieuses. Les médecins, pour leur part, modèlent leur conduite sur ce qu'ils estiment juste et éthique dans les circonstances, par rapport à leur expertise et aux standards fixés par leurs codes de déontologie. Pourtant, il semblerait logique et conforme à notre tradition que le droit, à un moment ou à un autre de son évolution, prenne position pour dire au personnel médical si telle ou telle pratique est acceptable pour lui. Il apparaît difficile dans une matière où la vie humaine est concernée, de constamment temporiser et de ne se contenter que d'hypothèses. Jamais, il est vrai, la loi ne pourra parler au singulier et donner une réponse claire, nette et précise à chaque médecin, à propos de chaque acte qu'il pose à l'égard de chacun de ses patients. Elle peut, par contre, parler au pluriel et fixer certains paramètres généraux, mais suffisamment précis dans le contexte actuel, pour dire ce qu'elle considère comme acceptable et ce qu'elle considère, au contraire, comme ne l'étant pas.

Ainsi, nombre de personnes se demandent à l'heure actuelle s'il est légal, pour employer une expression vernaculaire, de «débrancher» un individu. Il s'est, à cet égard, développé

dans les hôpitaux une pratique basée sur certaines normes éthiques et médicales. Le fait que ces pratiques existent partout, se soient multipliées depuis l'apparition des respirateurs et soient appliquées quotidiennement, sans interférence de la part de la loi, semble leur conférer *a priori* un caractère de légitimité et de légalité. Pour beaucoup, la question ne se pose même plus: la pratique est légale parce qu'elle existe, parce qu'elle se fait tous les jours et parce que le droit n'a jamais jugé bon d'intervenir. Le silence du droit est donc interprété comme un endossement ou un acquiescement tacite de sa part.

Il est probable que les pratiques hospitalières actuelles sur l'arrêt de respirateurs ne heurtent pas les principes juridiques fondamentaux. Par contre, il est d'autres cas où la chose est beaucoup moins certaine. Le nouveau-né qui souffre d'une trisomie 21*, qui n'est pas affecté d'autres difformités sérieuses, mais qui présente une atrésie* du tube digestif, pose un problème sérieux.

Laisser dans cette hypothèse des pratiques différentes se développer à travers le pays, à travers la même province ou la même ville est probablement inévitable dans une certaine mesure. Toutefois lorsque, comme dans le cas actuel, une vie humaine est en jeu, le droit doit tout faire pour éclairer le milieu et pour définir d'une façon beaucoup plus précise les limites minimales de ce que notre société juge acceptable.

La Commission croit donc que ce serait pratiquer la politique de l'autruche que de ne pas *au moins* se poser le problème de la nécessité d'une réforme, de ne pas voir *au moins* s'il n'est pas possible d'apporter une certaine amélioration à la situation et de lever, *au moins* en partie, le voile de l'incertitude et de l'ambiguïté.

II. Les objectifs de la réforme

Chercher à identifier dans un domaine aussi controversé le fruit qu'une réforme peut apporter à la communauté canadienne, c'est d'une part identifier le rôle que peut avoir la règle

* Voir Annexe II

34

de droit et d'autre part, et surtout, apprendre à en reconnaître les limites.

Comme l'a souvent énoncé la Commission dans les nombreux rapports et documents de travail qu'elle a produits depuis dix ans, le rôle du droit criminel ne se limite pas à punir l'individu. Ce rôle de sanction existe bien évidemment. Il est même probablement le plus éminemment visible. Toutefois, le droit criminel ne s'arrête pas seulement à la sanction du coupable.

Il exerce également un rôle de prévention qui, lorsque examiné dans le contexte de la pratique médicale, de la cessation de traitement et de l'aide au suicide, paraît particulièrement important. Le fait de punir le vol à main armée ou le meurtre avec sévérité n'empêchera probablement pas la perpétration de ces crimes. La société, quels que soient la sévérité ou le raffinement de la législation sur le sujet, doit s'attendre à ce que chaque année, un certain nombre d'inculpations sous ces chefs aient lieu. Par contre, lorsque le droit a affaire à une catégorie particulière de citoyens (les médecins, le personnel hospitalier) bien informés, ayant bénéficié d'une éducation leur permettant de comprendre peut-être plus facilement les tenants et aboutissants de la loi et dont la raison d'être est de poser des gestes altruistes, la probabilité paraît plus forte que leur conduite suive davantage la norme fixée par la loi, si celle-ci est suffisamment explicite. Par exemple, si le législateur ou un arrêt de jurisprudence décidait demain que ne pas opérer le nouveau-né trisomique qui ne souffre que d'une atrésie* constitue un acte criminel, il y a gros à parier que les médecins qui, à l'heure actuelle, suivent cette pratique, l'abandonneraient immédiatement.

Le droit pénal constitue aussi un outil d'éducation active. En théorie du moins, ses règles sont l'expression d'un certain consensus social. Changer la règle ou tenter de l'expliciter davantage, devrait permettre une discussion dans les milieux affectés par le changement et dans le public en général et donc une plus grande prise de conscience collective des enjeux

---

* Voir Annexe II

véritables des problèmes posés par la cessation de traitement, l'euthanasie et l'aide au suicide. De ces discussions et de la ventilation des diverses opinions sur le sujet, peut ensuite se dégager un certain nombre de règles basées sur un degré plus ou moins élevé de consensus social. Cette opération peut paraître inutile ou superflue à certains. La Commission la croit, au contraire, utile et nécessaire. C'était d'ailleurs l'un des objectifs clairement définis du projet de recherche sur la protection de la vie, dont le présent document est issu.

Par contre, il faut aussi être conscient que, dans une matière aussi complexe et aussi controversée, il est impossible d'espérer faire l'unanimité autour d'une réforme, quelle qu'elle puisse être. Les questions que ce document aborde ont en effet des racines très profondes dans la morale, la conduite, l'expérience vécue, et la psychologie de chaque individu. On ne doit donc espérer ni une solution miracle, ni une solution qui rallie tous les suffrages. Ce ne sont pas là cependant des raisons suffisantes pour renoncer au travail.

Enfin, une réforme législative ne constitue pas une fin en soi, mais plutôt le début de la véritable réforme. Changer la loi est une chose, changer les attitudes, les conduites, les modes de comportement en est une autre sur laquelle le législateur n'a parfois que bien peu d'emprise. Dans la matière qui fait l'objet de ce document, les suggestions de réforme législative ponctuelle doivent donc nécessairement s'accompagner de réforme de politique sociale et institutionnelle nécessaires pour pouvoir produire les résultats escomptés.

III. Les impératifs de la réforme

Réformer le droit criminel sur les questions qui ont été abordées dans le présent document, revient à poser trois questions concrètes et précises:

(1) Le législateur doit-il, d'une façon ou d'une autre, légaliser ou du moins décriminaliser certaines formes d'euthanasie active, comme le meurtre par compassion?

(2)   Le législateur doit-il décriminaliser l'aide au suicide en abrogeant l'article 224 du *Code criminel*?

(3)   Le législateur doit-il intervenir dans le cadre des articles 14, 45, 198 et 199, pour préciser les limites de la légalité du refus et de la cessation du traitement médical?

Les réponses à ces trois questions sont complexes et nécessairement nuancées. Le fond même de ces trois questions a de plus fait l'objet d'une abondante littérature. Il n'est pas dans l'intention de la Commission, encore une fois, de traiter de façon exhaustive et analytique de l'ensemble de ces questions. Il est par contre, dans son intention, de discuter les choix et les options de politique législative que le droit canadien pourrait prendre, eu égard à sa philosophie de base.

Pour conserver une indispensable logique interne à la réforme, il est apparu à la Commission qu'une première étape de réflexion était nécessaire, de façon à cerner les impératifs catégoriques de cette réforme. Il convient en d'autres termes de se poser la question suivante: quels sont les principes ou les règles fondamentales qui doivent inspirer une réforme éventuelle de la loi?

Ces impératifs sont de deux ordres. Les uns tiennent à la nature de la réforme, les autres à son contenu.

Sur le plan de la nature, le premier impératif catégorique est que la réforme doit être consciente des limites intrinsèques du droit criminel. Comme l'a maintes fois affirmé la Commission, le droit criminel n'est qu'un instrument de contrôle social parmi d'autres, et un instrument bien imparfait. On ne doit donc pas attendre d'une réforme du droit criminel qu'elle serve de panacée universelle; on ne doit donc pas attendre du droit criminel une solution miracle ou une solution éternelle. Le droit criminel n'est là que pour réprimer les abus les plus sérieux et les plus grossiers. Quelle que puisse être la réforme législative, elle devra se frotter à l'usage et à l'expérience jurisprudentielle qui seuls sauront lui conférer, avec le temps, sa véritable portée.

En second lieu, les solutions proposées doivent conserver une grande flexibilité de façon à s'adapter aux circonstances particulières de chaque espèce et à ne pas gêner l'évolution de la science, de la médecine et de la société. Il convient donc de se méfier des solutions extrêmes, des solutions trop tranchées et des solutions qui ne laissent pas suffisamment de marge au processus naturel d'adaptation.

En troisième lieu, il est préférable de rechercher des solutions qui, autant que faire se peut, s'insèrent harmonieusement dans le contexte socio-juridique actuel et ne constituent pas un bouleversement radical de l'ensemble des principes de base et des institutions de notre droit.

Sur le plan du contenu, un certain nombre de principes fondamentaux doivent guider le processus de réforme. La réforme ne doit pas être basée sur une catégorisation de concepts flous, non scientifiques, ou discriminatoires.

A. *La distinction entre la personne humaine et l'être non-humain*

Il paraît impensable tout d'abord, de fonder une réforme sur la reconnaissance de deux catégories d'êtres: ceux auxquels on reconnaîtrait le statut de personne humaine et ceux auxquels ce statut ne serait pas, au contraire, reconnu. L'histoire révèle trop bien les dangers d'une telle catégorisation. Qualifier un être de «non-humain» a souvent été le prétexte ou la justification pour le considérer également comme un hors-la-loi (au sens propre du terme), pour le situer en dehors du droit et donc pour refuser de lui appliquer les normes protectrices de base que la loi accorde aux humains. Pour en prendre un exemple concret, nier à un nouveau-né anencéphale* la qualité de personne humaine, pourrait justifier de lui nier aussi la protection de la loi, et donc permettre de justifier que de le tuer directement ou de ne pas le laisser vivre ne constitue ni un meurtre, ni un acte de négligence criminelle. L'histoire est

---

* Voir Annexe II

38

remplie de cas où des sorcières, des malades mentaux, des ethnies et des races entières ont été éliminés après d'abord avoir été catégorisés comme n'étant pas humains. La Commission estime que le droit doit continuer à être fondé sur la règle de base prévue à l'heure actuelle par notre droit criminel: est humain celui né de parents humains. Sur le plan de l'exercice des droits subjectifs, elle croit devoir continuer à respecter la règle de base du *Code criminel* à l'effet qu'un être humain est celui qui est entièrement sorti vivant du ventre de sa mère et doit rejeter carrément toute distinction entre, par exemple, une personne humaine et un «être non-humain». Toute personne humaine, quel que soit son degré de handicap, a droit à la protection de la loi. La chose est particulièrement importante dans le contexte du traitement médical. Ce point a d'ailleurs présidé à l'élaboration de la réforme proposée par la Commission sur les critères de détermination de la mort[18a].

B.   *La distinction entre mesures ordinaires et mesures extraordinaires*

Il ne paraît pas ensuite utile, dans une perspective de réforme, de faire sienne une distinction parfois couramment employée dans certains milieux: celle entre mesures ou soins ordinaires et extraordinaires.

Il est coutume de retracer l'origine de cette distinction dans un discours du Pape Pie XII à des anesthésistes en 1957. Le Pape, à cette occasion, émit l'opinion que le médecin n'était moralement obligé d'utiliser que les moyens ordinaires pour préserver la vie et la santé, c'est-à-dire les moyens n'emportant pas d'inconvénients sérieux pour le patient. Ces termes ont fait l'objet d'interprétations variées. La plus courante est d'y voir une différence entre le traitement strictement nécessaire, usuel et le traitement de pointe ou inusité dans les circonstances. Le médecin aurait donc le devoir d'utiliser tous les moyens usuels ou «ordinaires», mais non ceux qui sont inusités ou «extraordinaires».

Cette distinction voulait correspondre à un besoin de clarification. Elle demeure cependant entachée d'un certain degré

d'imprécision qui rend difficile son adoption comme critère dans une réforme éventuelle. Si l'on prend le mot «ordinaire» dans le sens le plus commun, celui d'usuel, on aboutit à un non-sens. La médecine n'est pas une science stable et fixe, mais au contraire une science en constante évolution. Ce qui est usuel de nos jours, ne l'était pas il y a quelques années. De plus, ce qui peut être usuel dans tel milieu ou tel centre hospitalier bien équipé ne l'est probablement pas dans tel autre milieu ou dans tel autre centre sous-équipé. Ainsi, il est probable, à l'heure actuelle, que placer une personne en état d'arrêt respiratoire dans un respirateur, serait objectivement considéré comme une procédure usuelle ou ordinaire. Tel n'était sûrement pas le cas dans les quelques années qui ont suivi la mise sur le marché de ces appareils. Tel n'est probablement pas le cas non plus dans un endroit reculé, éloigné d'un centre hospitalier moderne. Il est donc difficile de séparer ce qui est «usuel» de ce qui ne l'est pas et cette séparation comporte, en plus, une large part d'arbitraire. Si le médecin ne devait à son patient que les soins usuels, il serait irrémédiablement condamné au *statu quo* et donc à une pratique extrêmement conservatrice de la médecine. Les médecins ont d'ailleurs fort bien compris la difficulté, et pour eux le mot «ordinaire» désigne toujours ce qui est ordinaire dans les circonstances particulières à chaque espèce.

Certains ont alors proposé d'entendre les mots «ordinaire» et «extraordinaire» dans un sens qui ne soit pas un sens strictement objectif. Serait «ordinaire» le traitement qui offrirait un espoir *raisonnable* de réussite sans entraîner des souffrances ou inconvénients indus pour le patient. Serait par contre «extraordinaire» le traitement qui n'offrirait pas de perspectives raisonnables de guérison ou de soulagement ou qui entraînerait pour le patient des souffrances ou des inconvénients intolérables. À bien y penser, cette nouvelle formulation beaucoup plus proche de la réalité ne confère pas non plus une utilité particulière à la distinction sur le strict plan d'une réforme législative. Elle ne fait que décrire dans le premier cas le véritable traitement médical, dans le second l'acharnement thérapeutique. À notre avis, cette distinction reste trop ambiguë pour servir de base solide à une qualification précise de

l'intensité juridique de l'obligation du médecin à l'endroit du patient et pour fonder un axe véritable de réforme, même si elle garde son utilité sur d'autres plans.

C. *La présomption en faveur de la vie*

La préservation de la vie humaine est une valeur reconnue comme fondamentale par notre société. Sur ce point, notre droit criminel a au fond fort peu varié dans son histoire. Il sanctionne, d'une façon générale, le principe du caractère sacré de la vie humaine. Il a cependant, au cours des ans, été amené à apporter des nuances à l'absolutisme apparent du principe, à découvrir ses limites intrinsèques et à lui donner sa véritable dimension.

La Commission est d'avis que toute réforme portant sur la vie humaine doit au départ fermement admettre une présomption en faveur de celle-ci. Autrement dit, on ne doit jamais présumer qu'un patient en phase terminale entend renoncer à la vie à moins d'une expression claire, libre et informée de volonté contraire. Cette règle nous paraît d'une grande importance. En effet, il est parfois impossible de savoir si une personne désire ne pas continuer à vivre ou souhaite au contraire que l'on utilise à son égard tous les moyens pour prolonger une vie déjà sérieusement compromise. Il en est ainsi de ceux qui sont privés de la faculté d'exercer ce pouvoir décisionnel (par exemple le patient comateux). Dans tous ces cas, la seule politique d'orientation législative valable est de présumer ce que dicte le sens commun, c'est-à-dire que chaque être humain préfère la vie à la mort.

Il ne faut pas cependant, et c'est là où le problème devient difficile, que cette présomption en faveur de la vie ne serve de base à toute la pratique médicale. Il serait désastreux, par exemple, que cette présomption ait pour effet d'obliger le médecin à pratiquer l'acharnement thérapeutique dans les cas où le patient est incapable de manifester sa volonté. Une telle application du principe entraînerait des abus intolérables et créerait aussi un état de discrimination à l'endroit des personnes incapables ou handicapées, en les mettant dans une situation désavantageuse.

Cette présomption en faveur de la vie doit être précisée. Elle doit simplement signifier ceci: *si un traitement peut être raisonnablement appliqué pour préserver la vie ou la santé d'une personne, on doit présumer que la volonté de cette personne, si elle avait pu la manifester, eût été de recevoir le traitement et non de le refuser.* Sur le plan pratique cette règle est d'ailleurs appliquée tous les jours dans le cas des soins d'urgence. Lorsqu'un patient arrive inconscient à l'urgence d'un centre hospitalier, les médecins traitent. Ils ne peuvent présumer, même lorsqu'il s'agit apparemment d'une tentative de suicide, que la personne a vraiment renoncé à la vie. Par contre, toujours dans ce même cas, cette présomption en faveur de la vie ne les poussera pas aux extrêmes et ne les obligera donc pas à appliquer au patient inconscient un traitement qui, dans les circonstances, apparaît déraisonnable ou inutile. L'utilisation d'une telle présomption a pour effet concret de renverser le fardeau de la preuve et de le placer sur les épaules de celui qui invoque la légitimité d'un acte qui ne favorise pas le prolongement ou le maintien de la vie humaine.

D. *L'autonomie et l'autodétermination de la personne*

La loi doit aussi reconnaître, comme elle le fait d'ailleurs à l'heure actuelle de façon implicite, le principe de l'autonomie et de l'autodétermination de la personne, c'est-à-dire, le droit pour chaque être humain de voir sa volonté respectée lorsqu'il s'agit de décisions portant sur son corps. Il faut admettre, à notre avis, que chaque être humain est en principe maître de sa propre destinée. Il est libre toutefois, pour des raisons morales ou religieuses, de s'imposer des restrictions ou des limites à son droit d'autodétermination. Là n'est pas la question. Ces limites ne doivent pas lui être imposées par la loi en dehors des hypothèses où l'exercice de ce droit est susceptible de nuire à l'ordre public ou aux droits des autres, par exemple de constituer une menace pour la vie ou la sécurité d'autrui.

Notre droit à l'heure actuelle reconnaît d'ailleurs ce principe. L'admettre formellement comme axe de réforme n'est donc pas bouleverser la situation acquise. Depuis 1972, le droit criminel a aboli l'infraction de la tentative de suicide. Cette

mesure ne veut pas dire que le législateur approuve ou endosse un acte qui est profondément contre la nature humaine. Elle signifie simplement que le législateur ne considère pas l'acte comme suffisamment asocial pour mériter les foudres du droit criminel. Le législateur a adopté sur la question une attitude essentiellement pragmatique. Dans la tentative de suicide, en effet, le délinquant et la victime sont la même personne. Le châtiment pénal a dans ce cas quelque chose d'un peu odieux et d'inhumain, d'autant plus que fondamentalement la personne a plus besoin d'aide que de sanction. L'acte continue à être illicite au sens large du terme. Il n'est plus cependant illégal.

La tradition jurisprudentielle est dans le même sens lorsqu'elle établit la règle selon laquelle l'individu sain d'esprit et bénéficiant d'un consentement éclairé est libre de renoncer à un traitement. Le témoin de Jéhovah adulte qui refuse une transfusion sanguine, tout en sachant que c'est probablement là le seul moyen d'éviter la mort, exerce ce droit à l'autodétermination. Il en est de même du cancéreux qui renonce à un traitement susceptible de prolonger son existence. Dans son Document de travail n° 26 sur le traitement, la Commission a d'ailleurs recommandé la reconnaissance formelle de ce principe.

La Commission, encore une fois, estime que les choix de morale individuelle doivent être respectés par la règle de droit à condition qu'ils ne pêchent pas contre l'ordre public et les bonnes mœurs. Elle estime donc que la règle de droit ne doit pas imposer un caractère absolu au principe du caractère sacré de la vie. Elle doit, au contraire, continuer à respecter le droit d'autodétermination de l'homme sur sa propre existence, tout en assurant la protection et la promotion du maintien de la vie comme valeur fondamentale.

E. *Les critères de la qualité de la vie*

Comme nous l'avons déjà noté, notre droit criminel à l'heure actuelle considère la vie humaine essentiellement comme une valeur quantitative. Il punit sévèrement celui qui la

supprime ou l'abrège. Un document d'étude préparé dans le cadre du projet sur la protection de la vie a bien montré l'origine de cette conception[19], les changements qu'elle a subis et le caractère artificiel que revêt souvent la distinction entre la quantité et la qualité de vie, entre le caractère sacré de la vie et sa qualité. Nous référons donc le lecteur à ce document pour plus de détails.

La Commission estime que la réforme doit reconnaître à la vie humaine un aspect autre qu'un aspect simplement quantitatif. La réforme doit admettre que des considérations portant sur la qualité de la vie peuvent être légitimes dans les prises de décision et peuvent servir de critères valables pour justifier certains actes qui peuvent paraître attentatoires à la vie conçue comme valeur exclusivement quantitative.

En matière de droit médical, la reconnaissance de ce fait est déjà passée dans les mœurs et dans la pratique. C'est au nom de la qualité de leur vie que certains patients refusent un traitement et que ce libre choix est respecté par les médecins. C'est également au nom de la qualité de la vie de leur patient que certains médecins décident parfois d'interrompre ou de ne pas entreprendre un traitement particulier. Dans le cas de la personne autonome, c'est à elle qu'il appartient de définir ses propres priorités et exigences de qualité de vie. Celles-ci doivent être respectées par les autres. Dans le cas de la personne qui n'est pas autonome, c'est à d'autres qu'il appartient de les définir, en tenant compte de certains critères comme le bénéfice pour la personne, l'utilité de l'acte, ses effets possibles sur le plan physique et mental, etc.

En d'autres termes, dans la formulation d'une politique de réforme, le législateur ne doit pas systématiquement exclure les valeurs tenant à la qualité de vie au profit d'une valeur absolue qui serait la préservation quantitative de la vie. Le droit ne doit donc pas exclure *a priori* le choix du patient de refuser la continuation d'un traitement au nom de son droit de mourir dans la dignité et de vivre des derniers instants de qualité suffisante.

F. *La protection particulière des incapables*

La loi doit protéger tous les citoyens également. La loi est aussi là pour renforcer sa protection à l'endroit de ceux qui sont plus faibles ou dont les droits peuvent être plus facilement violés ou ignorés. On peut donc dire, dans une certaine mesure, que le droit doit avoir un préjugé favorable à leur égard. En matière de protection de la vie, ce préjugé doit être maintenu, sinon renforcé.

Sur le plan de la politique législative, un dilemme très sérieux apparaît quant aux droits de ceux qui sont incapables, par suite d'inconscience, de défaut d'âge ou de handicap mental, de jouir d'un pouvoir décisionnel véritable. Ces personnes ont besoin d'être protégées. Les lois fédérales et provinciales reconnaissent toutes ce fait et organisent des mécanismes de protection. L'une des caractéristiques de ces mécanismes est de prévoir qu'un autre (parent, tuteur, curateur) puisse donner un consentement à la place de l'incapable. La chose porte relativement peu à conséquences lorsqu'il s'agit de l'exercice de droits patrimoniaux ou économiques. Par contre, prendre une décision pour un autre lorsque cette décision affecte sa santé, son intégrité corporelle, ou sa vie, implique un ordre de grandeur et de valeur complètement différent. La Commission a d'ailleurs fait état de la complexité de cette question dans un document de travail sur la stérilisation des personnes souffrant d'un handicap mental[20].

Il faut noter également que la plupart des lois provinciales prévoient des mécanismes pour résoudre les conflits possibles, en matière de traitement, entre les parents et le médecin. Ainsi au Québec, la loi prévoit que si le consentement des parents, lorsqu'il est requis, est refusé ou ne peut être obtenu, un juge de la Cour supérieure peut alors trancher le débat. Ce même texte ajoute aussi que l'obtention de ce consentement n'est pas nécessaire lorsque la vie de l'enfant est en danger[20a]. Dans les provinces de common law, la loi prévoit aussi que l'enfant peut être placé sous la protection de la Cour[20b].

La principale difficulté vient du fait suivant: toute décision sur la santé ou la vie étant essentiellement personnelle, le

consentement substitué peut au départ être considéré comme un mécanisme inadéquat. Si on suit alors ce principe, on ne permettra pas à quelqu'un d'autre (le tuteur par exemple) de prendre de telles décisions. C'est, dès lors, créer pour l'incapable une situation différente de celle de la personne capable, situation qui peut entraîner des décisions contraires à ce qui peut apparaître, *a priori*, comme son meilleur intérêt. D'un autre côté, traiter l'incapable exactement sur le même pied d'égalité que la personne pleinement capable n'est pas non plus une solution valable, puisque l'incapable peut ne pas être en mesure de saisir la portée et les conséquences exactes des gestes qu'il pose ou des décisions qu'il prend.

Un exemple permettra d'illustrer le problème. Une personne capable prend la décision de ne pas entreprendre un traitement de chimiothérapie, parce qu'elle estime plus important de ne pas compromettre la qualité du temps de vie qui lui reste au profit d'une survie prolongée. Le médecin dans ce cas respectera la décision. S'il s'agit cependant d'une personne totalement incapable de donner un consentement valable, comme dans l'affaire *Saikewicz*, le dilemme est le suivant: ou le médecin traite, en ne tenant pas compte de la qualité de vie diminuée qui va en résulter pour l'incapable, ou le médecin ne traite pas et, dans ce cas, la décision risque d'être fondée sur le jugement de valeur personnel de ceux qui auront pris la décision. Il n'est pas certain en effet que telle aurait été ou aurait pu être la décision de l'intéressé.

La Commission est d'avis que la solution du dilemme se trouve dans l'élaboration de règles propres à assurer que la décision substituée soit prise dans le meilleur intérêt de l'incapable. Ce «meilleur» intérêt, dans certains cas, n'est pas *nécessairement* l'initiation ou la poursuite d'un traitement. Il importe toutefois, comme la Commission le signalait dans son document sur les stérilisations, que des règles de protection additionnelles soient mises en place. Si ces règles existent et sont adéquates, il devrait y avoir moins d'hésitation à permettre l'interruption d'un traitement chez un incapable, dans les mêmes circonstances où il paraîtrait légitime de le faire à l'égard d'une personne jouissant de toutes ses facultés. Toute-

fois, il faut être conscient du fait qu'aucune règle n'est parfaite et qu'il est strictement impossible d'éliminer toutes les erreurs. L'objectif doit être de réduire la possibilité de leur survenance au strict minimum.

QUATRIÈME PARTIE

La réforme

Comme nous le mentionnions au début de la troisième partie de ce document, sur le plan de la politique législative susceptible d'être suivie par le *Code criminel* canadien, le problème se résume à essayer de répondre à trois questions fondamentales:

(1) Le législateur doit-il, d'une façon ou d'une autre, légaliser ou du moins décriminaliser certaines formes d'euthanasie active, comme le meurtre par compassion?

(2) Le législateur doit-il décriminaliser l'aide au suicide en abrogeant l'article 224 du *Code criminel*?

(3) Le législateur doit-il intervenir dans le cadre général des articles 14, 45, 198 et 199, pour préciser les limites de la légalité du refus et de la cessation du traitement médical?

I. L'euthanasie

Avant d'entrer dans une discussion sur le sujet, il importe de donner quelques précisions sur le vocabulaire utilisé et sur le sens exact du mot «euthanasie», tel qu'il sera entendu ici. Ce terme est souvent utilisé, en effet, pour décrire des situations fort différentes les unes des autres.

On oppose en général l'euthanasie positive, directe ou active à l'euthanasie négative, indirecte ou passive. La différence qui sépare ces deux notions est celle que reflète l'acte par rapport à l'omission ou à l'inaction. Mettre fin aux jours de quelqu'un en lui administrant un poison est un acte d'euthanasie positive. Pour les fins de ce document, nous utiliserons le mot euthanasie dans un sens très précis pour désigner exclusivement l'acte positif de causer la mort de quelqu'un pour des raisons humanitaires.

On oppose également euthanasie volontaire à euthanasie involontaire, en prenant pour critère de distinction le fait que la «victime» a consenti ou non à la mort causée par acte positif ou par omission. Pour les fins de ce document, nous utiliserons le mot euthanasie pour désigner l'euthanasie volontaire uniquement, c'est-à-dire celle qui implique le consentement exprès ou implicite de l'intéressé eu égard aux circonstances et qui est faite apparemment pour le bénéfice du patient.

A. *La légalisation de l'euthanasie*

Des plaidoyers fort éloquents ont été faits pour inciter le législateur à permettre l'euthanasie positive à la demande du patient en phase terminale. Un texte de Glanville Williams est d'ailleurs, à cet égard, considéré comme un classique du genre[21]. Williams s'efforce de montrer que la loi et la société sont hypocrites d'une part, et d'autre part qu'elles sont inhumaines, en ne reconnaissant pas la possibilité pour une personne à l'agonie et qui souffre le martyre de demander à une autre de mettre fin à ses souffrances.

Ce type d'argumentation n'est pas nouveau. On le retrouve, par exemple, dans le célèbre livre allemand publié en 1920 par Binding et Hoche[22]. On le retrouve aussi à la base de tous les documents qui, en Angleterre, aux États-Unis ou dans les autres pays, ont prôné la reconnaissance ou du moins la décriminalisation de l'euthanasie. Ce type d'argumentation n'est pas non plus utilisé uniquement par des gens qui prônent

une «amélioration de la race» ou «l'élimination d'éléments sociaux inutiles ou indésirables». Il ne faut surtout pas empoisonner la discussion d'un problème aussi sérieux en se référant constamment aux abus atroces commis par certains régimes politiques comme celui de l'Allemagne nazie. Il ne faut pas pour autant les oublier, du moins en tant que leçons de l'histoire.

De très nombreux arguments ont été présentés en faveur de la législation de l'euthanasie positive. Il n'est pas dans notre intention de reprendre ici systématiquement tous et chacun d'entre eux. Le lecteur trouvera dans la littérature sur le sujet les éclairages supplémentaires qu'il pourrait désirer[23]. Certains points principaux méritent toutefois un examen plus attentif.

L'un des arguments le plus souvent utilisé consiste à souligner l'illogisme ou le cynisme des règles de droit actuelles. La société reconnaît le droit pour le patient de refuser un traitement ou de demander son interruption, de façon à ne pas prolonger une agonie. Le patient, dit-on, est maître des décisions sur son propre corps et sur sa vie. La plupart des régimes juridiques vont même jusqu'à sanctionner pénalement la conduite d'un médecin qui, passant outre à la volonté expresse de son patient, lui administrerait un traitement contre son gré. Si donc le droit actuel reconnaît l'autonomie décisionnelle et l'autodétermination et permet qu'elles servent à justifier une omission ou une absence d'action, pourquoi ne serait-il pas logique avec lui-même et ne reconnaîtrait-il pas aussi cette même justification pour l'acte positif? Quelle différence si fondamentale sépare, en effet, la renonciation à un traitement et l'injection mortelle à la demande d'un patient, pour que le droit absolve l'une et considère l'autre comme une infraction criminelle?

Bien plus, argumentent les partisans de l'euthanasie, puisque le droit ne punit plus la tentative de suicide, il permet implicitement au patient en phase terminale de s'ôter la vie. N'est-il pas plus humain, pour les gens qui veulent en finir, mais en sont physiquement incapables, et pour ceux qui désirent s'assurer de l'aide pour le faire dans les meilleures

conditions possibles, que la mort puisse être administrée d'une façon scientifique, médicalement sûre et humainement acceptable? Légaliser l'euthanasie active et volontaire n'est-ce pas, au fond, faire preuve de réalisme? N'est-ce pas respecter la liberté de chacun dans toutes ses conséquences?

Plusieurs projets législatifs légalisant l'euthanasie ont été proposés en Angleterre et aux États-Unis. Tous, sans exception, n'ouvrent le droit à l'euthanasie qu'à ceux qui souffrent d'une maladie incurable ou terminale. Tous également prennent grand soin de prévoir un système permettant de s'assurer de la volonté de la personne et de sa déclaration d'intention. La majorité prévoient des pénalités sévères pour celui qui crée l'impression qu'une autre personne désire l'euthanasie. La plupart enfin exigent que l'acte d'euthanasie soit pratiqué par un médecin ou sous surveillance médicale. Selon ces systèmes, si toutes les conditions posées sont respectées, le praticien agissant de bonne foi ne commet pas de meurtre et ne tombe pas sous le coup de la loi criminelle ou civile.

Les exemples les plus connus de ce type de législation sont le *British Voluntary Euthanasia Act* de 1936 et de 1969, le *Euthanasia Society of America Bill* (Nebraska 1938) et une série de projets déposés plus récemment devant les législatures des États de New York (1947), de l'Oregon (1973), de l'Idaho (1969), du Montana (1973) et de la Floride (1973, 1976).

La Commission reconnaît les intentions humanitaires qui sont à l'origine de ces recommandations. Cependant, si l'on transpose le problème au niveau des politiques législatives et donc des politiques de la société canadienne dans son ensemble, la Commission est d'avis qu'une législation légalisant la pratique de l'euthanasie active volontaire est totalement inacceptable.

Légaliser l'euthanasie serait dans l'état actuel de la société, faire courir des risques beaucoup trop élevés par rapport aux profits que cette même société et les individus qui la composent pourraient espérer en tirer. Il existe d'abord le risque d'erreurs et d'accidents puisque l'hypothèse d'un diagnostic erroné reste toujours présente. De plus, la possibilité

de la découverte d'un nouveau traitement ou de l'application nouvelle d'un traitement déjà existant permettant soit une survie, soit une guérison, ne peut jamais, quoi qu'on en dise, être totalement écartée. Ce sont là des arguments de poids et des arguments trop bien connus pour qu'il soit nécessaire de les développer davantage.

L'argument principal et déterminant pour la Commission reste, toujours sur le plan de la politique législative, celui touchant les abus possibles. Il existe, tout d'abord, un danger réel que la procédure mise au point pour permettre de tuer ceux qui se sentent un fardeau pour eux-mêmes, ne soit détournée progressivement de son but premier, et ne serve aussi éventuellement à éliminer ceux qui sont un fardeau pour les autres ou pour la société. C'est là l'argument dit du doigt dans l'engrenage qui, pour être connu, n'en est pas moins réel. Il existe aussi le danger que, dans bien des cas, le consentement à l'euthanasie ne soit pas vraiment un acte parfaitement libre et volontaire. L'opposition médicale à l'euthanasie a souvent repris, avec raison, ces deux arguments.

En effet, on peut s'interroger sérieusement sur la valeur psychologique et juridique de l'acte de volonté du patient en phase terminale. Le système que les partisans de l'euthanasie proposent n'est concevable que si, et seulement si, il est possible d'être toujours absolument assuré que la décision d'y recourir est libre, volontaire et éclairée. On raisonne donc toujours en fonction de l'exemple du malade en phase terminale, lucide, intelligent, informé et courageux. On oublie peut-être un peu trop facilement que si ce type de malade existe, il en existe d'autres qui ont, eux, leurs facultés affaiblies par la maladie ou les médicaments, qui sont angoissés, et qui peuvent aussi, à tort ou à raison, se sentir un fardeau pour leurs proches. Loin de nous la pensée que jamais un malade en phase terminale ne puisse prendre une décision éclairée. Par contre, nous pensons, quelles que puissent être les précautions dont la loi pourrait s'entourer, qu'il existe un danger certain et réel que la demande d'euthanasie ne reflète pas la véritable volonté de l'individu, ou soit trop facilement conditionnée par des circonstances et des pressions extérieures.

Un second argument, particulièrement bien développé par Kamisar[24] en réponse à Glanville Williams, est le suivant. Le patient qui désire l'euthanasie active n'entend évidemment pas prolonger son agonie. Il veut, au contraire, mettre fin à ses souffrances le plus vite possible. Or, tout projet de légalisation de l'euthanasie doit nécessairement prévoir un processus permettant de vérifier si le patient est véritablement atteint d'une maladie incurable d'une part et si, d'autre part, sa décision est libre, volontaire et éclairée. Les procédures doivent être bien contrôlées et ne doivent naturellement pas être prises à la légère. Tout ceci exige du temps et crée ces délais, que précisément le mouvement euthanasique désire éviter, et tend à bureaucratiser le processus de décision. De plus, le personnel médical est là pour rendre un service professionnel important et devrait le moins possible être impliqué dans ce genre de bureaucratie non productive.

Enfin, de l'avis de la Commission, un autre argument déterminant peut être apporté contre la légalisation de l'euthanasie positive. Dans tout changement d'orientation du droit, il doit exister une proportionnalité acceptable entre les maux que l'on veut éviter et les difficultés auxquelles on entend remédier d'une part et, d'autre part, les risques nouveaux que le changement est susceptible de générer. Cette proportionnalité, dans le cas de l'euthanasie, apparaît à la Commission comme clairement et manifestement inacceptable.

En premier lieu, il est faux de prétendre qu'il existe à l'heure actuelle dans la société canadienne une demande insistante ou une pression sociale forte pour la légalisation de l'euthanasie. L'expérience des autres pays montre également que les divers groupes ou mouvements réclamant la pratique de l'euthanasie ont été fort actifs mais n'ont pas, dans l'ensemble, réussi à mobiliser une proportion importante de la population en faveur de leur cause. Le phénomène reste un phénomène isolé, qui réapparaît d'ailleurs de façon presque cyclique. Il n'existe pas sur la question un degré d'unanimité sociale acceptable. Par contre, les risques et les dangers de l'opération sont énormes et toujours présents quelles que soient les précautions dont les projets de légalisation s'entourent.

La loi est là pour répondre à un besoin réel. La Commission reste persuadée, indépendamment de tous les autres arguments, qu'il n'existe pas, à l'heure actuelle, au Canada un problème ou un besoin suffisamment grand pour bouleverser une tradition bien établie fondée sur une morale séculaire. Il lui apparaîtrait peu responsable de légaliser une telle pratique eu égard au bénéfice réel de l'opération, comparé aux risques et aux dangers qu'elle présente. L'extraordinaire développement depuis quelques années des soins palliatifs, l'expérience positive des hospices en Angleterre et des unités spécialisées au Canada et aux États-Unis est, très certainement, une réponse meilleure et beaucoup plus positive au problème.

B. *La décriminalisation du meurtre par compassion*

Comme nous l'avons vu précédemment, le droit criminel canadien en matière d'homicide ne tient pas compte du motif qui a inspiré l'auteur de l'acte. Seul compte le fait que l'auteur ait eu ou non l'intention de causer la mort. Peu importe le motif derrière cette intention.

Le droit canadien suit en cela la tradition de common law et se démarque nettement de la plupart des systèmes de droit continentaux qui, au moins au niveau de la sentence, sinon de la classification de l'infraction elle-même, font une différence entre le meurtre commis pour un motif moralement blâmable (par exemple l'appât du gain) et celui commis pour un motif humainement excusable (par exemple la compassion devant la souffrance).

Au plan de la politique législative, le choix est donc clair. Il se résume à consacrer législativement l'une des trois options suivantes: continuer avec le système actuel et ne pas tenir compte du motif; créer d'une façon ou d'une autre une catégorie spéciale d'homicide pour tenir compte des cas où le motif est excusable; conserver enfin l'infraction actuelle, mais tenir compte de la motivation au niveau de la sentence.

Créer, tout d'abord, une catégorie spéciale d'homicide pour le meurtre par compassion ne paraît pas une solution

valable pour deux raisons. En premier lieu, on peut s'interroger sur la nécessité pratique d'une telle démarche. Que l'infraction soit en effet qualifiée d'homicide, de meurtre ou d'un autre nom, n'a, en fait, que peu d'importance pratique. La qualification n'a rien de magique en elle-même. Elle n'est intéressante que par les conséquences et les effets juridiques que le législateur peut y attacher. Or, en matière de meurtre par compassion, c'est bien évidemment au niveau de la criminalisation ou de la sentence que la question se pose. Le problème n'est donc pas de savoir si l'acte doit porter la qualification de meurtre, d'homicide, d'euthanasie ou autre, mais bien de déterminer si, dans ce cas, la loi doit prévoir un acquittement ou des circonstances atténuantes motivant une sentence moins sévère que pour un meurtre crapuleux.

En second lieu, la compassion devant un agonisant n'est probablement pas le seul motif valable que la loi devrait reconnaître en matière d'homicide. Que dire, par exemple, du meurtre passionnel, du meurtre commis par état de nécessité, du crime à caractère politique, etc.? Le problème dépasse donc de loin le seul cas de l'euthanasie active et c'est donc l'ensemble du droit sur l'homicide qu'il conviendrait de réviser de fond en comble. Dans l'hypothèse où cette révision permettrait de conclure que le motif *en général* doit être pris en considération pour l'homicide, il serait alors logique d'inscrire le motif humanitaire, parmi d'autres, comme excuse totale ou partielle à la prohibition de tuer.

Sous réserve donc des recommandations que la Commission pourra faire dans son prochain document de travail sur l'homicide, il lui apparaît, à l'heure actuelle, que créer une catégorie spécifique d'infraction pour le meurtre par compassion n'est pas apporter une solution pratique valable au problème dans le cadre du droit criminel canadien actuel.

Une seconde solution consiste à conserver le système actuel, mais à permettre au tribunal, au niveau de la peine, de réduire ou de faire disparaître la sentence obligatoire en tenant compte du motif de compassion ayant inspiré le geste de l'auteur ou de faire de l'acte un homicide du troisième degré.

Cette solution, comme nous l'avons vu, est celle que certains pays ont déjà adoptée. L'acte posé continue donc cependant à être considéré comme un meurtre.

Les quelques consultations préalables qu'a eues la Commission sur le sujet, montrent que c'est probablement là la solution qui rencontrerait le plus facilement l'adhésion du public. Celui-ci, en effet, ne porte pas sur les actes des autres un jugement strictement juridique. Il apprécie ces actes en fonction de leur résonance morale. Il a donc beaucoup de mal à accepter qu'un authentique meurtre par compassion, geste motivé essentiellement par l'altruisme, soit, sur le plan de la sentence, traité de la même façon qu'un meurtre par vengeance ou par appât du gain qui est lui un geste égoïste. À n'en pas douter, l'aménagement juridique de cette perception de la réalité rencontrerait l'approbation du public.

L'adoption d'une telle solution n'est cependant pas sans poser des problèmes complexes. En premier lieu, il est là aussi difficile d'isoler la compassion à l'endroit d'un malade en phase terminale, comme la seule et unique hypothèse où, en matière d'homicide prémédité, la loi devrait tenir compte du motif. Qu'en serait-il du meurtre ou crime passionnel? Qu'en serait-il du meurtre commis par une personne pour se libérer des mauvais traitements infligés par une autre, du meurtre commis dans la défense d'intérêts nationaux supérieurs, etc.? Là encore, force est de constater qu'il est inacceptable d'isoler le seul motif de compassion à l'égard d'un mourant. Pour être logique avec elle-même, la réforme devrait aussi tenir compte d'autres motifs ou d'autres raisons de valeur morale égale ou supérieure.

En second lieu, il est toujours fort difficile d'évaluer chez l'auteur d'un homicide les véritables motifs qui l'ont poussé à agir. On discute souvent du problème à partir d'un exemple qui ressemble un peu à une image d'Épinal: le mourant qui implore l'un de ses proches de mettre fin à ses souffrances et celui-ci qui, mettant de côté ses sentiments d'amour pour lui et dans un acte de courage sublime, lui donne la mort. La Commission ne nie pas que de telles hypothèses aient existé ou existent

encore. La Commission estime cependant qu'à côté de ces cas clairs, il existe d'autres cas où la pureté et le désintéressement du motif sont beaucoup moins facilement perceptibles. Infliger la mort peut être inspiré par des raisons infiniment plus complexes, par exemple par un mouvement de compassion, mais aussi par un désir de mettre fin, pour soi-même, à une période psychologiquement difficile et à des contraintes physiques parfois épuisantes. Qui peut, dès lors, avec certitude sinon avec probabilité, peser la complexité de la motivation humaine?

La troisième difficulté, toujours sur le plan de la politique législative, est la possibilité d'abus que risque d'entraîner en pratique, une diminution sensible de la protection traditionnelle de la loi à l'égard de la vie et de l'intégrité de la personne humaine. Le danger existe à deux niveaux. Le premier est que de véritables meurtres soient commis, mais déguisés ensuite en meurtres par compassion. Comme on peut présumer que dans la plupart des cas l'acte n'est pas un acte public, la justice ne pourra, au fond, jamais être certaine ni de la pureté du motif, ni du consentement de la victime. Admettre un système d'évaluation du motif dans la sentence, n'est-il pas encourager le meurtre véritable de personnes qui sont un fardeau pour l'auteur, ou dont celui-ci a un intérêt à se débarrasser? Le second danger, qui est à l'heure actuelle très difficile à évaluer, est celui de l'effet d'entraînement. Une libéralisation de la loi par le biais de l'importance accordée au motif ne risque-t-elle pas de produire un effet d'incitation? À son tour, cet effet ne risque-t-il pas d'engendrer des abus?

La Commission croit donc, pour l'instant, que l'introduction en droit criminel canadien de l'élément motif, même au niveau de la sentence, dans ce cas comporte des dangers. Elle réalise toutefois fort bien qu'un tel système est concevable et que certaines garanties et certaines mesures peuvent être prises pour en minimiser les risques. Par exemple, l'acte pourrait continuer à être traité comme un meurtre au niveau de la sentence, à moins que l'auteur lui-même ne démontre d'une façon convaincante que seule la compassion l'a guidé.

La Commission croit également qu'il importe de ne pas considérer seulement cette question dans la perspective du

Code criminel et des textes créant les infractions, mais aussi dans celle du système de justice criminelle dans son ensemble. Or, le système que nous connaissons comporte des mécanismes internes permettant de corriger ce que l'application stricte de la loi dans des cas individuels pourrait avoir d'inéquitable ou d'odieux. Comme on peut le constater à la lumière de l'expérience de certains pays qui offrent sur le plan juridique une certaine similitude avec le nôtre, les véritables cas de meurtre par compassion qui sont effectivement poursuivis, qui se terminent par un verdict de culpabilité et auxquels la pleine rigueur de la loi sur le plan sentenciel est appliquée sont rares, voire inexistants. L'opportunité de la poursuite, les plaidoyers de culpabilité à une infraction moindre sont deux moyens parmi d'autres, d'ajuster l'apparente rigueur de la loi. Certes, d'aucuns prétendront que la loi est alors hypocrite et qu'il est illogique de traiter formellement le meurtre par compassion comme un meurtre pur et simple, tout en refusant de le faire effectivement sur le plan de la pratique des poursuites. Ils ont probablement raison sur le plan théorique. Toutefois, la discrétion de ne pas poursuivre dans un cas de meurtre par compassion ne nuit pas pour autant à la crédibilité de la loi criminelle. Elle montre, au contraire, que dans l'application de la loi, la justice est, elle aussi, capable de considérer l'aspect humanitaire des choses.

La conclusion à laquelle en arrive donc la Commission est que le système actuel qui, en matière de meurtre par compassion, ne fait pas de différence basée sur le motif est probablement la moins mauvaise solution, eu égard au contexte général du droit criminel canadien. Il ne s'agit cependant pas là pour la Commission d'une condamnation et d'une prise de position définitive. La Commission serait donc particulièrement heureuse de continuer à bénéficier des réactions du public canadien sur ce point.

II.   L'aide au suicide

L'article 224 du *Code criminel* punit de quatorze ans de prison celui qui aide une personne à se donner la mort, l'encourage ou la conseille. Le fait de tenter de se donner la mort n'est plus cependant, depuis 1972, une infraction criminelle.

La décriminalisation de l'aide au suicide a souvent été considérée comme une bonne solution de compromis. Une personne qui désire en terminer avec la vie est libre de le faire sur le plan juridique, puisque le droit moderne, contrairement à l'ancien droit, ne la punit plus. Si elle est incapable de poser le geste elle-même (par exemple parce qu'elle est paralysée, ou ne peut avoir accès aux moyens nécessaires à la réussite de son entreprise), il est illogique, argumente-t-on, de traiter comme un criminel celui qui l'aide à réaliser son plan. Cette aide n'est pas un meurtre puisqu'il n'y a pas de geste positif causal. De plus, la personne reste toujours libre de renoncer à son projet. Pourquoi donc tant de sévérité?

Depuis quelques années, aux États-Unis, en Angleterre comme dans d'autres pays européens, et maintenant au Canada, certains groupes de pression réclament la décriminalisation de l'aide au suicide pour le patient en phase terminale. Il ne faut pas croire, comme d'aucuns l'ont affirmé, que ces mouvements prônent le suicide. Ils revendiquent tout simplement ce qui leur paraît être le corrolaire nécessaire du droit de la personne de disposer d'elle-même: celui de se faire aider. Ils n'exaltent nullement le droit à la mort d'une façon générale.

Il paraît, à première vue, fort incongru de criminaliser la participation à un acte qui n'est plus lui-même un acte criminel. C'est en droit pénal un exemple unique. De plus, quelle différence véritable y a-t-il sur le plan pratique entre regarder une personne en phase terminale avaler un poison qu'elle s'est procurée elle-même et qu'elle prend sans aucun secours, et avoir la même conduite, après avoir procuré le poison en question au patient? Dans les deux cas, argumentent certains moralistes, les deux actes sont blâmables ou ne le sont pas! Pourquoi le droit ferait-il une différence aussi importante entre deux types de comportements aussi proches? N'y a-t-il pas là un byzantinisme inacceptable?

La réponse sur le seul plan de la logique est extrêmement difficile. Il est, en effet, pratiquement impossible de justifier l'existence d'une différence ontologique entre ces deux comportements. Par contre, une réponse plus convaincante peut

être apportée en se plaçant sur le plan de la politique législative et des conséquences pratiques que pourrait avoir une décriminalisation de l'aide au suicide.

Tout d'abord, la prohibition de l'article 224 n'est pas restreinte au seul cas du patient en phase terminale, pour lequel on ne peut qu'éprouver de la sympathie, ni au seul cas de son médecin ou de l'un de ses proches qui l'aide à mettre fin à ses souffrances. L'article est beaucoup plus général. Il s'applique à une variété de situations pour lesquelles il est plus difficile d'éprouver une telle sympathie. Que dire par exemple, pour reprendre un fait qui s'est passé récemment, de l'incitation à un suicide collectif? Que dire de celui qui, profitant de l'état dépressif d'une autre personne, la pousse au suicide pour en tirer un bénéfice pécuniaire? Comment juger le geste de celui qui, connaissant les tendances suicidaires d'un adolescent, lui procure des médicaments en dose suffisante pour le tuer? On ne saurait affirmer dans ce cas que le «complice» n'est pas moralement blâmable. On ne saurait non plus conclure que le droit criminel devrait s'abstenir de sanctionner ces conduites. Décriminaliser complètement l'aide, le conseil et l'encouragement au suicide n'est donc probablement pas une politique législative valable sur un plan général. L'est-elle cependant lorsque l'on s'adresse à des individus en phase terminale?

Dans ce cas précis, on doit constater encore une fois que la raison probable qui a motivé le législateur à ne pas faire d'exception pour l'agonisant, est fondée sur la crainte des excès ou des abus qu'une libéralisation de la loi actuelle pourrait entraîner. Comme dans le cas du meurtre par compassion, une décriminalisation serait basée sur le caractère humanitaire du motif qui pousse la personne à fournir aide, conseil ou encouragement. Comme dans le cas du meurtre par compassion, la loi peut cependant légitimement craindre les difficultés qu'il peut y avoir à établir la motivation réelle de l'auteur de l'acte.

De plus, aide ou incitation au suicide d'une part et homicide d'autre part sont parfois extrêmement proches l'un de l'autre. Qu'en est-il, par exemple, du médecin qui tient le verre

contenant le poison et en verse le contenu dans la bouche du patient? Est-ce une aide au suicide? Est-ce plutôt un homicide, puisque le consentement de la victime à la mort est indifférent? Le législateur peut craindre que des cas d'homicide de personnes en phase terminale, pour des motifs peu nobles, ne puissent être facilement déguisés en aides au suicide.

Il convient, à cet égard, de se rappeler que les réactions législatives à ce problème sont variées. Certains pays, comme l'Angleterre et plusieurs États américains, font une infraction distincte de l'aide au suicide, la punissant moins sévèrement que l'homicide. D'autres ne connaissent pas d'infraction comme telle. Pourtant, ils punissent parfois ce comportement sous le chef de l'homicide, en étendant la notion de lien de causalité.

Il faut également, à propos de l'aide au suicide, se souvenir que, dans l'hypothèse où véritablement il s'agit d'une aide humanitaire apportée à un patient en phase terminale qui désire la mort, rarissimes sont les cas où la poursuite est intentée par les autorités.

La Commission, dans la perspective où le motif présidant à un homicide continue, selon la tradition actuelle, à être ignoré, n'est pas d'avis de créer une exception particulière pour décriminaliser l'aide, l'encouragement ou le soutien au suicide. Par contre, elle serait prête, de façon à renforcer législativement le système de réserve actuelle dans l'exercice de l'action pénale et à insister davantage sur le caractère exceptionnel que devraient avoir les poursuites pour une telle action, à recommander un amendement à l'article 224 du *Code criminel*, de façon à ce que la poursuite ne puisse être prise que par le procureur général sur autorisation donnée par écrit. Les modifications apportées en 1961 à la loi anglaise (*British Suicide Act*) comportent d'ailleurs cette soupape de sûreté.

III. L'interruption de traitement et la renonciation au traitement

Comme nous l'avons déjà noté dans ce document, il existe à l'heure actuelle sur le plan du droit criminel un écart considérable entre la réalité de la pratique médicale et ce que

pourrait révéler une interprétation littérale et restrictive des textes du *Code criminel* en matière de traitement. Comme nous l'avons également noté, l'absence quasi-complète de jurisprudence sur la question, crée un état d'incertitude et d'ambiguïté tant pour le juriste que pour les membres du personnel médical et pour le public. La loi, pense la Commission, ne peut pas parler par énigme, surtout sur une question aussi importante, sans risquer de perdre crédibilité et respect de la part de tous ceux auxquels elle s'adresse.

La Commission a déjà discuté, dans un document de travail publié en 1980, du traitement médical en général. Elle a, à ce propos, émis un certain nombre d'idées et soumis un certain nombre de propositions de réforme. Il n'est pas dans son intention de revenir sur celles-ci dans le présent document. Elle entend donc seulement apporter un complément à cette analyse, sous l'angle très particulier de l'interruption au traitement et de la renonciation au traitement. C'est au niveau d'un rapport au Parlement qu'elle proposera une réforme d'ensemble. Il convient de discuter des solutions au problème, d'une part à partir de la situation normale, soit celle du patient capable d'exprimer sa volonté, et d'autre part à partir de la situation plus exceptionnelle du patient qui, pour une raison ou pour une autre, est dans l'impossibilité de le faire.

A. *La personne capable*

Dans son Document de travail n° 26 sur le traitement médical, la Commission a émis et défendu l'opinion que le patient capable doit être considéré par la loi comme le maître absolu des décisions sur son propre corps. En ce faisant, la Commission ne formulait pas une règle nouvelle et révolutionnaire, mais préconisait une simple reconnaissance de la règle de common law. La Commission n'a pas changé d'avis sur ce point. Elle estime qu'une personne capable doit avoir et doit conserver le droit de refuser un traitement quel qu'il soit et d'exiger qu'un traitement entrepris soit interrompu de façon temporaire ou définitive.

Or, la loi actuelle, en raison des distinctions qu'elle fait entre l'acte et l'omission et en raison du fait qu'elle impose, en

principe, la continuation d'un traitement entrepris si son interruption constitue une menace pour la vie, crée, sans aucun doute, certaines pressions en faveur de l'acharnement thérapeutique ou du moins un climat juridique susceptible de le favoriser.

Le devoir premier de la médecine est de se battre pour la vie et contre la mort. Nul ne contestera sérieusement ce fait. La médecine, comme la loi d'ailleurs, doit cependant reconnaître qu'à un certain moment le traitement optimal du patient n'est plus de lutter pour maintenir une vie purement végétative ou clinique, mais de laisser la mort se produire, tout en entourant l'individu des soins nécessaires pour soulager la douleur. La personne consciente et capable d'exprimer une volonté éclairée doit être le seul maître de cette décision.

Ce principe est souvent exprimé par le concept de la «mort dans la dignité». Le patient, maître de sa vie dans certaines limites et sous certaines conditions, doit également être maître de sa mort. Il doit pouvoir exercer un choix constant sur la façon dont il entend mourir et surtout sur la façon dont il entend vivre ses derniers moments. L'acharnement thérapeutique non consenti par le patient viole ce droit, en lui imposant une contrainte qui ne tient précisément pas compte de sa volonté et de ses désirs. La loi doit clairement en établir les corrolaires: le médecin, tout d'abord, ne doit pas encourir de responsabilité criminelle du seul fait qu'il respecte la volonté du patient d'interrompre ou de ne pas entreprendre un traitement médical. Le médecin, ensuite, qui persiste à traiter malgré la volonté contraire clairement exprimée de son patient, doit tomber sous les dispositions du *Code criminel* concernant les voies de fait, sans parler bien entendu des autres sanctions civiles ou disciplinaires. Ces deux règles sont apparemment les règles du droit actuel, mais ne sont pas législativement exprimées.

Les reconnaître ne signifie pas pour autant admettre l'euthanasie. Il existe, en effet, une différence fondamentale, comme nous l'avons vu, entre le fait d'infliger la mort par un acte positif et délibéré et le fait de retirer un traitement à un

patient qui le demande. Le premier acte doit continuer à faire l'objet d'une sanction criminelle et est inacceptable moralement et juridiquement; le second est, au contraire, parfaitement justifié au nom de l'autonomie de la personne et de son droit à l'autodétermination. Le respect de ce principe exige sur le plan juridique que le droit criminel actuel ne puisse être interprété comme imposant au médecin une obligation de traiter qui entre en conflit avec le droit du patient de refuser un traitement. Il importe de lever l'ambiguïté actuellement existante.

Pour ce qui est donc de la personne capable de prendre une décision par elle-même, *la Commission est d'avis que la loi lui reconnaisse de façon formelle et claire le droit absolu de refuser un traitement médical ou d'exiger son interruption.* Ce refus ou cette interruption doit, en tous les cas, avoir préséance sur l'obligation du médecin d'entreprendre ou de continuer un traitement déjà entrepris.

B. *La personne incapable*

C'est à l'endroit de la personne incapable de manifester sa volonté que les problèmes vraiment complexes se posent. Par personne incapable, nous entendons ici tout être humain qui, par la suite d'un défaut d'âge, d'un état d'inconscience temporaire ou permanente, ou d'un handicap, est dans l'impossibilité de manifester sa volonté et de prendre une décision éclairée et perd donc ainsi sa faculté de choisir. Avant de rentrer plus avant dans la discussion de ce problème, un certain nombre d'observations préliminaires doivent être faites.

En premier lieu, la Commission estime que la loi doit éviter un effet discriminatoire probablement involontaire à l'égard de ces personnes. Elle pense que l'acharnement thérapeutique n'est pas plus justifié dans le cas d'un incapable que dans le cas d'une personne capable. En d'autres termes, l'incapacité d'un individu ne doit pas servir de base ou de prétexte pour lui nier les droits fondamentaux ou une faculté de choix reconnus à la personne capable. Il serait, par exemple, regrettable et absurde que parce qu'une personne est incapable, le médecin traitant se voie obligé, légalement, de continuer ou

d'entreprendre un traitement inutile et soit tenu de prolonger inutilement l'agonie de cette personne. Il serait inadmissible que le droit de mourir dans la dignité soit enlevé, dès l'instant où la personne devient incapable de manifester sa volonté.

Toutefois, nul ne peut le contester, l'incapable a besoin d'une protection accrue. D'ailleurs, à l'heure actuelle, tous les systèmes juridiques tant en droit criminel qu'en droit civil ont mis sur pied des mécanismes de protection, notamment en lui nommant un curateur ou un gardien et en entourant les décisions prises au nom de ces personnes de certaines exigences formelles. Le problème est donc, puisque nous touchons ici à des valeurs suprêmes de vie et de mort, dans le développement de mesures de protection laissant le moins de place possible à l'arbitraire et à l'erreur. Le problème ne se situe pas dans la reconnaissance d'une différence d'essence ou de nature, entre la personne capable et la personne incapable. L'incapacité doit continuer à être une mesure de protection; elle ne doit pas servir à retirer des droits à cette personne, ni surtout à aggraver sa situation face à la mort.

En second lieu, le droit doit reconnaître ce qui est maintenant une réalité médicale et scientifique. Il doit admettre que la cessation ou la non-initiation d'un traitement qui n'offre aucune chance de succès est *une bonne décision et relève d'une saine pratique médicale*. Le traitement est une mesure destinée à aider le patient à guérir de sa maladie, à en enrayer temporairement la progression ou à en soulager les symptômes. Il est conçu, préparé et administré dans le but de sauvegarder ou de prolonger la vie. Le patient capable doit être libre, nous l'avons vu, de renoncer aux bénéfices du traitement. Face à un patient capable, le médecin a le loisir de lui expliquer le pronostic et les chances de succès du traitement. Avec l'incapable, la situation est évidemment différente puisque ce dialogue est parfois impossible. Le médecin ne peut donc pas compter sur la communication de la volonté du patient.

D'aucuns en concluent que, puisque la présomption en faveur de la vie doit toujours exister (ce que la Commission ne conteste pas), le devoir le plus strict du médecin dans le cas de

l'incapable est d'instituer le traitement et de continuer à traiter dans tous les cas. Agir dans le sens contraire serait, dit-on, pratiquer l'euthanasie négative. De l'avis de la Commission, cette prise de position est fausse. Fausse parce qu'elle oublie qu'à la base de toute décision médicale le principe essentiel à respecter n'est pas la vie en tant que telle et en tant que valeur suprême, mais le *bien* du patient. Ce bien coïncide, il est vrai, la plupart du temps avec le maintien de la vie. Il n'en est pas cependant toujours ainsi. Il n'en est pas ainsi lorsque le prolongement de la vie est devenu purement artificiel. Il n'en est pas ainsi lorsque le maintien de la vie ne peut se faire que par une prolongation indue de l'agonie. Il n'en est pas ainsi lorsque le maintien de la vie passe par le fait d'infliger des souffrances supplémentaires. En d'autres termes, il n'en est pas ainsi lorsque le traitement est détourné de sa finalité propre et ne fait que prolonger le «mourir» plutôt que de prolonger la vie. Le patient capable prend une décision en fonction de ses intérêts. Il peut exceptionnellement souhaiter d'être maintenu en vie artificiellement, ou de prolonger son agonie ou de souffrir. Dans ce cas, le médecin n'a presque pas le choix: il doit respecter la volonté exprimée par le patient en phase terminale; il doit traiter ou continuer de traiter, indépendamment de ses vues personnelles, si les circonstances s'y prêtent, c'est-à-dire si cette continuation n'est pas déraisonnable.

Par contre, dans le cas de l'incapable il n'est pas exact, ni sain d'ailleurs, de transposer une situation exceptionnelle en une situation générale et d'agir comme si, parce que la personne est incapable, elle aurait souhaité être maintenue artificiellement, voir prolonger son agonie, ou continuer de souffrir. Pour ce faire, la loi doit donc reconnaître que, même dans le cas d'une personne incapable, la cessation ou la non-initiation d'un traitement médical peut constituer objectivement une bonne pratique médicale et ne doit pas être sanctionnée par la loi criminelle.

En troisième lieu, une autre règle mérite d'être reconnue. Il est indispensable de faire une distinction, en matière d'interruption de traitement chez l'incapable, entre deux situations que l'on a malheureusement souvent confondues. La

première est celle dont nous venons tout juste de parler et qui consiste à interrompre ou à ne pas entreprendre un traitement parce que celui-ci n'offre pas d'espoir raisonnable d'amélioration et ne ferait donc que prolonger le «mourir» plutôt que la vie. Dans ce cas, comme nous l'avons dit, l'interruption ou la non-initiation du traitement est légitime et doit être reconnue comme légale. La seconde est celle où un traitement n'est pas entrepris ou continué uniquement parce que la situation chez le patient incapable présente des aspects négatifs par rapport à la norme acceptée. Un exemple permettra d'illustrer cette différence.

Décider de ne pas entreprendre de traitement dans le cas d'un nouveau-né anencéphale* est médicalement justifié. Il n'existe aucun traitement, à l'heure actuelle, permettant de remédier à cette condition. Procéder à une opération pour réparer une atrésie* du tube digestif dans un tel cas serait inutile et équivaudrait peut-être même à prolonger l'inévitable agonie d'un être humain. Le devoir le plus strict du médecin dans un tel cas est de voir à ce que la mort inévitable se déroule dans les meilleures conditions possibles. Il ne s'agit pas d'aider la nature, mais de laisser la nature suivre son cours tout en administrant au nouveau-né des soins palliatifs adéquats.

Par opposition, il est évident que le devoir le plus strict du médecin devant un nouveau-né normal par ailleurs, mais qui souffre d'une atrésie*, est de procéder à la chirurgie corrective qui lui permettra de s'alimenter.

Enfin, que doit-on décider dans le cas de l'enfant qui, à la naissance, présente les caractéristiques d'une trisomie 21 (Syndrome de Down ou mongolisme)* et souffre aussi d'une atrésie* du tube digestif? De l'avis de la Commission, cet enfant doit être traité pour l'atrésie*. Abandonner l'enfant et le laisser mourir de faim est inacceptable et contraire aux normes du droit criminel. Le refus de traitement dans un tel cas n'est pas en effet basé sur l'absence d'espoir d'amélioration (la réparation de l'atrésie* va au contraire régler le problème). Il est

---

* Voir Annexe II

68

fondé sur le fait que le traitement ne changera pas la déficience de l'enfant. La décision est donc basée sur un jugement de valeur sur la qualité de vie actuelle ou future du nouveau-né. Elle équivaut à une condamnation à mort fondée sur l'incapacité dont souffre l'enfant. La Commission est cependant consciente des douloureux problèmes que pose la naissance d'un enfant souffrant de malformations sérieuses, des conséquences tragiques que celle-ci peut avoir sur le couple et sur la famille. Ce n'est pas cependant une façon légitime de régler le problème que de le faire disparaître. La réponse se trouve beaucoup plus dans les moyens de prévention par le diagnostic prénatal et dans l'aide et le soutien matériel que la société tout entière doit apporter aux parents dans l'éventualité d'une telle naissance.

Une précision importante doit cependant être apportée. Si le nouveau-né trisomique et souffrant d'atrésie* a en plus d'autres malformations importantes pour lesquelles un traitement est inutile ou inapproprié dans les circonstances particulières de l'espèce, la décision de ne pas traiter doit alors être considérée comme légitime. Elle n'est pas prise alors en fonction de l'existence de la trisomie*, mais bien en fonction du non-prolongement d'un processus de mortalité déjà engagé comme dans la première hypothèse. La Commission pense donc que l'on doit accepter comme fondamental le principe de la non-discrimination entre la personne capable et la personne incapable d'une part et d'autre part, la règle qu'en cas d'impossibilité d'expression de volonté, tout traitement médicalement utile et nécessaire pour sauver la vie doit être administré.

Le problème, si ces principes sont pris pour acquis, devient alors celui-ci: comment s'assurer de la volonté présumée de l'incapable? Sur quelle base et en vertu de quels critères une autre personne peut-elle ou doit-elle prendre pour lui une décision d'interruption ou de non-initiation de traitement, lorsque celui-ci paraît inutile? À notre avis, il importe de faire une distinction (qui ne reflète peut-être pas une véritable différence cependant) entre les personnes incapables qui antérieurement

* Voir Annexe II

69

ont eu la possibilité d'exprimer leur volonté et celles qui n'ont jamais pu ou ne pourront jamais le faire.

Dans la première catégorie, on peut ranger l'adulte qui, à un moment ou à un autre, est devenu inconscient ou incapable, mais qui antérieurement a exprimé sa volonté sur le sujet. Celle-ci peut avoir été le fruit d'un échange avec le médecin ou avec ses proches. Elle peut avoir été exprimée d'une manière plus formelle dans une lettre ou un écrit du type «testament de vie». Dans une telle hypothèse, il nous paraît que cette volonté doit être respectée et que le médecin est tenu alors de se placer dans la même position que si son patient était conscient et capable. Par traitement, bien entendu, il faut comprendre ici le traitement qui n'offre plus d'espoir raisonnable de guérison ou d'amélioration de l'état du malade. Si le traitement au contraire offre cet espoir, le médecin a alors le devoir de l'entreprendre ou de le continuer, à moins d'une défense très claire de la part du patient. Décider autrement est tomber dans un cercle vicieux et risquer d'aboutir à une situation absurde, qui a d'ailleurs été en grande partie responsable du développement des systèmes instaurant un testament de vie: dès que le patient est inconscient ou incapable, quel que soit son état ou sa volonté antérieure, le médecin aurait l'obligation de poursuivre ou d'entreprendre les traitements, même inutiles!

La situation semble différente dans l'hypothèse où le patient, par suite d'un défaut d'âge ou d'un handicap mental, est dans l'impossibilité absolue d'exprimer sa volonté. C'est le cas du nouveau-né; c'est le cas du retardé sévère; c'est aussi le cas du comateux qui n'a jamais auparavant exprimé sa volonté. Dans ces cas, la situation est pour ainsi dire «neutre», en ce sens qu'on ne peut avoir aucune indication sur ce que pourrait être ou aurait pu être la volonté de la personne en question. Cette contrainte impose le seul système rationnel et possible dans les circonstances: la décision doit être prise par un autre. La difficulté vient alors de savoir qui est cet autre, et quels sont les critères qui peuvent ou doivent servir à la prise de décision.

Trois systèmes sont concevables. À l'intérieur de chacun peuvent naturellement exister des différences d'aménagement

et de modalités. Le premier est de laisser le tout à la décision du médecin. C'est conférer à ce dernier le soin de juger de chaque cas en regard des circonstances particulières de l'espèce et de prendre seul la décision ultime. Certes, il peut et doit même s'entourer de toute l'expertise que commande le cas particulier. Il doit aussi évidemment consulter les proches et la famille, si faire se peut, et les engager dans la dynamique même du processus décisionnel.

Certains s'opposent de façon plus ou moins véhémente à cette solution pour deux raisons. La première est qu'ils voient en elle une sorte de blanc-seing que la société toute entière donne à la science médicale, sans garantie que le résultat soit objectivement valable. C'est, prétend-on, donner au médecin un pouvoir pratiquement divin. C'est, par-delà, attribuer à la médecine un rôle qui n'est pas le sien. Cette première objection tient beaucoup plus à une attitude ou à une question de confiance ou de méfiance à l'égard de la pratique médicale en général et des médecins en particulier. Cette objection part aussi du principe que donner le pouvoir de décider au médecin est automatiquement enlever à la société tout pouvoir de contrôle. Cette conclusion est inexacte. Donner le pouvoir décisionnel final au médecin ne veut pas dire pour autant lui conférer une immunité absolue pour les conséquences des décisions qu'il prend. Le droit criminel est précisément là pour sanctionner les abus et n'est qu'un des nombreux mécanismes de contrôle.

On objecte, en second lieu, que cette solution ne fait que maintenir la situation actuelle. Les pratiques médicales et hospitalières variant considérablement d'un lieu à un autre, d'un individu à un autre, on craint que les décisions ne continuent à se prendre dans un subjectivisme total d'une part et, d'autre part, que certaines pratiques condamnables comme l'acharnement thérapeutique ne se perpétuent.

La réponse à cette deuxième série d'objections est multiple. Tout d'abord, il faut reconnaître et admettre qu'il est de toute façon impossible de se débarrasser complètement de toute subjectivité ou jugement individuel. La chose n'est d'ailleurs

pas souhaitable. La médecine ne doit pas être normalisée, pas plus que les décisions médicales. La qualité de la pratique en dépend. Ensuite, on peut expliquer en bonne partie, à notre avis, les différences de pratique actuelle par l'incertitude qui entoure l'état du droit. On peut, en effet, soupçonner que si l'acharnement thérapeutique continue à se pratiquer, il est probablement dû beaucoup plus à la crainte de poursuites et donc à l'exercice d'une prudence qui commande de traiter, qu'à la transposition délibérée et voulue des attitudes et de la philosophie personnelles du médecin. On peut donc raisonnablement espérer qu'à la levée de ces ambiguïtés et incertitudes correspondra une uniformisation accrue des pratiques médicales.

Le second système possible est de «judiciariser» les mécanismes décisionnels. Cette seconde option est susceptible de beaucoup de variations. On peut, par exemple, concevoir un système dans lequel toute prise de décision sur la continuation ou la cessation du traitement d'un incapable doive nécessairement et obligatoirement faire l'objet d'une décision judiciaire ou quasi-judiciaire d'un tribunal ou d'un organisme administratif. On a proposé aussi parfois de créer des comités de «sages», des ombudsman au sein des hôpitaux, etc.

Sur le plan technique, plusieurs systèmes peuvent être envisagés. Le premier serait qu'un comité hospitalier soit mis sur pied dans chaque hôpital. Ce comité aurait pour fonctions de constater et de vérifier pour le patient capable comme pour le patient incapable les conditions de l'interruption ou de la non-entreprise d'un traitement. Le second serait de s'assurer simplement qu'un ou deux autres médecins indépendants participent à la décision. Le système du comité a des avantages mais aussi des inconvénients sur le plan pratique. La Commission n'a pris aucune décision ferme sur cette question, préférant la réserver pour ses recommandations finales. Elle invite donc les médecins, les membres du personnel hospitalier et le public en général à lui faire connaître leur position sur ce problème.

La Commission ne songe naturellement pas à nier le rôle primordial des décisions judiciaires dans le règlement des

conflits. Celles-ci offrent les garanties d'impartialité et de justice naturelle. Par contre, elle hésite fortement à encombrer les tribunaux, en leur référant d'une façon systématique toutes et chacune des décisions qui doivent être prises quant aux incapables en matière de cessation de traitement. La chose apparaît irréaliste. Elle hésite aussi à judiciariser et donc à «adversariser» un processus décisionnel qui devrait plus relever du modèle du consensus que de celui de la confrontation. La décision judiciaire est nécessaire lorsqu'il y a conflit véritable. Elle est peut-être superflue lorsqu'elle ne vise qu'à formaliser une décision déjà prise et à propos de laquelle personne ne se plaint ou à propos de laquelle une dispute, une controverse ou un conflit n'existe pas vraiment. Si, pour en prendre un exemple, le médecin décide en s'appuyant sur son meilleur jugement médical que dans les circonstances le maintien du traitement est inutile et que de son côté la famille du patient s'oppose formellement à son retrait, alors et alors seulement, la seule façon véritable de trancher paraît être une décision judiciaire. Chacune des deux parties, en effet, interprète de façon différente l'intérêt de l'incapable. Seul un tiers arbitre peut choisir. Le fait que la décision soit judiciaire donne aussi à penser qu'elle prendra à cœur les meilleurs intérêts de l'incapable et que progressivement l'accumulation de ces décisions permettra de faire ressortir un certain nombre de critères décisionnels qui, à l'heure actuelle, peuvent apparaître encore flous. La Commission estime donc que le modèle judiciaire est valable, mais seulement avec les aménagements et dans les limites qu'elle vient de mentionner.

La troisième possibilité est de laisser les proches, la famille ou celui (curateur, gardien, tuteur) qui représente l'incapable prendre seul la décision. Cette solution peut apparaître la moins mauvaise à première vue. Ces personnes, en effet, connaissent le patient et sont donc mieux que toutes autres en mesure d'apprécier les éléments subjectifs du cas d'espèce. On peut présumer aussi qu'elles auront toujours à cœur de défendre les meilleurs intérêts du malade. Tout ceci est exact. Cependant, deux objections sont régulièrement apportées à ce troisième système. La première est que prendre une telle décision entraîne en général l'apparition d'un sentiment de culpabilité et ce,

quelle que soit la décision effectivement prise. On peut donc se demander s'il est vraiment juste d'imposer ce fardeau à des personnes qui, à la différence du médecin, ne sont pas, par leur profession même, spécialement préparées à y faire face. La seconde est que, dans le cas d'une personne incapable, il peut paraître préférable que la décision soit prise par une personne indépendante, moins en raison de conflits d'intérêts (ceux-ci peuvent cependant être réels), qu'en raison de la nécessité d'entourer la prise de décision du plus grand degré d'objectivité possible et de la protection la plus stricte des droits de l'incapable. Toutefois, la Commission reconnaît, encore une fois, que ces personnes doivent être engagées à une étape ou à une autre dans le processus décisionnel.

La Commission en définitive constate qu'il n'existe malheureusement pas en la matière de solution miracle susceptible de pallier tous les inconvénients, de supprimer toutes les difficultés et de rallier tous les suffrages. Le choix est donc limité. Il s'agit de trouver une solution qui, dans notre contexte particulier, est la moins mauvaise. La première possibilité nous paraît à l'heure actuelle rencontrer ce critère.

À cette étape, il est peut-être important de résumer les conclusions provisoires auxquelles la Commission est arrivée jusqu'ici. Ces conclusions sont les suivantes:

(1) *la loi doit donner tout son effet à la volonté du patient capable et donc respecter celle-ci lorsqu'il exige la cessation ou la non-initiation d'un traitement;*

(2) *la loi doit clairement affirmer que le médecin agit légalement lorsqu'il décide d'interrompre ou de ne pas initier un traitement inutile qui n'offre plus d'espoir raisonnable, à moins que son patient n'ait manifesté sa volonté contraire;*

(3) *la loi doit reconnaître que la prolongation de la vie n'est pas une valeur en soi et donc que le médecin n'agit pas illégalement lorsqu'il ne prend pas les*

mesures pour le faire, si ces mesures sont inutiles ou vont contre la volonté ou l'intérêt du patient;

(4) *la loi doit reconnaître que le médecin qui continue à traiter, malgré la volonté contraire de son patient, est sujet aux dispositions du* Code criminel;

(5) *la loi doit admettre que l'incapacité d'une personne de manifester sa volonté n'est pas une raison suffisante pour obliger le médecin à l'administration de traitements de prolongation inutiles;*

(6) *la loi doit reconnaître que dans le cas du patient inconscient ou incapable, le médecin n'encourt pas de responsabilité criminelle en interrompant un traitement devenu inutile.*

CINQUIÈME PARTIE

La formulation de la réforme

Il n'est peut-être pas inutile, au terme de cette analyse et avant de présenter une formule possible de réforme, de rappeler encore une fois certaines réalités. La réforme, quelle qu'elle soit, ne peut en aucune façon régler tous les problèmes. La loi ne peut pas fournir au public ou au médecin un guide complet, permettant de prendre des décisions de vie ou de mort au moyen de critères entièrement objectifs. La chose est rigoureusement impossible. La réforme ne peut à cet égard tout au plus que dissiper certaines ambiguïtés.

La réforme sur le plan du droit criminel ne peut, de façon réaliste, judiciariser le processus décisionnel pour faire déterminer *a priori* si telle ou telle décision d'entreprendre ou de cesser un traitement est valable. Comme nous l'avons mentionné antérieurement, le droit criminel n'est là que pour sanctionner les abus les plus flagrants. Le contrôle de la légalité ou de l'illégalité du geste posé doit donc demeurer généralement un contrôle *a posteriori*. Dans ce sens la loi n'est pas et ne peut pas être rassurante pour le médecin ou celui qui prend la décision. Celui-ci doit prendre la décision au meilleur de ses connaissances, de ses capacités et de son jugement médical, éthique et juridique, et s'attendre, si celle-ci est abusive ou mauvaise, à subir les foudres de la loi. S'il est impossible et irréaliste de vouloir changer ce processus, il reste possible, par contre, de lui indiquer les bases fondamentales sur lesquelles le droit estime que ces décisions doivent être prises.

La réforme, du moins celle qui est proposée dans les pages qui suivent, ne rencontrera sûrement pas l'approbation de tout

le monde. D'ailleurs, le but du présent document n'est pas tellement de dégager un consensus sur une question aussi controversée, mais plutôt de proposer pour fin de discussion un certain nombre de solutions qui paraissent raisonnables et de les confronter à la critique, avant de faire des recommandations finales au Parlement du Canada.

Enfin, la réforme proposée ne doit pas être évaluée de façon «désincarnée». La loi ne peut pas, par des textes, codifier la pratique médicale ou hospitalière. Elle peut tout simplement tenter de l'influencer et de créer un climat propice à l'épanouissement de certains droits et principes fondamentaux pour l'homme. Le lecteur ne doit donc pas espérer trouver dans les suggestions de réforme qui suivent un tableau complet. Il doit replacer ces suggestions dans le contexte social, culturel et médical actuel.

I. L'euthanasie

Comme l'a énoncé la Commission, elle n'est pas en faveur de la reconnaissance de l'euthanasie active sous aucune de ses formes. *Elle recommande donc que les prohibitions actuelles du* Code criminel *concernant l'homicide soient maintenues.* Quant au problème du meurtre par compassion, la Commission est d'avis que celui-ci doit continuer à être sanctionné par la loi. Si, par contre, dans la réforme que la Commission proposera bientôt sur l'homicide, elle en venait à la conclusion que, contrairement au système et à la tradition actuels, le motif devrait entrer en ligne de compte, alors et alors seulement, estime-t-elle que le motif de compassion pourrait, dans ce cadre nouveau, être pris en considération au niveau d'une réduction possible de la sentence.

II. L'aide au suicide

Pour les raisons exprimées plus haut, *la Commission est d'avis qu'une décriminalisation complète de l'aide ou de l'incitation au suicide serait inopportune et dangereuse dans*

le contexte actuel. En ce faisant, la Commission n'entend nullement nier le droit à l'autonomie de la personne, ni le principe de son autodétermination. Elle entend simplement, sur le plan de la politique législative générale du droit du *Code criminel* canadien, maintenir la prohibition face aux possibilités d'abus sérieux qu'une décriminalisation pourrait entraîner.

Par contre, pour permettre de mieux tenir compte de l'aspect humanitaire indéniable dans certains cas, de l'aide fournie par un proche à un parent en phase terminale et parce qu'elle n'est pas convaincue que dans un tel cas, l'imposition d'une sentence criminelle soit la mesure appropriée, *la Commission propose l'addition à l'article 224 du* Code criminel *actuel d'un second paragraphe se lisant comme suit*:

> *224. (2) Nul ne peut être poursuivi pour une infraction prévue au présent article sans l'autorisation du procureur général lui-même, donnée par écrit.*

III.   L'interruption de traitement et la renonciation au traitement

Sur le problème de l'interruption de traitement, la Commission s'est longuement penchée sur l'optique de réforme prise par certains États américains, notamment la Californie, et donc sur la possibilité de suggérer l'adoption, au Canada, d'un équivalent du *Natural Death Act.*

Elle a cependant rejeté cette option pour les raisons suivantes. Il lui paraîtrait malheureux d'inverser ce qui lui semble être ou devoir être une règle générale, à savoir qu'il ne doit pas exister d'obligation de traiter ou de maintenir un traitement lorsque celui-ci est inutile. La solution californienne part du principe contraire, puisqu'elle exige que la volonté du patient soit formalisée et exprimée par écrit pour autoriser le médecin à ne pas prolonger l'agonie et la mort. Cette démarche qui, en raison de certaines conditions particulières à la Californie est peut-être logique là-bas, ne l'est pas dans le contexte canadien qui nous est propre.

La décision de ne pas traiter ou d'interrompre un traitement inutile est une bonne décision médicale et doit être reconnue comme telle. La loi ne doit donc pas partir du principe que le médecin qui ne prolonge pas la vie agit illégalement, mais au contraire du principe que le médecin agit légalement s'il ne prolonge pas la mort.

De l'avis de la Commission donc, ce principe reconnu en pratique à l'heure actuelle par le common law, peut et doit tout simplement être formulé dans le cadre du *Code criminel* actuel. De même, pour reprendre dans le cadre du présent document une suggestion contenue dans le Document de travail nº 26, la Commission estime également que le droit criminel doit, pour lever toute ambiguïté, formaliser la reconnaissance du principe selon lequel une personne capable a le droit de refuser un traitement ou d'exiger que celui-ci soit interrompu.

Pour ce qui est de la personne incapable de manifester sa volonté, la Commission est d'avis que la décision d'interrompre ou de ne pas entreprendre un traitement doit se fonder sur une double critériologie soit, d'une part sur un critère d'ordre médical touchant l'utilité ou la non-utilité de l'administration du traitement, et d'autre part sur celui des volontés de la personne avant de devenir incapable, ou sur ses meilleurs intérêts dans le cas où la personne n'a pas ou n'a jamais été en mesure d'exprimer sa volonté. La Commission estime que les «meilleurs intérêts» de la personne peuvent, dans certains cas, être la prolongation de la vie et dans d'autres, au contraire, l'interruption d'un traitement de façon à conserver à la personne incapable son droit à une mort paisible et dans la dignité. En cas de conflit d'appréciation sur la question de savoir quels sont les meilleurs intérêts de la personne (par exemple entre le médecin traitant et la famille), le tribunal devrait, comme la chose se fait d'ailleurs aujourd'hui, être appelé à trancher. *Sur ce point la Commission suggère donc le maintien du droit et de la pratique actuels.*

Enfin, pour ce qui est du problème touchant l'administration des soins palliatifs, la Commission est d'avis que jamais le médecin ne doit refuser l'administration au patient en phase

terminale de médicaments, de drogues antidouleur ou d'autres traitements, lorsqu'à son avis ils sont médicalement utiles pour atténuer ou supprimer la douleur, pour la seule raison que leur administration répétée peut hâter la mort.

La Commission suggère donc l'addition au *Code criminel* des textes suivants:

1. *Rien, dans les articles 14, 45, 198 et 199 du* Code criminel *ne doit être interprété comme créant une obligation pour un médecin*

a) de continuer à administrer ou d'entreprendre un traitement médical, lorsque la personne à laquelle ce traitement s'adresse a clairement exprimé sa volonté du contraire;

b) de continuer à administrer ou d'entreprendre un traitement médical, lorsque ce traitement est médicalement inutile et n'est pas dans le meilleur intérêt de la personne à laquelle il s'adresse, à moins que cette personne n'ait clairement exprimé sa volonté du contraire.

2. *Rien, dans les articles 14, 45, 198 et 199 du* Code criminel *ne doit être interprété comme empêchant un médecin d'entreprendre ou d'interrompre l'administration de soins palliatifs et de mesures destinées à éliminer ou à atténuer les souffrances d'une personne pour la seule raison que ces soins ou ces mesures sont susceptibles de raccourcir l'expectative de vie de cette personne.*

Renvois

1. Les documents de travail sont: *Les critères de détermination de la mort*, document de travail n° 23; *Stérilisation*, document de travail n° 24; *Le traitement médical et le droit criminel*, document de travail n° 26. Les documents d'étude sont: *Le consentement à l'acte médical* et *Le caractère sacré de la vie ou la qualité de la vie*.

2. *Les critères de détermination de la mort*, rapport n° 15.

3. E. Keyserlingk, *Le caractère sacré de la vie ou la qualité de la vie*, document d'étude, Commission de réforme du droit du Canada, Ottawa, Approvisionnements et Services Canada, 1979.

4. Voir à ce sujet, Commission de réforme du droit du Canada, *Les critères de détermination de la mort*, rapport n° 15, Ottawa, Approvisionnements et Services Canada, 1981.

5. Voir entre autres, le code d'éthique de l'Association médicale canadienne.

6. *Globe and Mail*, 16 août 1978, "Probe continues in death of baby at B.C. hospital". Dans ce cas, toutefois, il nous a été impossible de déterminer avec précision le degré exact de malformation de l'enfant. Voir *In re B (A Minor)* (1981) 1 W.L.R. 1421.

7. Commission de réforme du droit du Canada, *Le traitement médical et le droit criminel*, document de travail n° 26, Ottawa, Approvisionnements et Services Canada, 1980.

8. Voir *Le traitement médical et le droit criminel*, *op. cit.*, note 7, p. 28 à 30.

9. Pour une analyse plus détaillée de ces dispositions, voir *Le traitement médical et le droit criminel*, *op. cit.*, note 7, p. 28 et suivantes.

10. H. Picard, *Legal Liability of Doctors and Hospitals in Canada*, Toronto, Carswell, 1978, p. 298.

11. *R. v. St-Germain* (1976) C.A. 185. Dans cette affaire, rappelons-le, un médecin avait été accusé de négligence criminelle pour avoir refusé de traiter un patient en état grave à l'urgence d'un hôpital de Montréal.

11a. *La Reine* v. *Milliard*, Cour des Sessions de la Paix, Montréal, n° 01-001050-803, 7 mars 1980.

11b. H. Palmer, "Dr. Adams' Trial for Murder" (1957) *Cr. Law Rev.* 365, p. 375.

12. Sur l'historique de ces mouvements en Grande-Bretagne et aux États-Unis, voir R. Kaplan, "Euthanasia Legislation: A Survey and a Model Act" (1976) 2 *Am. J. of Law and Med.* 41, p. 52 et suivantes.

13. G. Williams, *The Sanctity of Life and the Criminal Law*, Londres, Faber and Faber, 1958; aussi, "Euthanasia" (1973) 41 *Medicolegal Journal* 14.

14. California Health and Safety Code #7185 et suivantes (1976).

15. Oregon, Nouveau-Mexique, Nevada, Arkansas, Caroline du Nord, Idaho et Texas.

16. Projet de loi (privé) n° 3 intitulé "An Act Respecting the Withholding or Withdrawal of Treatment where Death Is Inevitable", 4ᵉ session, 30ᵉ Législature de l'Ontario (1973).

17. Pour les détails concernant ces diverses législations, voir H. Silving, "Euthanasia: A Study in Comparative Criminal Law" (1954) 103 *U. of Pen. Law Rev.* 350 et D. Maguire, *Death by Choice*, New York, Schocken, 1975.

18. Voir Maguire, *ibid.*, ch. 2, p. 22.

18a. Voir, Commission de réforme du droit, rapport n° 15.

19. E. Keyserlingk, *Le caractère sacré de la vie ou la qualité de la vie*, Commission de réforme du droit du Canada, Ottawa, Approvisionnements et Services Canada, 1979.

20. Commission de réforme du droit du Canada, *La stérilisation*, document de travail n° 24, Ottawa, Approvisionnements et Services Canada, 1979.

20a. *Loi sur la protection de la santé publique*, L.R.Q. 1977, ch. P-35, art. 42 et 43.

20b. Voir, par exemple, le *Child Welfare Act*, R.S.O. 1970, ch. 64; le *Child Welfare Act*, R.S.A. 1970, ch. 45.

21. Voir note 13.

22. K. Binding et A. Hoche, *The Release of the Destruction of Life Devoid of Value*, Los Angeles, R. Sassone, 1975 (Édition allemande originale publiée en 1920).

23. Voir *infra* Annexe I, pour une bibliographie sommaire.

24. Y. Kamisar, "Some Non-Religious Views against Proposed 'Mercy-Killing' Legislation" (1958) 42 *Min. Law Rev.* 969.

ANNEXE I

Bibliographie sommaire

BARRIÈRE, I., et LALOU, E., *Le dossier confidentiel de l'euthanasie*, Paris, Stock, 1962.

BEAUCHAMP, T., et DAVIDSON, R., "The Definition of Euthanasia" (1979) 4 *J. of Medicine and Philosophy* 294.

BEHNKE, J. A., et BOK, S., éds., *The Dilemmas of Euthanasia*, New York, Anchor Books, 1975.

BINDING, K., et HOCHE, A., *The Release of the Destruction of Life Devoid of Value*, Los Angeles, R. Sassone, 1975 (Édition allemande originale publiée en 1920).

CHORON, J., *Suicide*, N.Y., Scribners, 1972.

COMMISSION DE RÉFORME DU DROIT DU CANADA, *Le traitement médical et le droit criminel*, document de travail n° 26, Ottawa, Approvisionnements et Services Canada, 1980.

Les critères de détermination de la mort, rapport au Parlement n° 15, Ottawa, Approvisionnements et Services Canada, 1981.

Définition de la mort — Euthanasie, document préparé par l'Institut de recherche sur l'interprétation contemporaine de l'homme, Université de Sudbury, 1975.

CRANE, D., "Physicians Attitudes toward the Treatment of Critically Ill Patients" (1973) 23 *Bio. Sc.* 471.

DELAGLANDE, J., et ARNAUD, R., «Réflexions sur l'euthanasie» (1962) *Études* 305.

DICKENS, B., "The Role of the Family in Surrogate Medical Consent" (1980) 1 *Health Law in Canada* 49.

"The Right to Natural Death" (1981) 26 *McGill Law Journal* 847.

DOWNING, A., éd., *Euthanasia and the Right to Death*, Londres, Owen, 1977.

FLETCHER, G., "Prolonging Life" (1967) 42 *Wash. L. Rev.* 999.

FLETCHER, John, "Attitudes toward Defective Newborns" (1974) 2 *Hastings Center Studies* 21.

"Abortion, Euthanasia and Case of Defective Newborns" (1975) 292 *New England Journal of Medicine* 75.

FLETCHER, Joseph, "Ethics and Euthanasia" dans Robert H. Williams, éd., *To Live and to Die: When, Why and How*, New York, Springer-Verlag, 1973, p. 113 et suivantes.

"The 'Right' to Live and the 'Right' to Die: A Protestant View of Euthanasia" (1974) 34 *Humanist* 12.

GARLAND, M., "Politics, Legislation and Natural Death" (1976) 6 *Hastings Center Report* 5.

HARRISON, C., "Medicine, Terminal Illness and the Law" (1977) 3 *Can. Med. Ass. J.* 177.

HORAN, D., et MALL, D., *Death, Dying and Euthanasia*, Washington D.C., University Publications of America, 1977.

HUNTER, R., "Euthanasia" (1980) 25 *Can. J. Psych.* 439.

JARETZKI, A., "Death with Dignity — Passive Euthanasia: Guide to the Physician dealing with Dying Patients" (1976) 76 *N.Y. St. J. of Med.* 539.

JONAS, H., "The Right to Die" (1978) 8 *Hastings Center Report* 35.

KAMISAR, Y., "Some Non-Religious Views against Proposed 'Mercy-Killing' Legislation" (1958) 42 *Min. Law Rev.* 969.

KAPLAN, R., "Euthanasia Legislation: A Survey and a Model Act" (1976) 2 *Am. J. of Law and Med.* 41.

KENNEDY, I., "The Legal Effects of Requests by the Terminally Ill and Aged not to Receive further Treatment from Doctors" (1976) *Crim. L. Rev.* 217.

86

KEYSERLINGK, E., *Le caractère sacré de la vie ou la qualité de la vie*, document d'étude, Commission de réforme du droit du Canada, Ottawa, Approvisionnements et Services Canada, 1979.

«Le testament de vie» (1979) 14 *Méd. du Québec* 63.

KLUGE, E., *The Practice of Death*, Newhaven, Yale Univ. Press, 1975.

The Ethics of Deliberate Death, Port Washington N.Y., National University Publications, 1981.

KOHL, M., *The Morality of Killing*, Londres, Owen, 1974.

KOZA, P., "Euthanasia: Some Legal Considerations" (1976) 1 *Essence* 79.

KRAUSS, A., "Patients Who Want to Die: A Survey" (1977) *Can. Fam. Physician* 63.

KUBLER-ROSS, E., *On Death and Dying*, N.Y., MacMillan, 1969.

LEVASSEUR, G., «Suicide et euthanasie en regard du droit pénal» (1957) 32 *Lumière et Vie* 183.

LOUISELL, D., "Euthanasia and Biothanasia: On Dying and Killing" (1973) 22 *Cath. U. L. Rev.* 723.

MAGUIRE, D., *Death by Choice*, N.Y., Schocken, 1975.

MANTOUT, P., «L'Euthanasie» (1973) 2 *Vie Méd.* 136.

MORRIS, A., "Voluntary Euthanasia" (1970) 45 *Wash. L. Rev.* 247.

NOLAN-HALEY, J., "Defective Children, Their Parents and the Death Decision" (1976) 4 *J. of Leg. Med.* 9.

NOTE, "The Tragic Choice: Termination of Care for Patients in a Permanent Vegetative State" (1976) 51 *N.Y.U. Law Rev.* 285.

PICARD, H., *Legal Liability of Doctors and Hospitals in Canada*, Toronto, Carswell, 1978.

RAMSEY, P., "Prolonged Dying: Not Medically Indicated" (1976) *Hastings Center Report* 14.

REICH, W., "On the Birth of a Severely Handicapped Infant" (1973) 9 *Hastings Center Report* 10.

ROBERTSON, J., "Involuntary Euthanasia of Defective Newborns: A Legal Analysis" (1975) 27 *Stanford Law Rev.* 213.

SANDERS, J., "Euthanasia: None Dare Call It Murder" (1969) 60 *J. Crim. L. C. and P. S.* 351.

SILVING, H., "Euthanasia: A Study in Comparative Criminal Law" (1954) 103 *U. of Pen. L. Rev.* 350.

SKEGG, P., "Informed Consent to Medical Procedures" (1975) 15 *Med. Sc. and Law* 124.

SPORKEN, P., *Le droit de mourir*, Paris, Dexlée de Brower, 1974.

STARKMAN, B., "The Control of Life: Unexamined Law and the Life Worth Living" (1973) 11 *Osgoode Hall L.J.* 175.

"A Defence to Criminal Responsibility for Performing Surgical Operations: Section 45 of the *Criminal Code*" (1981) 26 *McGill Law Journal*, 1048.

STEINBERG, M., "The California Natural Death Act — A Failure to Provide for Adequate Patient Safeguards and Individual Autonomy" (1977) 9 *Conn. Law Rev.* 203.

STEINFELS, P., et VEATCH, R., *Death Inside Out*, N.Y., Harper and Row, 1974.

TROWELL, H., *The Unfinished Debate on Euthanasia*, Londres, S.C.M. Press, 1973.

VAUGHAN, N.L., "The Right to Die" (1974) 10 *Cal. West. L. Rev.* 613.

VEATCH, R., "Death and Dying: The Legislative Option" (1977) *Hastings Center Report* 5.

WILLIAMS, G., "Euthanasia" (1973) 41 *Med. Leg. J.* 14.

The Sanctity of Life and the Criminal Law, Londres, Faber and Faber, 1958.

ANNEXE II

Glossaire de termes médicaux

Anencéphale: Personne atteinte d'anencéphalie.

Anencéphalie: Absence de cerveau.

Atrésie du tube digestif: Obstruction totale ou partielle du tube digestif.

Mongolisme: État d'anomalie consécutif à la trisomie 21.

Spina bifida: Malformation congénitale de la colonne vertébrale consistant en une hernie d'une partie du contenu du canal rachidien.

Syndrôme de Down: Ensemble des symptômes caractéristiques de la trisomie 21.

Trisomie 21:   Anomalie congénitale caractérisée par l'apparition d'un chromosome supplémentaire dans une paire. Cette anomalie entraîne l'état dit de mongolisme.

THE ATTACK
ON AMERICA:
SEPTEMBER 11, 2001

Other books in the At Issue series:

THE ATTACK
ON AMERICA:
SEPTEMBER 11, 2001

William Dudley, *Book Editor*

Daniel Leone, *President*
Bonnie Szumski, *Publisher*
Scott Barbour, *Managing Editor*

GREENHAVEN PRESS
SAN DIEGO, CALIFORNIA

GALE GROUP

™
THOMSON LEARNING

Detroit • New York • San Diego • San Francisco
Boston • New Haven, Conn. • Waterville, Maine
London • Munich

Library of Congress Cataloging-in-Publication Data

The attack on America: September 11, 2001 / William Dudley, book editor.
  p. cm. — (At issue) (An opposing viewpoints series)
  Includes bibliographical references and index.
  ISBN 0-7377-1292-9 (lib. bdg. : alk. paper) —
ISBN 0-7377-1293-7 (pbk. : alk. paper)
  1. info. I. Dudley, William, 1964– . II. Series: At issue (San Diego, Calif.) III. Series: Opposing viewpoints series (Unnumbered)

  x   2002
  —dc21   2001
                                                           CIP

Copyright © 2002 by Greenhaven Press,
an imprint of The Gale Group
10911 Technology Place, San Diego, CA 92127

Printed in the U.S.A.

Contents

Introduction

On September 11, 2001, four passenger planes were hijacked by terrorists. Two of the planes were flown into the twin towers of the World Trade Center (WTC) in New York City, causing huge fires that led to the collapse of the towers less than two hours later. One plane crashed into the Pentagon building in Washington, D.C. The last plane crashed in a field in Pennsylvania; it is believed the hijackers had planned to also crash this plane into a building or landmark, but were foiled by the actions of the plane's passengers. Many of these horrific events, including the second plane's crash into the World Trade Center and the collapse of the towers, were witnessed live by millions of television viewers. It was by far the worst terrorist attack on American soil; conservative columnist George F. Will labeled it "the most lethal terrorism in human experience."

As the dust settled in New York and Washington, Americans were left to ponder what the attacks meant for the nation. In search of a historical precedent or point of comparison, many Americans reached back to Japan's surprise assault on Pearl Harbor on December 7, 1941, another "day of infamy" in which the United States was suddenly attacked. In both instances, a seemingly secure nation was jolted by massive assaults on its own soil. "As Pearl Harbor snapped America out of a false sense of security," NBC news anchor and author Tom Brokaw writes, "September 11 had a similar effect on young Americans."

The comparisons Brokaw and others made between the two dates dealt not only with the attacks themselves, but also how the American people responded to them. Many people wondered whether the resolve and unity shown by the American people in 1941 would be matched in 2001. Others wondered whether September 11 would become a defining experience for this current generation of Americans, much as Pearl Harbor had been for members of a previous generation. In attempting to answer these questions, it is instructive to note both the parallels and differences between the two events.

Casualties and perpetrators

Both Pearl Harbor and the September 11 attacks resulted in a large loss of human life. The attack on Pearl Harbor killed 2,388 people. The September 11 carnage was even larger, although an exact number was difficult to ascertain at first. In the initial weeks following September 11, the rough media consensus for the total number of fatalities at the WTC, the Pentagon, and in Pennsylvania was six or seven thousand (numbers cited by some of the articles in this volume). As weeks and months went by, that number consistently shrank, eventually reaching three thousand.

The September 11 casualties were not only numerically larger than those of Pearl Harbor, they were also different in nature. Pearl Harbor was a military attack against American military targets. Most of the casualties were sailors or soldiers; of the 2,388 people killed, forty-eight were civilians. For the most part, the September 11 attacks were directed not at soldiers or military targets, but at civilians going about their everyday jobs. For many, the fact that the September 11 terrorists targeted civilians made these acts even more outrageous and horrific than the events of 1941.

Another important difference between the two events was the identities of the attackers. On December 7, 1941, Americans knew who the enemy was—the Japanese Empire—and what its intentions were—to wage war against the United States. On September 11, 2001, Americans knew they had been attacked and perhaps were even at war, but they did not know who the enemy was or what their future intentions were.

In the days following September 11, 2001, some answers to these questions were found. Investigators from the Federal Bureau of Investigation (FBI) and other law enforcement agencies identified the nineteen air passengers that they believed were responsible for the attacks. The presumed terrorists were all men from Middle Eastern countries, including Egypt and Saudi Arabia. Suspicion quickly zeroed in on an organization called al-Qaida (the base), a terrorist network led by Osama bin Laden, a Saudi Arabian exile who had taken up residence in Afghanistan.

Thus, Americans were facing significantly different enemies in 1941 and 2001. Historian and World War II veteran Frank Mathias notes that Japan was a powerful nation with 191 infantry divisions and a large navy, as well as the support of Germany and Italy, while al-Qaida had "no navy, no organized army, no airforce." However, the absence of such resources did not prevent the shadowy terrorist organization from inflicting the damage of September 11.

America's response

In both 1941 and 2001, Americans responded quickly and patriotically, but were called upon to do different things. In 1941 Americans swamped military recruiting stations or waited for draft notices and sacrificed personal comforts for the war effort. In 2001 Americans expressed support for the paid professionals of the U.S. military and were called upon to spend the United States out of economic recession. Both eras were marked by upswings of patriotism and unity that extended to the federal government. Following the Pearl Harbor attacks, U.S. president Franklin D. Roosevelt addressed Congress and called for a declaration of war against Japan. Congress, previously divided and strongly isolationist, passed a war declaration with only one dissenting vote. Following the September 11 attacks, President George W. Bush addressed Congress, argued that the evidence pointed to al-Qaida, and called for a "war on terror" that "will not end until every terrorist group of global reach has been found, stopped, and defeated." He issued an ultimatum against the Taliban regime in Afghanistan, which he accused of harboring bin Laden and his network of terrorists. Congress, which earlier in 2001 had been preoccupied with domestic issues and partisan disputes, passed (again with one dissenting vote) a resolution authorizing Bush to use military force.

America's war against Japan in 1941 resulted in victory in 1945. America's war against terrorism is incomplete. On October 7, 2001, after marshaling diplomatic support worldwide, the United States began a bombing campaign in Afghanistan. By the end of 2001, Afghan rebels, assisted by U.S. bombing and special forces, had toppled the Taliban regime, and numerous al-Qaida officials were either killed or captured (Osama bin Laden himself, however, remained at large).

The successful yet inconclusive results of America's initial military campaign again highlight the differences between 1941 and 2001. America's war against Japan not only had a clear enemy, but a clear objective—Japan's defeat and official surrender. America's war against terrorism promised no such clear-cut solution. Even if Osama bin Laden were to be captured or killed, that would not necessarily signal the end of terrorism's threat to America. Bin Laden's followers and other terrorists hiding in nations such as Pakistan, Somalia, and the Philippines will likely prove to be elusive targets.

Patriotism and dissent

Both the Pearl Harbor and September 11 attacks resulted in an upsurge of patriotism. Following September 11, Americans purchased and proudly displayed the national flag. Hundreds of millions of dollars of charitable contributions flowed to organizations and individuals to help the families of those killed. Partisan differences in Washington were temporarily put aside to pass national security legislation. But the unity of spirit that the United States showed in the days, weeks, and months following September 11 did not necessarily translate into uniformity of opinion. Virtually all American and foreign observers condemned the actions as horrible and unjustified. Differences of opinion remained, however, on the difficult question of *why* these particular individuals did something so horrible (at the cost of their own lives).

Even commentators who see parallels between Pearl Harbor and September 11 disagree on the meaning of these events. Military historian Victor Davis Hanson writes that the lessons Americans learned from Pearl Harbor and September 11 are essentially the same: "There is no quarter to be given criminals, whether they be fascist states or murderous fundamentalists," and the American people, "self-absorbed" in times of peace, are quickly roused to eradicate enemies when attacked. Religious studies professor Ira Chernus, on the other hand, argues that just as Pearl Harbor needs to be seen in the context of American foreign policy in Asia, September 11 needs to be analyzed in light of U.S. actions in the Muslim world. He asserts that it is a "myth" that the United States was "naïve and innocent, isolated from the world" prior to Pearl Harbor and that the Japanese were simply "the devil incarnate" with "no possible rational motive" for attacking. It is a similar myth to portray the September 11 terrorists simply as "agents of the devil, doing evil for evil's sake, as if their own history and the world's history had nothing to do with it."

A point of agreement between Hanson and Chernus is that Americans cannot ignore events beyond their borders—in times of peace or war. The events of September 11, 2001, much as Pearl Harbor before it, will color how the United States interacts with the global community for years to come. The articles in this volume provide opinions and views on the causes, meaning, and potential consequences of the events of September 11, 2001, for the United States and the world.

1

Enemies of Freedom Committed an Act of War Against America

George W. Bush

George W. Bush is president of the United States. Nine days after the September 11, 2001, attack, he made this televised address to Congress and the American people.

The United States has been victimized by an act of war carried out by terrorists. Evidence indicates that the attack was organized and carried out by the al-Qaida [al Queda] terrorist network. This organization is led by Osama bin Laden, who is being sheltered by the Taliban government in Afghanistan. The enemies of freedom who have attacked America will not prevail. The spirit of the American people remains unbroken, and the United States will do whatever is necessary to defend itself against further attacks and to defeat and destroy global terrorists. The fight against terrorism is not just America's struggle, but one that calls on all civilized nations.

O n September the 11th, enemies of freedom committed an act of war against our country. Americans have known wars—but for the past 136 years, they have been wars on foreign soil, except for one Sunday in 1941. Americans have known the casualties of war—but not at the center of a great city on a peaceful morning. Americans have known surprise attacks—but never before on thousands of civilians. All of this was brought upon us in a single day—and night fell on a different world, a world where freedom itself is under attack.

Americans have many questions tonight. Americans are asking: Who attacked our country? The evidence we have gathered all points to a collection of loosely affiliated terrorist organizations known as al Qaeda. They are the same murderers indicted for bombing American embassies in Tanzania and Kenya, and responsible for bombing the USS Cole.

Al Qaeda is to terror what the mafia is to crime. But its goal is not

Excerpted from George W. Bush's "Address to a Joint Session of Congress and the American People," September 20, 2001.

10

making money; its goal is remaking the world—and imposing its radical beliefs on people everywhere.

The terrorists practice a fringe form of Islamic extremism that has been rejected by Muslim scholars and the vast majority of Muslim clerics—a fringe movement that perverts the peaceful teachings of Islam. The terrorists' directive commands them to kill Christians and Jews, to kill all Americans, and make no distinction among military and civilians, including women and children.

This group and its leader—a person named Osama bin Laden—are linked to many other organizations in different countries, including the Egyptian Islamic Jihad and the Islamic Movement of Uzbekistan. There are thousands of these terrorists in more than 60 countries. They are recruited from their own nations and neighborhoods and brought to camps in places like Afghanistan, where they are trained in the tactics of terror. They are sent back to their homes or sent to hide in countries around the world to plot evil and destruction.

Al Qaeda and Afghanistan

The leadership of al Qaeda has great influence in Afghanistan and supports the Taliban regime in controlling most of that country. In Afghanistan, we see al Qaeda's vision for the world.

Afghanistan's people have been brutalized—many are starving and many have fled. Women are not allowed to attend school. You can be jailed for owning a television. Religion can be practiced only as their leaders dictate. A man can be jailed in Afghanistan if his beard is not long enough.

The United States respects the people of Afghanistan—after all, we are currently its largest source of humanitarian aid—but we condemn the Taliban regime. It is not only repressing its own people, it is threatening people everywhere by sponsoring and sheltering and supplying terrorists. By aiding and abetting murder, the Taliban regime is committing murder.

And tonight, the United States of America makes the following demands on the Taliban: Deliver to United States authorities all the leaders of al Qaeda who hide in your land. Release all foreign nationals, including American citizens, you have unjustly imprisoned. Protect foreign journalists, diplomats and aid workers in your country. Close immediately and permanently every terrorist training camp in Afghanistan, and hand over every terrorist, and every person in their support structure, to appropriate authorities. Give the United States full access to terrorist training camps, so we can make sure they are no longer operating.

These demands are not open to negotiation or discussion. The Taliban must act, and act immediately. They will hand over the terrorists, or they will share in their fate.

America's enemy

I also want to speak tonight directly to Muslims throughout the world. We respect your faith. It's practiced freely by many millions of Americans, and by millions more in countries that America counts as friends. Its teachings are good and peaceful, and those who commit evil in the name of Allah blaspheme the name of Allah. The terrorists are traitors to their own faith, trying, in effect, to hijack Islam itself. The enemy of America is not our many Muslim friends; it is not our many Arab friends. Our enemy is a radical network of terrorists, and every government that supports them.

Our war on terror begins with al Qaeda, but it does not end there. It will not end until every terrorist group of global reach has been found, stopped and defeated.

Americans are asking, why do they hate us? They hate what we see right here in this chamber—a democratically elected government. Their leaders are self-appointed. They hate our freedoms—our freedom of religion, our freedom of speech, our freedom to vote and assemble and disagree with each other.

They want to overthrow existing governments in many Muslim countries, such as Egypt, Saudi Arabia, and Jordan. They want to drive Israel out of the Middle East. They want to drive Christians and Jews out of vast regions of Asia and Africa.

On September the 11th, enemies of freedom committed an act of war against our country.

These terrorists kill not merely to end lives, but to disrupt and end a way of life. With every atrocity, they hope that America grows fearful, retreating from the world and forsaking our friends. They stand against us, because we stand in their way.

We are not deceived by their pretenses to piety. We have seen their kind before. They are the heirs of all the murderous ideologies of the 20th century. By sacrificing human life to serve their radical visions—by abandoning every value except the will to power—they follow in the path of fascism, and Nazism, and totalitarianism. And they will follow that path all the way, to where it ends: in history's unmarked grave of discarded lies.

The coming war

Americans are asking: How will we fight and win this war? We will direct every resource at our command—every means of diplomacy, every tool of intelligence, every instrument of law enforcement, every financial influence, and every necessary weapon of war—to the disruption and to the defeat of the global terror network.

This war will not be like the war against Iraq a decade ago, with a decisive liberation of territory and a swift conclusion. It will not look like the air war above Kosovo two years ago, where no ground troops were used and not a single American was lost in combat.

Our response involves far more than instant retaliation and isolated strikes. Americans should not expect one battle, but a lengthy campaign, unlike any other we have ever seen. It may include dramatic strikes, visible on TV, and covert operations, secret even in success. We will starve terrorists of funding, turn them one against another, drive them from place to place, until there is no refuge or no rest. And we will pursue nations that provide aid or safe haven to terrorism. Every nation, in every region, now has a decision to make. Either you are with us, or you are with the terrorists. From this day forward, any nation that continues to harbor or support terrorism will be regarded by the United States as a hostile regime.

Our nation has been put on notice: We are not immune from attack. We will take defensive measures against terrorism to protect Americans. Today, dozens of federal departments and agencies, as well as state and local governments, have responsibilities affecting homeland security. These efforts must be coordinated at the highest level. So tonight I announce the creation of a Cabinet-level position reporting directly to me— the Office of Homeland Security.

Our war on terror . . . will not end until every terrorist group of global reach has been found, stopped and defeated.

And tonight I also announce a distinguished American to lead this effort, to strengthen American security: a military veteran, an effective governor, a true patriot, a trusted friend—Pennsylvania's Tom Ridge. He will lead, oversee and coordinate a comprehensive national strategy to safeguard our country against terrorism, and respond to any attacks that may come.

These measures are essential. But the only way to defeat terrorism as a threat to our way of life is to stop it, eliminate it, and destroy it where it grows.

Many will be involved in this effort, from FBI agents to intelligence operatives to the reservists we have called to active duty. All deserve our thanks, and all have our prayers. And tonight, a few miles from the damaged Pentagon, I have a message for our military: Be ready. I've called the Armed Forces to alert, and there is a reason. The hour is coming when America will act, and you will make us proud.

Civilization's fight

This is not, however, just America's fight. And what is at stake is not just America's freedom. This is the world's fight. This is civilization's fight. This is the fight of all who believe in progress and pluralism, tolerance and freedom.

We ask every nation to join us. We will ask, and we will need, the help of police forces, intelligence services, and banking systems around the world. The United States is grateful that many nations and many international organizations have already responded—with sympathy and with support. Nations from Latin America, to Asia, to Africa, to Europe, to the Islamic world. Perhaps the NATO Charter reflects best the attitude of the world: An attack on one is an attack on all.

The civilized world is rallying to America's side. They understand that if this terror goes unpunished, their own cities, their own citizens may be next. Terror, unanswered, can not only bring down buildings, it can threaten the stability of legitimate governments. And you know what— we're not going to allow it.

What Americans must do

Americans are asking: What is expected of us? I ask you to live your lives, and hug your children. I know many citizens have fears tonight, and I ask you to be calm and resolute, even in the face of a continuing threat.

I ask you to uphold the values of America, and remember why so many have come here. We are in a fight for our principles, and our first responsibility is to live by them. No one should be singled out for unfair treatment or unkind words because of their ethnic background or religious faith.

I ask you to continue to support the victims of this tragedy with your contributions. Those who want to give can go to a central source of information, libertyunites.org, to find the names of groups providing direct help in New York, Pennsylvania, and Virginia.

The thousands of FBI agents who are now at work in this investigation may need your cooperation, and I ask you to give it.

I ask for your patience, with the delays and inconveniences that may accompany tighter security; and for your patience in what will be a long struggle.

What is at stake is not just America's freedom. This is the world's fight.

I ask your continued participation and confidence in the American economy. Terrorists attacked a symbol of American prosperity. They did not touch its source. America is successful because of the hard work, and creativity, and enterprise of our people. These were the true strengths of our economy before September 11th, and they are our strengths today.

And, finally, please continue praying for the victims of terror and their families, for those in uniform, and for our great country. Prayer has comforted us in sorrow, and will help strengthen us for the journey ahead.

New challenges

Tonight I thank my fellow Americans for what you have already done and for what you will do. And ladies and gentlemen of the Congress, I thank you, their representatives, for what you have already done and for what we will do together.

Tonight, we face new and sudden national challenges. We will come together to improve air safety, to dramatically expand the number of air marshals on domestic flights, and take new measures to prevent hijacking. We will come together to promote stability and keep our airlines flying, with direct assistance during this emergency.

We will come together to give law enforcement the additional tools it needs to track down terror here at home. We will come together to strengthen our intelligence capabilities to know the plans of terrorists before they act, and find them before they strike.

We will come together to take active steps that strengthen America's economy, and put our people back to work.

Tonight we welcome two leaders who embody the extraordinary

spirit of all New Yorkers: Governor George Pataki, and Mayor Rudolph Giuliani. As a symbol of America's resolve, my administration will work with Congress, and these two leaders, to show the world that we will rebuild New York City.

America's future

After all that has just passed—all the lives taken, and all the possibilities and hopes that died with them—it is natural to wonder if America's future is one of fear. Some speak of an age of terror. I know there are struggles ahead, and dangers to face. But this country will define our times, not be defined by them. As long as the United States of America is determined and strong, this will not be an age of terror; this will be an age of liberty, here and across the world.

Great harm has been done to us. We have suffered great loss. And in our grief and anger we have found our mission and our moment. Freedom and fear are at war. The advance of human freedom—the great achievement of our time, and the great hope of every time—now depends on us. Our nation—this generation—will lift a dark threat of violence from our people and our future. We will rally the world to this cause by our efforts, by our courage. We will not tire, we will not falter, and we will not fail.

It is my hope that in the months and years ahead, life will return almost to normal. We'll go back to our lives and routines, and that is good. Even grief recedes with time and grace. But our resolve must not pass. Each of us will remember what happened that day, and to whom it happened. We'll remember the moment the news came—where we were and what we were doing. Some will remember an image of a fire, or a story of rescue. Some will carry memories of a face and a voice gone forever.

And I will carry this: It is the police shield of a man named George Howard, who died at the World Trade Center trying to save others. It was given to me by his mom, Arlene, as a proud memorial to her son. This is my reminder of lives that ended, and a task that does not end.

I will not forget this wound to our country or those who inflicted it. I will not yield; I will not rest; I will not relent in waging this struggle for freedom and security for the American people.

The course of this conflict is not known, yet its outcome is certain. Freedom and fear, justice and cruelty, have always been at war, and we know that God is not neutral between them.

Fellow citizens, we'll meet violence with patient justice—assured of the rightness of our cause, and confident of the victories to come. In all that lies before us, may God grant us wisdom, and may He watch over the United States of America.

2

The Attacks Were God's Punishment for America's Actions Against Islam

Osama bin Laden

Osama bin Laden, a wealthy native of Saudi Arabia, is the head of al-Qaida ("The Base"), a terrorist network. Believed to be responsible for organizing two 1998 bombings of U.S. embassies in Africa, he was an immediate prime suspect for masterminding the September 11, 2001, attacks on America. The following is a translation of taped remarks that aired on an Arab television station on October 7. The remarks were first broadcast shortly after American and British forces began bombing operations that day in Afghanistan, where bin Laden has resided since 1996.

What America has experienced is God's just punishment for the sufferings they have inflicted on the world of Islam. It is good America is full of fear. The United States will not know peace until the infidels (Americans) leave the land of Muhammad (Saudi Arabia) and peace is secured in Palestine.

I bear witness that there is no God but Allah and that Mohammad is his messenger.

There is America, hit by God in one of its softest spots. Its greatest buildings were destroyed, thank God for that. There is America, full of fear from its north to its south, from its west to its east. Thank God for that.

What America is tasting now is something insignificant compared to what we have tasted for scores of years. Our nation (the Islamic world) has been tasting this humiliation and this degradation for more than 80 years. Its sons are killed, its blood is shed, its sanctuaries are attacked, and no one hears and no one heeds.

When God blessed one of the groups of Islam, vanguards of Islam, they destroyed America. I pray to God to elevate their status and bless them.

Millions of innocent children are being killed as I speak. They are being killed in Iraq without committing any sins, and we don't hear condemnation or a fatwa (religious decree) from the rulers. In these days, Israeli tanks infest Palestine—in Jenin, Ramallah, Rafah, Beit Jalla, and other places in the land of Islam, and we don't hear anyone raising his voice or moving a limb.

American hypocrisy

When the sword comes down (on America), after 80 years, hypocrisy rears its ugly head. They deplore and they lament for those killers, who have abused the blood, honor and sanctuaries of Muslims. The least that can be said about those people is that they are debauched. They have followed injustice. They supported the butcher over the victim, the oppressor over the innocent child. May God show them His wrath and give them what they deserve.

I say that the situation is clear and obvious. After this event, after the senior officials have spoken in America, starting with the head of infidels worldwide, Bush, and those with him. They have come out in force with their men and have turned even the countries that belong to Islam to this treachery, and they want to wag their tail at God, to fight Islam, to suppress people in the name of terrorism.

What America is tasting now is something insignificant compared to what we have tasted for scores of years.

When people at the ends of the earth, Japan, were killed by their hundreds of thousands, young and old, it was not considered a war crime, it is something that has justification. Millions of children in Iraq is something that has justification. But when they lose dozens of people in Nairobi and Dar es Salaam (capitals of Kenya and Tanzania, where U.S. embassies were bombed in 1998), Iraq was struck and Afghanistan was struck. Hypocrisy stood in force behind the head of infidels worldwide, behind the cowards of this age, America and those who are with it.

These events have divided the whole world into two sides. The side of believers and the side of infidels, may God keep you away from them. Every Muslim has to rush to make his religion victorious. The winds of faith have come. The winds of change have come to eradicate oppression from the island of Muhammad, peace be upon him.

To America, I say only a few words to it and its people. I swear by God, who has elevated the skies without pillars, neither America nor the people who live in it will dream of security before we live it in Palestine, and not before all the infidel armies leave the land of Muhammad, peace be upon him.

God is great, may pride be with Islam. May peace and God's mercy be upon you.

3

Osama bin Laden Wants to Drive the West from the Islamic World

James S. Robbins

James S. Robbins is an international relations professor at National Defense University.

Osama bin Laden's statement released on October 7, 2001, reveals some clues as to his motives behind his endorsement and alleged planning of the World Trade Center and Pentagon terrorist attacks. He wishes to rid the Middle East of Western influence and to overthrow regimes in Saudi Arabia and Jordan that trace their roots to post–World War I European diplomacy. His comments calling on Muslims everywhere to resist the United States reveal that America's war against terrorism is not against one man or regime, but against an ideology that is diametrically opposed to the American way of life.

Osama bin Laden's statement Sunday [October 7, 2001] after the first Allied air strikes in Afghanistan was mostly what one would expect, the usual denunciations of the United States and "the chief infidel Bush," but did contain two curious passages: "Our nation has undergone more than 80 years of this humiliation . . ."; and: "When the sword reached America after 80 years . . ." Eighty years? 1921? Is he saying that this whole thing is Warren G. Harding's fault?

Bin Laden is talking about the 1920 Treaty of Sèvres imposed on the Turks after World War One, which detached their Arab provinces and spelled the end of the Ottoman Empire. The Ottomans had ruled the region for 600 years or so, and brought varying degrees of political harmony under the Sultanate and religious unity under the Caliphate [Islamic realm ruled by the caliphs, successors to Mohammad]. The 1920 treaty did away with the political order, and the Caliphate was banned by Kemal Ataturk in 1924. The European powers saw to the disposition of the Arab lands, the route to British India was secured from Russian expansionism, France was given an interest in Syria, and the Mideast oil supplies were safe.

Old news? Well, we are dealing with people with long historical memory. Ayman Zawahri, leader of the Egyptian Jihad, stated on October 7 that his group "will not tolerate a recurrence of the Andalusia tragedy in Palestine." (The Andalusia tragedy is the end of Moorish rule in Spain in 1492.)

So the World Trade Towers had to come down because some psychopath can't come to grips with the end of World War I? Basically, yes. In bin Laden's universe, that was when everything started to go wrong. Viewed in that context, his plots against the Saudi and Jordanian monarchies make perfect sense. They are products of this original sin, the establishment of the political order of the Middle East by the Allied powers 80 years ago. The founding of Israel ("the Zionist entity") is an echo of the same Western interference. Iraq's annexation of Kuwait in 1991 was an attempt to right things—Kuwait was part of the same administrative division as Iraq within the Ottoman Empire, so it is only just that it be reclaimed. Hence, Western opposition to Saddam's invasion is a key event to bin Laden. He mentions this specifically in his 1998 *fatwa* [decree issued by an Islamic religious leader] against Americans, and also in his most recent statement in which he says there will be no peace until, among other things, "and all infidel armies depart from the land of Mohammad," i.e., Americans leave Saudi Arabia.

Comprehending our enemy

It is important to understand these dates and events to comprehend the adversary we face. Bin Laden looks back to what he believes was a golden age in which Western influence in the Mideast was minimal and there was no interference in Muslim affairs by "atheists." If he and his followers could recreate that environment, they could construct a theocratic utopia after the blueprint of Taliban Afghanistan. The main impediments to that vision are the Arab monarchies and autocracies that do business with the west. Bin Laden must first drive out the infidels who prop up these regimes, then topple them and replace them with pure Islamic states (that is, Islam *ala* Osama).

Bin Laden looks back to what he believes was a golden age in which Western influence in the Mideast was minimal.

Those who see poverty at the root of all conflict should note well that Osama bin Laden and the members of Al Qaeda are the products of affluence. The September 11 suicide hijackers were more familiar with the discos of Berlin than the slums of Ramallah. We are not dealing with politicians who can be bought off with an increased minimum wage and comprehensive national health care plan. These are idealists violently promoting a comprehensive and exclusive worldview. Bin Laden said Sunday, "These events have divided the world into two parts: a part that espouses faith and is devoid of hypocrisy, and an infidel part, may God protect us from it." As an Al Qaeda spokesman put it, "There are only two sides and no third one. Either you chose the side of faith or that of atheism." There can be no compromise; this is war to the death.

The scope of the current war is vast. It is not a struggle against one demented man, or one radical regime. It is a war against an idea, an ideology antithetical to our way of life and to the western conception of freedom. Afghanistan is the nerve center of this ideology, a state that has supplied safe haven to its theorists, and a test bed for its practitioners. But the tendrils of this network reach far; to Indonesia, the Philippines, western China, Chechnya, the Balkans, Nigeria, and Colombia to name a few. It is a global web tied to organized crime, narcotics, and arms smuggling. Its lifeblood is money, much of which is obtained through illegal activity. But it also does commerce in mercenaries, and supplies tactical training and ideological indoctrination. This is not the type of threat our national-security apparatus is organized to defeat, but it is the one with which we must now come to grips.

New strategies

The United States doesn't formulate 80- or even eight-year strategies. Our approach to problems is to wait until they get serious, go in, fix them, and leave. We thought we did this in Iraq in 1991; clearly we did not. Likewise with Afghanistan—after Soviet forces withdrew in 1989 we were done with that country and let it fall into chaos. We figured our friends the Pakistanis would take care of it, and they certainly did. Their answer was the Taliban, which gave Afghanistan more stability than it had seen in years. True, it was the stability of the graveyard, but that served Pakistan's interests. And when it became clear that serious problems were developing in Afghanistan, the Clinton administration responded by placing sanctions on Pakistan for engaging in nuclear testing and feebly launching cruise missiles into the Afghan mountains. The single most significant diplomatic move in the current conflict was lifting the sanctions and detaching Pakistan from the Taliban. The Afghan regime has no hope of survival without its Pakistani patrons, and without the Taliban the Al Qaeda network has no cover. One hopes that when the smoke clears and Afghanistan is liberated the United States will not revert to its traditional regional attention deficit disorder.

The opening shots of this war were not fired October 7, but the instant President Bush responded on September 11. The United States is now formulating a new type of warfighting strategy. Military force is a necessary and powerful part of the solution, but there are important roles to be played by law enforcement, intelligence, diplomacy, international financial agreements, covert operations, foreign aid—almost every tool at the disposal of the government must be utilized to win this struggle. It will take time, steady leadership, and strategic vision. Bin Laden may die tomorrow—*inshallah* [if Allah wills]—but we have a long way to go.

4

The Attacks Were Part of Militant Islam's War Against America

Daniel Pipes

Daniel Pipes is the director of the Middle East Forum, a think tank that works to define and promote American interests in the Middle East. He is the author of numerous books and articles on the region.

The September 11, 2001, terrorist attacks against the World Trade Center towers and the Pentagon were the latest in a long series of actions that comprise militant Islam's war against the United States. Previous attacks include 1983 bombings against the U.S. embassy and marine barracks in Lebanon, bombings of embassies in Africa, and killings of Americans in New York and other places. Future attacks by militant Islamists may be even worse, involving weapons of mass destruction.

All four of the plane crashes on September 11 occurred in the northeastern United States, where I live. According to the latest *Newsweek* poll, a massive two-thirds of my neighbors feel "less safe" than they did before that day.

I beg to disagree. This particular American now feels more secure. The reason? Those terrible events alerted my fellow citizens to the fact that militant Islam is engaged in fighting a war on the United States.

War began in 1979

That war began, not as people seem to think, in September 2001 but in February 1979, when Ayatollah Khomeini took power in Iran. Already by November 1979, Khomeini had seized the US Embassy in Teheran and held nearly 60 captives for 444 days. Eight American soldiers (the first casualties in this war) died in the failed US rescue attempt in 1980.

The Islamists' initial major act of violence against Americans, killing 63, took place in 1983 when they attacked the US Embassy in Beirut. As the analyst David Makovsky notes, Washington "beat a hasty exit, and Islamic militants saw this as a vindication that suicide bombing was . . . deadly effective." Then followed a rapid sequence of attacks on Americans in Lebanon (the embassy a second time, a Marine barracks, airline passengers, university presidents), plus other Middle Eastern countries.

This assault persisted for the next 18 years. Prominent targets included American soldiers in Saudi Arabia (twice), two embassies in East Africa, and a warship in Yemen. Further afield, Islamists killed Americans in Israel, Pakistan, Kashmir, and the Philippines.

Militant Islam seeks to destroy the United States.

Attacks on US soil began with the 1980 murder of an anti-Khomeini Iranian resident in the Washington, DC, area. Subsequent killings included a Muslim religious figure in Tucson, Arizona, a Jewish leader in New York City, and CIA employees waiting in their cars to enter the agency headquarters. A rash of murders took place at New York landmarks—the World Trade Center, the Brooklyn Bridge, the Empire State Building.

Washington threatened retribution ("You can run but you can't hide") for attacks against Americans, but hardly ever carried through. Rather, the preferred US response was to hunker down behind concrete barriers, thick walls, and security checks. Intelligence and defense capabilities remained inadequate. Actual perpetrators were sometimes caught and tried in court, but the apparatus that trained and dispatched them remained unscathed.

America awakes

The sad fact is, 22 years and 600 dead did not get the country's attention. Americans blithely ignored those specialists on militant Islam and terrorism who pleaded for vigilance and warned of horrors to come. This national obliviousness explains how Americans found themselves so embarrassingly unprepared for the events of September 11. "Scandal" is how one Israeli pilot correctly describes the military's inability to protect the World Trade Center or the Pentagon.

Nearly 7,000 deaths in one day did, at least, finally awake the country.

And I feel safer now, as the FBI is engaged in the largest operation in its history, armed marshals will again be flying on US aircraft, and the immigration service has placed foreign students under increased scrutiny. I feel safer when Islamist organizations are exposed, illicit money channels closed down, and immigration regulations reviewed. The amassing of American forces near Iraq and Afghanistan cheers me. The newfound alarm is healthy, the sense of solidarity heartening, the resolve is encouraging.

But will it last? Are Americans truly ready to sacrifice liberties and lives to prosecute seriously the war against militant Islam? I worry about US constancy and purpose.

One thing is very sure: should the thousands of deaths of fellow citizens not inspire Americans to extirpate the threat of militant Islam, then this will be back, and more dangerous next time. September's carnage was limited to the destruction of things crashing into each other, but future Islamist attacks are likely to involve weapons of mass destruction. Should that happen, the death toll could be in the millions, not the thousands.

So, let this warning be clear: Militant Islam seeks to destroy the United States (as well as Europe, Israel, and many other societies) as presently constituted. Islamists have shown resolve, tenacity, and tactical brilliance. Unless Westerners take this threat very much to heart, Islamists will be back, dispensing far worse punishments.

5

The Terrorist Attacks Were Not the Result of U.S. Actions

Peter Beinart

Peter Beinart is editor of the New Republic, *a weekly journal of opinion.*

Some people have blamed the September 11 terrorist attacks on "blowback"—the unintended consequences of U.S. foreign policy actions. They have argued that the rise of Osama bin Laden, believed to be the mastermind behind the attacks, was in part the result of American intervention in the war between Afghanistan and the Soviet Union in the 1980s. But a careful reading of history indicates otherwise. Bin Laden's rise is attributable to America's disengagement from Afghanistan, not its intervention there.

When America goes to war, Americans ask a historical question: How did we get ourselves into this? Doves usually answer: imperialism. If we didn't do such nasty things around the world, we wouldn't be attacked. But the connection between our misdeeds and their attacks can be rather tenuous. And so more sophisticated doves offer a more sophisticated answer: "blowback." Our foreign policy doesn't just create enemies in a general sense, it creates them in a very specific sense: We fund and train the people who later attack us. During the Panama invasion, doves gleefully noted Manuel Noriega's ties to the CIA. During the Gulf war [against Iraq], they gleefully noted America's semi-support for Saddam [Hussein] as a counterweight to Iran. And today antiwar commentators instruct us that the CIA, through its support for the Afghan war against the Soviet Union, created Osama bin Laden.

At first glance, blowback might not seem like a good historical argument for doves to make. After all, by condemning the U.S. for getting into bed with Noriega and Saddam and bin Laden in the past, doves acknowledge that they are worthy of condemnation—which might suggest that America should atone for its past wrongs by opposing them now. But doves aren't making a point about America's enemies; they are making a point about America. The assumption behind blowback is that the U.S. *can't* atone—that as long as it intervenes around the world, it will foster evil. To go to war against bin Laden today will only create more bin Ladens tomorrow.

The case of Afghanistan

Which makes it of more than mere historical interest that, as applied to the United States and Afghanistan, the blowback theory is dead wrong. American intervention in the Afghan war didn't create Osama bin Laden. In fact, if the United States bears any blame for bin Laden's terrorist network today, it's because in the 1980s and '90s, we didn't intervene in Afghanistan aggressively *enough*.

As bizarre as it may sound to the antiwar left, the CIA was deeply wary of U.S. involvement in Afghanistan. The Agency didn't think the mujahedin rebels could beat Moscow, and it feared that if it ran the war, it would take the blame if things went awry. As Vincent Cannistraro, who led the Reagan administration's Afghan Working Group from 1985 to 1987, puts it, "The CIA was very reluctant to be involved at all. They thought it would end up with them being blamed, like in Guatemala." So the Agency tried to avoid direct involvement in the war, and to maintain plausible deniability. For the first six years following the 1979 Soviet invasion, the U.S. provided the mujahedin only Eastern-bloc weaponry, so the rebels could claim they had captured it from Soviet troops rather than received it from Washington. And while America funded the mujahedin, it played barely any role in their training. To insulate itself, the U.S. gave virtual carte blanche to its allies, Pakistan and Saudi Arabia, to direct the rebel effort as they saw fit.

American intervention in the Afghan war didn't create Osama bin Laden.

This is where bin Laden comes in. After Moscow invaded, he and other Arab militants went to defend Afghanistan in the name of Islam. The Pakistani government allowed them in, and the Saudis gave them money, hoping to foster a Sunni Islamist network to counter the Shia network of rival Iran. Riyadh thought the network would espouse the monarchy's brand of conservative, rather than revolutionary, fundamentalism. And that idea seemed less naive in the 1980s when bin Laden was still a loyal Saudi subject, and before Islamist rebellions had broken out in Algeria and dramatically intensified in Egypt.

Had the U.S. been present on the ground in Afghanistan, it would have known about this. And it probably would have tried to stop it—if only because the Arab volunteers were aiding a virulently anti-Western Afghan rebel leader named Abdul Rasul Sayyaf, who opposed not only the Soviets, but the Western-backed mujahedin as well. But the U.S. wasn't present on the ground, and it had only the vaguest knowledge of the Arabs' presence and aims. In retrospect, that might seem hard to believe. But remember, contrary to bin Laden's later boasts, the Arabs were few in number (most came *after* the war, once bin Laden's network was established) and played virtually no military role in the victory over the Soviets. And the skittish CIA, Cannistraro estimates, had less than ten operatives acting as America's eyes and ears in the region. Milton Bearden, the Agency's chief field operative in the war effort, has insisted that "[T]he CIA had nothing to do with" bin Laden. Cannistraro says that when he coordinated Afghan policy from Washington, he never once heard bin Laden's name.

U.S. disengagement

And if U.S. disengagement contributed to the formation of bin Laden's network during the war, it contributed to it after the war was over as well. In 1992 the Communist regime in Kabul finally fell. Afghanistan needed foreign aid to reconstruct its shattered infrastructure, and an intense diplomatic effort to force its fractious mujahedin leaders to lay down their arms. The logical source of that financial assistance and political intervention was the U.S., which enjoyed the goodwill of many mujahedin leaders. But by all accounts, once Afghanistan's troubles lost their cold war significance, the [George H.] Bush and Clinton administrations paid them virtually no high-level attention. Neither administration tried seriously to negotiate a truce between the parties, and U.S. aid, which had totaled roughly $3 billion in the 1980s, dropped, by the end of 1994, nearly to zero.

For two more hideous years, mujahedin factions fought each other and preyed on an already brutalized population. Had ordinary Afghans not been desperate for the civil war to end, and for a leadership with at least some moral code, they would not have backed the Taliban, the religious students coming from the Pakistani border. And had Afghanistan not faced a political vacuum, Pakistan would not have armed those students in the hope that through them, it could dominate its neighbor to the northwest.

America's abandonment of Afghanistan was of a piece with its abandonment of countries like Liberia, Somalia, and Congo, which also disintegrated after cold war dictators fell. In Liberia the resulting anarchy produced the murderous Charles Taylor. In Somalia it produced the murderous Mohamed Farah Aideed. In Congo it produced the genocidal Hutu refugee camps. And in Afghanistan it produced the Taliban. Except that the Taliban didn't just harbor tribal killers, they harbored Al Qaeda, which brought its savagery all the way to America's shores.

No blowback

So the doves are wrong. There was no blowback. America's involvement in Afghanistan in the 1980s didn't help create Osama bin Laden; Saudi Arabia's involvement in Afghanistan in the 1980s helped create Osama bin Laden, in large part because the United States was too timid to direct the war itself. Similarly, it wasn't America's intervention in Afghanistan in the 1990s that created the Taliban; it was Pakistan's intervention and America's non-intervention. Doves might consider this as they counsel the U.S. to respond to September 11 by leaving the rest of the world to its own devices. After all, it was leaving the rest of the world to its own devices that got us into this in the first place.

6

U.S. Policies in Islamic Lands Are a Root Cause of the Terrorist Attacks

Faisal Bodi

Faisal Bodi is a British Muslim writer.

In asking the question of why they were the target of terrorists, Americans must look at U.S. policies in the Middle East. By supporting totalitarian regimes in Middle East nations, imposing economic sanctions on Iraq, and supporting Israel against the Palestinian people, the United States has contributed to the deaths of many innocent people and has become a symbol of terror and oppression for many Muslims. The September 11, 2001, terrorist attacks were in part a result of American abuses of human rights abroad.

As Americans wake from the nightmare of September 11th's onslaught against their key commercial and political buildings, two questions are likely to be on their lips: who and why?

The who is the easy part. Only a well-financed, well-oiled and militarily sophisticated body could pull off such an audacious assault against a world superpower. All fingers point in one direction, to the mountains of Afghanistan where Osama bin Laden, multimillionaire and the leader of the international Muslim army, called al-Qaeda, has his lair.

Why is America a target?

The harder and more crucial question is why. Why does the US continue to be a target for Islamist attacks? The US marine barracks in Beirut in 1983, the World Trade Centre in 1993, the al-Khobar bombings in 1996, the USS Cole bombing in 2000, what is it about the US that makes it a magnet for Muslim militants?

President Bush and secretary of state Colin Powell gave their own take September 11. They blamed extremists bent on damaging democracy and western civilisation. Disturbingly, their views will likely wash with an audience whose grasp of international affairs is so dumbed down as to prevent them separating loaded representation from reality.

But much as the attacks on civilian structures might suggest otherwise, democracy is not the intended target here, and neither is freedom. Inside America, the Trade Centre, the Pentagon, Camp David, and Capitol Hill are all seen as symbols of global US power and prestige, of the triumph of democracy. Outside, in the Muslim world, they are popularly regarded as symbols of terror and oppression.

If the dark cloud of Muslim terrorism has a silver lining one prays it is an internal review of US foreign policy.

Since 1991, American-led sanctions against Iraq and the effects of depleted uranium have killed 1 million children. Who knows if the attackers intended all flights inside the US to come to a halt, but for a day at least they succeeded in turning the tables on the no-fly zone in force over Iraq. Since the Palestinian uprising started in September 2000, American Apache helicopters, F-16s and M-16 rifles have been responsible for killing 700 Palestinians and injuring 25,000 more. Since CNN isn't there, by design rather than accident, to capture every smashed skull and charred corpse, westerners remain ignorant of US terrorism.

These are only the more visible examples of US abuses in Muslim lands. As it waves the flag of democracy in one hand, Washington pours billions of dollars into upholding totalitarian regimes in Egypt, Jordan, Saudi Arabia, Algeria, among others, to make sure its people are prevented from exercising their collective will. The US Fifth Fleet sails menacingly around the Gulf in a warning to dissidents that it will use force to protect its client rulers and an uninterrupted supply of oil. And the presence of US troops in Saudi Arabia cocks a snook at Muslim sensibilities about their holy places.

Support for Israel

But it is the unqualified US support for Israel that most enrages Muslims. Camp David [the rumored target of the fourth hijacked plane] was no random choice. The site of the first peace agreement between a Muslim state [Egypt] and Israel in 1978, is still seen by many as a capitulation and a sell-out of the Palestinians. Official US aid to Israel in 2001 amounts to a non-repayable $6 billion. In September 2001 Israel announced it was to exercise an option to buy 50 more F-16s in order to keep up its military superiority over all its Arab neighbours. That it is almost exclusively the US in the firing line and not other western countries suggests that for the militants, silence in the continued oppression of the Palestinians is excusable, direct complicity is not.

It is unlikely this will happen, but if the dark cloud of Muslim terrorism has a silver lining one prays it is an internal review of US foreign policy, especially with regards to Israel. Yesterday's attacks are the chickens of America's callous abuse of others' human rights coming home to roost.

Though it is a minority view in Islam that countenances retaliatory attacks on civilians, it is one that US policy is encouraging. Terrorism begets terrorism. This is not to excuse the perpetrators but to offer a way out of the spiral of tit for tat terror.

But if previous bombings have not shocked the US into self-reflection it is unlikely that even this, the biggest attack on its shores since Pearl Harbour, will do so. The likelihood is that Washington will order its spin doctors to steer the public gaze well away from itself and towards intensified military efforts to snuff out Bin Laden. That would be the most terrifying outcome of all. One living Bin Laden is better than a martyr who spawns a hundred more.

7

The Terrorists Were Waging a War the United States Began

Samuel Francis

Samuel Francis is a conservative syndicated columnist.

Most media accounts and editorials have described the September 11 attacks as acts of war against the United States. The truth that has been obscured in media coverage is that the United States has already been at war with Middle East nations and organizations for years, dating back at least to 1991 when America launched and led a war against Iraq. That war and subsequent economic sanctions have killed thousands of civilians. In addition, former president Bill Clinton launched bombing and missile raids against civilians in the Middle East and Afghanistan to deflect attention from his domestic scandals. The attacks on Washington and New York were payback for American actions.

"We're at war," the young waitress, her voice catching, informed me when I first heard of the terrorist attacks on the World Trade Center and the Pentagon this week.

She was hardly the only one. "America at War," the *Washington Times'* lead editorial pronounced the next day. "It's WAR," screamed its editorial cartoon. A "new kind of war has been declared on the world's democracies," the *Wall Street Journal's* editorial pontificated. "The War Against America" was the subject of the *New York Times* editorial. "A state of war," the *Washington Post* called it. "This is war," pronounced columnist Charles Krauthammer. "They were acts of war," confirmed the president of the United States.

Well, it probably is—except that, even as everyone from waitresses to the president was declaring war or howling for it, nobody was exactly sure who we were at war with.

The usual suspect was the shadowy Osama bin Laden, though some experts said the attacks didn't fit his profile, and even if we were sure, no one seemed able to say how we should wage the war, how we could win it or what would constitute victory. Mainly, what most Americans wanted to do—entirely understandably—was to blow the hell out of somebody or something. No doubt, in time, we will.

A U.S. war

But the blunt truth is that the United States has been at war for years—at least a decade, since we launched a war against Iraq in 1991, even though Iraq had done absolutely nothing to harm the United States or any American. Our bombing attacks on Iraq certainly caused civilian casualties, and if they were not deliberate, nobody beating the war drums at the time felt much regret for them.

The terrorists attacked us because they were paying us back for what we started.

For 10 years, we have maintained economic sanctions on Iraq that have led to the deaths of hundreds of thousands of civilians, and we have repeatedly bombed it whenever it failed to abide by standards we imposed on it.

Under Bill Clinton, we again launched bombing raids against civilians—once against so-called "terrorist training camps" supposedly under bin Laden's control in Afghanistan and at the same time against a purported "chemical weapons factory" in Sudan that almost certainly was no such thing. The attacks just happened to occur on the same day as Monica Lewinsky's grand jury testimony that she had engaged in sex with the president. [In 1998 Clinton was embroiled in a sex scandal involving Lewinsky, an intern, and testimony regarding a sexual harassment suit by Arkansas state employee Paula Jones; the scandal eventually led to his impeachment.]

"This is unfortunately the war of the future," Secretary of State Madeleine Albright said in justifying the U.S. raids, officially launched in retaliation for terrorist attacks on American embassies.

Later the same year [1998], Clinton ordered (but later countermanded) yet more missile attacks on Iraq—the day after the Paula Jones sex scandal was settled in court. Later yet again, Clinton ordered more bombings in Iraq the day before Congress was scheduled to vote on his impeachment. Then there are the Balkans, where the United States has waddled forth to war for no compelling reason and where it has also slaughtered civilians with its unprovoked bombings.

Why terrorists attack

In all the buckets of media gabble about the terrorist attacks in New York and Washington, not once have I heard any journalist ask any expert the simple question, "Why did the terrorists attack us?"

There is, of course, an implicit answer to the unasked question: It's because the terrorists are "evil"; they "hate democracy"; they are "fanatics," "barbarians" and "cowards." Those, of course, are answers that can satisfy only children. Some day it might actually dawn on someone in this country that the grown-up but unwelcome answer is that the terrorists attacked us because they were paying us back for what we started.

Let us hear no more about how the "terrorists" have "declared war on America." Any nation that allows a criminal chief executive to use its military power to slaughter civilians in unprovoked and legally unauthorized attacks for his own personal political purposes can expect whatever the "terrorists" dish out to it. If, as President Bush told us, we should make no distinction between those who harbor terrorists and those who commit terrorist acts, neither can any distinction be made between those who tolerate the murderous policies of a criminal in power and the criminal himself.

The blunt and quite ugly truth is that the United States has been at war for years—that it started the war in the name of "spreading democracy," "building nations," "waging peace," "stopping aggression," "enforcing human rights" and all the other pious lies that warmongers always invoke to mask the truth, and that it continued the war simply to save a crook from political ruin.

What is new is merely that in September 2001, for the first time, the war we started came home—and all of a sudden, Americans don't seem to care for it so much.

8

"Blowback" from U.S. Foreign Policy Is Partially to Blame for the Attacks

Chalmers Johnson

Chalmers Johnson is the author of a dozen books concerning East Asia and political violence, including Revolutionary Change *and* Blowback: The Costs and Consequences of American Empire.

The terrorist attacks against the World Trade Center and the Pentagon were an example of "blowback"—a term created by the Central Intelligence Agency (CIA) to describe unintended consequences of U.S. activities abroad. Terrorist network leader Osama bin Laden was in part the creation of the United States, which funded his efforts against the Soviet Union in the 1980s. Rather than continue with foreign policy as usual, the United States needs to make a serious effort to analyze and curb its global military activities.

For Americans who can bear to think about it, those tragic pictures from New York of women holding up photos of their husbands, sons and daughters and asking if anyone knows anything about them look familiar. They are similar to scenes we have seen from Buenos Aires and Santiago. There, too, starting in the 1970s, women held up photos of their loved ones, asking for information. Since it was far too dangerous then to say aloud what they thought had happened to them—that they had been tortured and murdered by US-backed military juntas—the women coined a new word for them, *los desaparecidos*—"the disappeareds." Our government has never been honest about its own role in the 1973 overthrow of the elected government of Salvador Allende in Chile or its backing, through "Operation Condor," of what the State Department has recently called "extrajudicial killings" in Argentina, Paraguay, Brazil and elsewhere in Latin America. But we now have several thousand of our own disappeareds, and we are badly mistaken if we think that we in the United States are entirely blameless for what happened to them.

The suicidal assassins of September 11, 2001, did not "attack America," as our political leaders and the news media like to maintain; they attacked American foreign policy. Employing the strategy of the weak, they killed innocent bystanders who then became enemies only because they had already become victims. Terrorism by definition strikes at the innocent in order to draw attention to the sins of the invulnerable. The United States deploys such overwhelming military force globally that for its militarized opponents only an "asymmetric strategy," in the jargon of the Pentagon, has any chance of success. When it does succeed, as it did spectacularly on September 11, it renders our massive military machine worthless: The terrorists offer it no targets. On the day of the disaster, President George W. Bush told the American people that we were attacked because we are "a beacon for freedom" and because the attackers were "evil." In his address to Congress on September 20, he said, "This is civilization's fight." This attempt to define difficult-to-grasp events as only a conflict over abstract values—as a "clash of civilizations," in current post-cold war American jargon—is not only disingenuous but also a way of evading responsibility for the "blowback" that America's imperial projects have generated.

Unintended consequences

"Blowback" is a CIA term first used in March 1954 in a recently declassified report on the 1953 operation to overthrow the government of Mohammed Mossadegh in Iran. It is a metaphor for the unintended consequences of the US government's international activities that have been kept secret from the American people. The CIA's fears that there might ultimately be some blowback from its egregious interference in the affairs of Iran were well founded. Installing the Shah in power brought twenty-five years of tyranny and repression to the Iranian people and elicited the Ayatollah Khomeini's revolution. The staff of the American embassy in Teheran was held hostage for more than a year. This misguided "covert operation" of the US government helped convince many capable people throughout the Islamic world that the United States was an implacable enemy.

Osama bin Laden . . . is no more (or less) "evil"
than his fellow creations of our CIA.

The pattern has become all too familiar. Osama bin Laden, the leading suspect as mastermind behind the carnage of September 11, is no more (or less) "evil" than his fellow creations of our CIA: Manuel Noriega, former commander of the Panama Defense Forces until George H. Bush in late 1989 invaded his country and kidnapped him, or Iraq's Saddam Hussein, whom we armed and backed so long as he was at war with Khomeini's Iran and whose people we have bombed and starved for a decade in an incompetent effort to get rid of him. These men were once listed as "assets" of our clandestine services organization.

Osama bin Laden joined our call for resistance to the Soviet Union's

1979 invasion of Afghanistan and accepted our military training and equipment along with countless other mujahedeen "freedom fighters." It was only after the Russians bombed Afghanistan back into the stone age and suffered a Vietnam-like defeat, and we turned our backs on the death and destruction we had helped cause, that he turned against us. The last straw as far as bin Laden was concerned was that, after the Gulf War, we based "infidel" American troops in Saudi Arabia to prop up its decadent, fiercely authoritarian regime. Ever since, bin Laden has been attempting to bring the things the CIA taught him home to the teachers. On September 11, he appears to have returned to his deadly project with a vengeance.

Globalization and America

There are today, ten years after the demise of the Soviet Union, some 800 Defense Department installations located in other countries. The people of the United States make up perhaps 4 percent of the world's population but consume 40 percent of its resources. They exercise hegemony over the world directly through overwhelming military might and indirectly through secretive organizations like the World Bank, the International Monetary Fund and the World Trade Organization. Though largely dominated by the US government, these are formally international organizations and therefore beyond Congressional oversight.

As the American-inspired process of "globalization" inexorably enlarges the gap between the rich and the poor, a popular movement against it has gained strength, advancing from its first demonstrations in Seattle in 1999 through protests in Washington, DC; Melbourne; Prague; Seoul; Nice; Barcelona; Quebec City; Göteborg; and on to its violent confrontations in Genoa earlier this year [2001]. Ironically, though American leaders are deaf to the desires of the protesters, the Defense Department has actually adopted the movement's main premise—that current global economic arrangements mean more wealth for the "West" and more misery for the "rest"—as a reason why the United States should place weapons in space. The US Space Command's pamphlet "Vision for 2020" argues that "the globalization of the world economy will also continue, with a widening between the 'haves' and the 'have-nots,'" and that we have a mission to "dominate the space dimension of military operations to protect US interests and investments" in an increasingly dangerous and implicitly anti-American world. Unfortunately, while the eyes of military planners were firmly focused on the "control and domination" of space and "denying other countries access to space," a very different kind of space was suddenly occupied.

On the day after the September 11 attack, Democratic Senator Zell Miller of Georgia declared, "I say, bomb the hell out of them. If there's collateral damage, so be it." "Collateral damage" is another of those hateful euphemisms invented by our military to prettify its killing of the defenseless. It is the term Pentagon spokesmen use to refer to the Serb and Iraqi civilians who were killed or maimed by bombs from high-flying American warplanes in our campaigns against Slobodan Milosevic and Saddam Hussein. It is the kind of word our new ambassador to the United Nations, John Negroponte, might have used in the 1980s to explain the slaughter of peasants, Indians and church workers by American-backed right-wing death squads in El Salvador, Guatemala, Honduras and Nicaragua while he was ambassador to Honduras. These activities made the Reagan years the worst decade for Central America since the Spanish conquest.

Massive military retaliation with its inevitable "collateral damage" will, of course, create more desperate and embittered childless parents and parentless children, and so recruit more maddened people to the terrorists' cause. In fact, mindless bombing is surely one of the responses their grisly strategy hopes to elicit. Moreover, a major crisis in the Middle East will inescapably cause a rise in global oil prices, with, from the assassins' point of view, desirable destabilizing effects on all the economies of the advanced industrial nations.

What America should do

What should we do? The following is a start on what, in a better world, we might modestly think about doing. But let me concede at the outset that none of this is going to happen. The people in Washington who run our government believe that they can now get all the things they wanted before the trade towers came down: more money for the military, ballistic missile defenses, more freedom for the intelligence services and removal of the last modest restrictions (no assassinations, less domestic snooping, fewer lists given to "friendly" foreign police of people we want executed) that the Vietnam era placed on our leaders. An inevitable consequence of big "blowback" events like this one is that, the causes having been largely kept from American eyes (if not Islamic or Latin American ones), people cannot make the necessary connections for an explanation. Popular support for Washington is thus, at least for a while, staggeringly high.

Nonetheless, what we *should* do is to make a serious analytical effort to determine what overseas military commitments make sense and where we should pull in our horns. Although we intend to continue supporting Israel, our new policy should be to urge the dismantling of West Bank Israeli settlements as fast as possible. In Saudi Arabia, we should withdraw our troops, since they do nothing for our oil security, which we can maintain by other means. Beyond the Middle East, in Okinawa, where we have thirty-eight US military bases in the midst of 1.3 million civilians, we should start by bringing home the Third Marine Division and demobilizing it. It is understrength, has no armor and is not up to the standards of the domestically based First and Second Marine Divisions. It has no deterrent value but is, without question, an unwanted burden we force the people of this unlucky island to bear.

A particular obscenity crying out for elimination is the US Army's School of the Americas, founded in Panama in 1946 and moved to Fort Benning, Georgia, in 1984 after Panamanian President Jorge Illueca called it "the biggest base for destabilization in Latin America" and evicted it. Its curriculum includes counterinsurgency, military intelligence, interrogation techniques, sniper fire, infantry and commando tactics, psychological warfare and jungle operations. Although a few members of Congress have long tried to shut it down, the Pentagon and the White House have always found ways to keep it in the budget. In May 2000 the Clinton Administration sought to provide new camouflage for the school by renaming it the "Defense Institute for Hemispheric Security Cooperation" and transferring authority over it from the Army Department to the Defense Department.

The school has trained more than 60,000 military and police officers from Latin American and Caribbean countries. Among SOA's most illustrious graduates are the dictators Manuel Noriega (now serving a forty-year sentence in an American jail for drug trafficking) and Omar Torrijos of Panama; Guillermo Rodrigues of Ecuador; Juan Velasco Alvarado of Peru; Leopoldo Galtieri, former head of Argentina's junta; and Hugo Banzer Suarez of Bolivia. More recently, Peru's Vladimiro Montesinos, SOA class of 1965, surfaced as a CIA asset and former President Alberto Fujimori's closest adviser.

More difficult than these fairly simple reforms would be to bring our rampant militarism under control. From George Washington's "farewell address" to Dwight Eisenhower's invention of the phrase "military-industrial complex," American leaders have warned about the dangers of a bloated, permanent, expensive military establishment that has lost its relationship to the country because service in it is no longer an obligation of citizenship. Our military operates the biggest arms sales operation on earth; it rapes girls, women and schoolchildren in Okinawa; it cuts ski-lift cables in Italy, killing twenty vacationers, and dismisses what its insubordinate pilots have done as a "training accident"; it allows its nuclear attack submarines to be used for joy rides for wealthy civilian supporters and then covers up the negligence that caused the sinking of a Japanese high school training ship; it propagandizes the nation with Hollywood films glorifying military service (*Pearl Harbor*); and it manipulates the political process to get more carrier task forces, antimissile missiles, nuclear weapons, stealth bombers and other expensive gadgets for which we have no conceivable use. Two of the most influential federal institutions are not in Washington but on the south side of the Potomac River—the Defense Department and the Central Intelligence Agency. Given their influence today, one must conclude that the government outlined in the Constitution of 1787 no longer bears much relationship to the government that actually rules from Washington. Until that is corrected, we should probably stop talking about "democracy" and "human rights."

In Saudi Arabia, we should withdraw our troops, since they do nothing for our oil security.

Once we have done the analysis, brought home most of our "forward deployed" troops, refurbished our diplomatic capabilities, reassured the world that we are not unilateralists who walk away from treaty commitments and reintroduced into government the kinds of idealistic policies we once pioneered (e.g., the Marshall Plan), then we might assess what we can do against "terrorism." We could reduce our transportation and information vulnerabilities by building into our systems more of what engineers call redundancy: different ways of doing the same things—airlines and railroads, wireless and optical fiber communications, automatic computer backup programs, land routes around bridges. It is absurd that our railroads do not even begin to compare with those in Western Europe or

Japan, and their inadequacies have made us overly dependent on aviation in travel between US cities. It may well be that some public utilities should be nationalized, just as safety aboard airliners should become a federal function. Flight decks need to be made genuinely inaccessible from the passenger compartments, as they are on El Al. In what might seem a radical change, we could even hire intelligence analysts at the CIA who can read the languages of the countries they are assigned to and have actually visited the places they write about (neither of these conditions is even slightly usual at the present time).

If we do these things, the crisis will recede. If we play into the hands of the terrorists, we will see more collateral damage among our own citizens. Ten years ago, the other so-called superpower, the former Soviet Union, disappeared almost overnight because of internal contradictions, imperial overstretch and an inability to reform. We have always been richer, so it might well take longer for similar contradictions to afflict our society. But it is nowhere written that the United States, in its guise as an empire dominating the world, must go on forever.

9

The Financial Backing of Terrorist Groups Must Be Targeted

Jim Hoagland

Jim Hoagland is a Pulitzer Prize–winning columnist for the Washington Post.

A key to the war against the terrorist organizations behind the September 11 attacks is to go after their money supply. International banks and financial institutions must crack down on money laundering practices that terrorists can exploit for their benefit. In addition, the United States should act against Islamic charities that may have supported terrorist groups.

Money sets Osama bin Laden apart from other Middle Eastern fanatics and murderers. A fortune derived from Saudi Arabia's vast oil revenues buys his organization survival and "success."

Finding and destroying the money trails to bin Laden is essential to finding and destroying his group. The Bush administration must penetrate and take apart the nexus of terror that surrounds bin Laden and his Afghan and Arab allies. The nexus is geographical, ideological and religious as well as financial. But without the money, the rest would not be enough to enable these mass murderers to hatch and conceal their plots for years and then spring them on a sunny Tuesday morning of their choosing.

That agents suspected of working for this son of a Saudi billionaire struck at the World Trade Center and brought down a visible symbol of international capitalism was certainly no accident. Revenge against easy money, money that has undermined the traditional way of life in the Arabian peninsula, had a place along with revenge against America on the terrorists' twisted agenda.

It is enough to make you think that Lenin got the general idea right but the details wrong. The first Soviet leader predicted that the merchants of America and Britain would gladly sell communists the rope with which

From "Dry Up the Money Trail," by Jim Hoagland, *The Washington Post*, September 30, 2001. Copyright © 2001 by The Washington Post Company. Reprinted with permission.

to hang the world's capitalists. But the West's symbolic weak link turns out to be oil—and the floods of money it has poured on economically primitive lands—not rope.

Finding and destroying the money trails to bin Laden is essential to finding and destroying his group.

It was jet fuel that caused the Trade Center's twin towers to burn and implode on Sept. 11. And it was oil money that enabled bin Laden to buy sanctuary first in Sudan and then Afghanistan, to assemble a small army to protect him and to field well-equipped and trained agents around the world.

Freezing assets

The White House fired a modest first shot at bin Laden's enablers last week [September 24, 2001] by freezing the U.S. assets of individuals and organizations with financial links to him. Probably more important, the Treasury Department turned on a dime from fighting significant international cooperation on dirty money havens to threatening retribution against foreign banks that did not follow the U.S. lead on bin Laden.

The Bank of International Settlements is now said to be coordinating a daily listing of suspect institutions and persons operating in the world's 10 richest countries and encouraging banking centers to sort for transactions involving them.

The U.S. list included Islamic foundations, such as the Al Rashid Trust of Pakistan and the Wafa Humanitarian Organization of Saudi Arabia. They are only the tip of an iceberg of other Islamic charity fronts that wittingly and unwittingly provide cover for bin Laden's activities in desolate, starving places such as Afghanistan and Yemen.

International banks

But going after the regional fronts is only part of the financial task. This crisis offers Washington the need and the opportunity to force American and international banks to clean up money concealment and laundering practices they now tolerate or encourage, and which terrorism can exploit.

"It is a major security problem to have the huge amount of money we know is being hidden in this system and not know who controls it," says Robert Morgenthau, New York's district attorney and a man who has thought deeply and consistently over the years about the damage the international banking system inflicts on capitalism in the pursuit of short-term profit.

In the past three years [1998–2001], bank deposits in the tiny and unregulated Cayman Islands have grown from $500 billion to $800 billion, says Morgenthau, who notes that "47 of the world's largest banks are licensed to operate" in a setting where banks are used to hide assets, launder proceeds of crimes and pay out bribes to foreign officials.

Morgenthau has tenaciously pursued difficult and time-consuming investigations into banking crimes that other prosecutors have avoided. He has found "terrorist accounts" offshore in the past—and also found little interest in Washington in pressing the banking industry to curb the secrecy and excesses that enable those accounts to be established.

"Congress is putting $40 billion into the national recovery effort," Morgenthau says. "They could recover that and more by preventing these tax havens and banks from hiding assets. We have to do our part to make taxpayers see the system is fair."

The Bush administration has put a toe into the offshore water where banks help bad guys manipulate them for evil and for mutual profit. The feds should wade in vigorously and prepare for a long struggle against all the enablers, even those in bankers' pinstripes.

10

The United States Should Seek Alternatives to Military Action

Joyce Neu

Joyce Neu is executive director of the Joan B. Kroc Institute for Peace and Justice at the University of San Diego.

Americans are justifiably angry at the terrorists behind the September 11 attacks. Many call for military reprisals. However, war has failed to deter terrorism and inevitably kills innocent bystanders and civilians. The United States should reject calls for war and revenge and instead seek out alternative ways of bringing the terrorists to justice and work to remove the underlying causes of terrorism. By responding with restraint and magnanimity, America can help prevent terrorism in the future.

In the last decade, I have seen firsthand the consequences of armed conflict in Bosnia, Congo, Georgia, Rwanda, Sudan and Uganda. As a professional in the field of conflict resolution, I have met with government and rebel leaders who argued eloquently, in the words of Bob Dylan's famous sixties song, that "God was on their side."

While each conflict may be different in its history and causes, each conflict is the same in causing the deaths of innocents. Of the several million people who have been killed in wars in the last decade, estimates are that 80 percent to 90 percent of these are civilians. No matter how just the cause, these people did not deserve to die.

As a result of the tragic events of Sept. 11, our government is examining possible responses, including military action. Polls show that most Americans favor military action; but there are those of us who believe the United States is capable of being held to a higher standard. If we believe, like the terrorists who struck the World Trade Center, the Pentagon, and a field in Pennsylvania, that our cause is just, and that innocent lives may have to be lost to extract "justice," then we become moral cowards, defining justice in terms of retribution and revenge and we perpetuate a cycle

From "Extracting Vengeance or Building a Lasting Peace," by Joyce Neu, *San Diego Union-Tribune*, September 27, 2001. Copyright © 2001 by Union-Tribune Publishing Company. Reprinted by permission of the author.

of violence all too familiar to those who perpetrated the brutal actions of Sept. 11.

The tragic loss of life of Sept. 11 has torn the mask of civility off many of our faces. We are justifiably angry and frustrated at our inability to have predicted or prevented the deaths on our soil of so many good people, Americans and others from around the world.

Responding magnanimously to violence

What kind of response can we have that will demonstrate to the world that we mean business in fighting this campaign against terrorism? Rather than look to military might as our answer, we might seek more creative, sustainable ways to ensure justice is done and that the causes for such violence are extinguished. As patriotic Americans, we may want to demonstrate to the world the power of a free society by acting internationally the way we see firefighters, police officers, and volunteers acting in response to the World Trade Center destruction—with perseverance, generosity and concern.

Why would we choose to respond magnanimously instead of militarily? Would this be seen as weakness? While military power serves as a deterrent to the threat of war between nations, it clearly has not served as a deterrent to terrorism.

Children growing up in the developing world look to the developed world, particularly the United States, as a model. Will Afghan and Iraqi children, having been subjected to hunger, disease and oppression, look at the United States as a model of what they want for their country or as the enemy on whom to seek revenge? This is within our power to decide. Responding magnanimously will sow the seeds of friendship; striking their homelands will give rise to a new generation of terrorists.

Perhaps just as importantly, if we respond militarily, what does it say about us as a people? Does it say that because we have the power to destroy, we must do so? That faced with an attack against us, we have no recourse but to respond in similar fashion? Wouldn't restraint reveal our true nature better?

That our ability to develop sophisticated weaponry does not mean that we are eager to use it? We should be clear that no matter how powerful our military is, it cannot guarantee that we can go into Afghanistan or Iraq without incurring the deaths of our own troops and those of innocent civilians.

Difficult choices

We are a nation of the people and by the people, and we are facing difficult choices: do we rationalize the deaths of innocents abroad as the cost of fighting terrorism? Do we make clear to the world that we hold human life sacred only if it is American life? Or do we find ways to safeguard our lives and property in a way that honors the foundations of our society: rule of law, human rights, and the dignity of each person?

The reactions of families whose loved ones were killed or are still missing seems to be that they do not want a military action taken in the name of their loved ones. They do not see that violence will get anything but more families torn apart in grief.

Americans should demonstrate that we are not like the terrorists and do not take the lives of innocents. We need the strength of character and moral authority to pursue a campaign to eradicate the causes of terrorism. While it may involve determining those responsible, routing them out and seeing that they are brought to justice, the campaign against terrorism must seek to pull out the roots that spread the hatred, fear and desperation that give rise to suicide and destruction.

We must begin a campaign of inoculating people against despair by taking on the economic and social disparities that give rise to hopelessness and frustration, whether in our country or outside. Americans are a generous people. The TV images of the work of firefighters, police officers and volunteers in New York City make us all proud to be Americans. We need to take this selflessness to those in need in our own country as well as outside our country.

Helping others

Just as we export goods, so should we export our know-how, our decency, and our conviction that working together, we can make a difference. One part of our covert campaign against terrorism therefore should consist of rebuilding schools and hospitals, providing training and skills for responsible leadership, and in the short-term, making sure that there are refugee camps ready with food and shelter to accept people fleeing from the feared U.S. military attacks.

Another part of the campaign is to make clear the distinction between religion and fanaticism. Just as many wars are supposedly waged in the name of religion, there are usually other, more material reasons for the violence. Islam is not the enemy just as Arab countries are not the enemy. These acts were the acts of terrorists. Not Islamic terrorists, not Arab terrorists—just terrorists. Our leaders have started to make this clear and we need to continue to emphasize that these acts had nothing to do with any religion or belief system. God was not on their side just as God is not on the side of anyone who perpetrates the killing and destruction of innocent people.

> *Polls show that most Americans favor military action; but there are those of us who believe the United States is capable of being held to a higher standard.*

The United States should also re-engage in the dialogue to establish a permanent International Criminal Court. Although discussions in the United Nations and other international arenas often take positions that the U.S. government believes are antithetical to ours, if we are not part of the debate, then we cannot complain when we do not like the outcome.

The United States has gained a reputation for walking out of difficult discussions, as we did at the U.N. Conference on Racism and Related Intolerance. We should have stronger stomachs and stay engaged. These terrorist acts are abundant evidence that if we won't deal with the problems in the world, they will come to us.

Without an International Criminal Court, we will have to create ad hoc tribunals for people like Osama bin Laden. The world deserves a permanent, standing court where terrorists and war criminals, regardless of country or conflict, can be tried.

Finally, we need to take time to mourn the dead and the missing. Before we react in a manner that undermines our character as a strong and proud people who believe in the rule of law and justice, our leaders should take the time to remember the lessons of U.S. involvement in Japan and Germany post-World War II.

By helping those countries and peoples rebuild and develop, we gained loyal allies that are still with us today. Let us create new allies out of enemies so that our children and grandchildren will remember Sept. 11, 2001 and its victims as giving rise to new understandings and tolerance, not to more violence and death.

11

The Terrorist Attacks Should Be Treated as Acts of War

Gary Dempsey

Gary Dempsey is a foreign policy analyst at the Cato Institute, a libertarian public policy think tank.

Some people have described the September 11 terrorist incidents in New York and Washington as "crimes against humanity" and have argued that the perpetrators should be captured, charged, and tried in an international court. However, treating terrorism as a criminal justice problem has failed in the past to deter terrorists or to hold foreign governments responsible for harboring or sponsoring terrorists. The terrorist assaults were acts of war against the American people. The U.S. government must respond accordingly by going to war against the perpetrators of those acts in order to protect Americans from more attacks.

A global coalition of human rights groups described the ghastly terrorist attacks on the World Trade Center and the Pentagon as "crimes against humanity." They added that the incidents proved the United States should reconsider its opposition to the creation of a standing international criminal court. Never mind that the international community has yet to agree on a legal definition of international terrorism or that a global court could open a Pandora's box of legal mischief—treating terrorism as a criminal justice matter is wrongheaded.

President Bill Clinton's responses to terrorism

Yet that is the way the Clinton administration chose to deal with the problem. Indeed, the 2000 bombing of the USS Cole (which killed 17 and wounded 33), the 1998 bombing of two U.S. embassies in east Africa (which killed 224 and wounded more than 4,000), and the 1993 bombing of the World Trade Center (which killed six and wounded more than 1,000), were all pursued as criminal justice matters. America's law enforcement agencies conducted investigations and eventually made some arrests. The result: 12 men involved in the 1993 World Trade Center bombing were convicted in November 1997, four years after their attack, and four men involved in the 1998 embassy bombings were convicted in May 2001, three years after their attack. The mastermind of the bombings, Osama bin Laden, remained at-large and was put on the FBI's 10 Most Wanted list. No one has yet been convicted for the Cole attack.

Treating terrorism as a criminal justice matter is wrongheaded.

According to a former Clinton administration official, the goal in treating international terrorism as a legal matter was to "depoliticize" and "delegitimize" it by defining it as criminal activity instead of warfare. Resorting to indictments, extraditions, and trials, it was argued, was the best course. "We are not a nation that retaliates just in order to get vengeance," exclaimed then-secretary of state Madeleine Albright after the U.S. embassy bombings. "America does not forget our own legal system while searching for those who harmed us." Such thinking continues today. University of Illinois law professor Francis Boyle, for example, says that Osama bin Laden "is a fugitive from justice and this should be handled as a matter as other fugitives from justice of international law enforcement."

But defining what happened in New York and Washington as crimes misses the point. One of the primary constitutional responsibilities of the U.S. government is to defend the American people from external attack. It's striking, then, that the last [Clinton] administration and its defenders were so willing to use the U.S. military for social work and peacekeeping around the world—mostly on missions that had little to do with the direct security of America—but treated the slaughter of American citizens and destruction of U.S. property by international terrorists as a law enforcement issue.

That approach has hardly proven a model of deterrence. It has neither held foreign governments sufficiently accountable for harboring, let alone sponsoring, terrorist organizations, nor confronted the root causes of what drives terrorists to target America in the first place.

That said, the magnitude of the attacks on New York and Washington and the perpetrators' demonstrable willingness to keep escalating their efforts (perhaps biological, chemical, or nuclear weapons next time) make it clear that countering terrorism can no longer be primarily a matter for the law enforcement or even the intelligence communities. The prospect of jail time is not a substitute for defense policy.

Acts of war

Sadly, even a radical shift in America's Middle East and Persian Gulf policies at this point is unlikely to reverse the built-up momentum of the terrorist threat. That means the United States has little choice now but to respond to the recent attacks as only the initial acts of war and to defend its citizens by taking the war back to bin Laden and whomever else supports him.

It wouldn't be the first time the United States has gone to war against non-state actors. In 1801, President Thomas Jefferson went to war against the Barbary pirates, who preyed upon European and American shipping in both Mediterranean and Atlantic waters. James Madison supported Jefferson's efforts, which proved successful by 1805.

Jefferson, unfortunately, operated without a formal declaration of war from Congress. He later admitted that he was "unauthorized by the Constitution, without the sanction of Congress, to go beyond the line of defense," and that it was the prerogative of Congress to authorize "measures of offense also." Lamentably, Congress last week [on September 14, 2001] sidestepped its duty to formally declare war and instead granted the president the authority "to use all necessary force."

Of course, formally declaring war would not mean that U.S. bombers must immediately launch air strikes or that the Marines must eventually conduct a full-scale land invasion. Rather, it would signify that a profound threshold has been crossed and that there are certain things Americans absolutely will not tolerate happening to their fellow citizens.

12

The Terrorist Attacks Should Be Treated as International Crimes

David Held

David Held is a professor of political science at the London School of Economics and author of Democracy and the Global Order *and other works.*

The terrorism of September 11 was an attack on fundamental and global principles of justice and law. The response to them must be careful and measured, and should not contradict these fundamental principles of civilization. While war and bombing are one option, another is the creation of an international commission on global terrorism under the auspices of the United Nations. Criminalizing terrorism on an international basis can foster global cooperation in capturing and bringing those responsible for the September 11 attack to justice. In addition, nations must work together to address social justice issues and underlying grievances that may contribute to the rise of terrorist groups.

The greatest Enlightenment philosopher, Immanuel Kant, wrote over two hundred years ago that we are 'unavoidably side by side'. A violent abrogation of law and justice in one place has consequences for many other places and can be experienced everywhere. While he dwelt on these matters and their implications at length, he could not have known how profound and immediate his concerns would become.

Since Kant, our mutual interconnectedness and vulnerability have grown rapidly. We no longer live, if we ever did, in a world of discrete national communities which have the power and capacity alone to determine the fate of those within them. Instead, we live in a world of overlapping communities of fate. The trajectories and futures of nation-states are now heavily enmeshed with each other. In our world, it is not only the violent exception that links people together across borders, the very nature of everyday problems and processes joins people in multiple ways.

From the movement of ideas and cultural artifacts to the fundamental issues raised by genetic engineering, from the conditions of financial stability to environmental degradation, the fate and fortunes of each of us
are thoroughly intertwined.

The story of our increasingly global order is not a singular one. There
are many myths about globalisation and one in particular is pernicious;
that is, that the age is increasingly defined by global markets, economic
processes and social forces which necessarily escape the control of states
and politicians. The spread of markets for goods, services and finance has,
indeed, altered the political terrain. But the story of globalisation is not
just one of the expansion of markets, neoliberal deregulation and the ab-
dication of politics; for it is also one of growing aspirations for international law and justice. From the UN system to the EU [European Union],
from changes to the law of war to the entrenchment of human rights,
from the emergence of international environmental regimes to the foundation of the International Criminal Court, there is also another narrative
being told—the narrative which seeks to reframe human activity and entrench it in law, rights and responsibilities.

This is why the 11th September is a defining moment for humankind. The terrorist violence was an atrocity of extraordinary proportions;
it was a crime against America and against humanity; it was an outrage
that ranks amongst the worlds most heinous crimes; and it was, make no
mistake about it, an attack on the fundamental principles of freedom,
democracy, the rule of law and justice.

Fundamental global principles

These principles are not just western principles. Elements of them had
their origins in the early modern period in the West, but their validity ex-
tends much further than this. For these principles are the basis of a fair,
humane and decent society, of whatever religion or cultural tradition. To
paraphrase the American legal theorist Bruce Ackerman, there is no nation
without a woman who yearns for equal rights, no society without a man
who denies the need for deference and no developing country without a
person who does not wish for the minimum means of subsistence so that
they may go about their everyday lives. The principles of freedom, democracy and justice are the basis for articulating and entrenching the equal liberty of all human beings, wherever they were born or brought up.

---

*The 11th September is a defining moment for
humankind.*

The intensity of the range of responses to the atrocities of 11th September is fully understandable from any perspective. There cannot be
many people in the world (despite media images of celebrations in some
quarters) who did not experience shock, revulsion, horror, disbelief, anger
and a desire for vengeance. This emotional range is perfectly natural
within the context of the immediate events. But it cannot be the basis for
a more considered and wise response.

The founding principles of our society, the very principles under attack on 11th September, dictate that we pause for reflection; that we do not overgeneralise our response from one moment and one set of events; that we do not jump to conclusions based on concerns that emerge in one particular country; and that we do not re-write and re-work history from one place.

The fight against terror must be put on a new footing. There can be no going back to the haphazard and complacent approach to terrorism of 10th September. Terrorists must be brought to heel and those who protect and nurture them must be brought to account. Zero tolerance is fully justified in these circumstances. Terrorism negates our most cherished principles and ambitions.

The fight against terror must be put on a new footing.

But any defensible, justifiable and sustainable response to the 11th September must be consistent with our founding principles and the aspirations of international society for security, law, and the impartial administration of justice—aspirations painfully articulated after the Holocaust and the Second World War. If the means deployed to fight terrorism contradict these principles, then the emotion of the moment might be satisfied, but our mutual vulnerability will be deepened. We will be set on yet another step backwards from a more secure and just world order. This could easily involve the growth of intolerance of all attempts to protest over and change political circumstances, even if they are law abiding and peaceful in their orientations.

Another option

War and bombing are one option for the immediate future; but another is an International Commission on global terrorism which might be modelled on the Nuremberg and Tokyo war tribunals, working under the authority of a reenergised and revitalised United Nations. Such a commission could be empowered to investigate those responsible for the new mass terrorism and to bring them to justice. Backed by the capacity to impose economic, political and military sanctions—and supported by UN and NATO military capacities, among others—it might be the basis of an investigation and system of punishment which commands global support. It could be the basis not only for the strengthening of existing legal and multilateral arrangements, but the basis for helping to define a new just, accountable and democratic order. The means would be consistent with the defence of the principles under threat. Terrorism must be criminalised on an international basis, not eradicated through arbitrary violent action.

I am not a pacifist. The motivation for these recommendations is not the avoidance of the use of coercive force under all circumstances. Rather, it is anchored on the wish to build on the more humane and just elements of our global order which have been set down in the last several decades, and to entrench them in such a way that could command the respect and loyalty of all peoples, everywhere.

But to borrow a phrase, we must be tough not just on crime but on the causes of crime. Whoever the perpetrators were of the terrorism of 11th September, we know that there will always be volunteers for suicide missions, suicide bombings, and for terrorist groupings if we do not concern ourselves with the wider issues of peace and social justice in the global community. In our global age shaped by the flickering images of television and new information systems, the gross inequalities of life chances found in many of the world's regions feed a frenzy of anger, hostility and resentment. Without a just peace in the Middle East and without an attempt to anchor globalisation in meaningful principles of social justice, there can be no durable solution to the kind of crimes we have just seen.

Of course, such crimes may often be the work of the simply deranged and the fanatic and so there can be no guarantee that a more just world will be a more peaceful one in all respects. But if we turn our back on these challenges altogether, there is no hope of ameliorating the social basis of disadvantage often experienced in the poorest and most dislocated countries. Gross injustices, linked to a sense of hopelessness born of generations of neglect, feed anger and hostility. Popular support against terrorism depends upon convincing people that there is a legal and pacific way of addressing their grievances.

Kant was right; the violent abrogation of law and justice in one place ricochets across the world. We cannot accept the burden of putting justice right in one dimension of life—security—without at the same time seeking to put it right everywhere.

13

Bombing Afghanistan Is the Wrong Response to the Terrorist Attacks

Matthew Rothschild

Matthew Rothschild is editor of the Progressive, *a monthly magazine that champions peace and social justice.*

President George W. Bush's October 7, 2001, decision to bomb Afghanistan was a risky and unjustified move. The people of Afghanistan were not responsible for the September 11 terrorist attacks and should not be killed by American bombs. Bush is embarking on a doomed crusade that will likely create as many terrorists as it destroys. The United States should instead get at the root causes of terrorism, including Third World poverty and repression.

By bombing Afghanistan, George W. Bush has rolled the bombs as if they were dice. And for all his protestations to the contrary, he has treated the people of Afghanistan as if they were playthings.

When the United States and Britain bombed Kabul, a city of more than two million people, and at least three other cities—Kandahar, Herat, and Jalalabad—they guaranteed that innocent Afghans would lose their lives. These Afghans did not fly planes into the World Trade towers or the Pentagon. They did nothing to deserve death at the hands of Washington.

How many innocent Afghans ultimately die in this war we will not know.

But what we do know is that Bush calculated that their deaths were worth it.

They are not.

Killing innocent people is never justified.

Making America less safe

And this war will not make the United States any safer; it will make this country more imperiled.

Already, the government is warning us of additional, and perhaps imminent, terrorist attacks on our soil.

Already, the government is nervous that Pakistan may fall to forces allied with the Taliban, and that Pakistan's nuclear weapons may not be secure.

Already, there is great anxiety in Washington about the negative response this war will spark in the rest of the Muslim world.

War is a terribly risky and dangerous game. But Bush was eager to play it.

Like his father in the Gulf War, George W. spurned a last minute offer to negotiate. The Taliban offered to release the eight Americans under arrest and apprehend Osama bin Laden and try him under Islamic law; the United States didn't give it a second thought.

Bush has vowed to wage an unlimited war. "You will have every tool you need," he assured his soldiers on Sunday [October 7, 2001], echoing his words of September 20, when he said the United States would use "every necessary weapon of war."

Does that include nuclear weapons?

The war is also unlimited in time and in location.

It was not reassuring to hear Bush say on Sunday that this war in Afghanistan was just "phase one."

How many phases does he have in mind?

This war will not make the United States any safer; it will make this country more imperiled.

"Today, we focus on Afghanistan, but the battle is broader," he said. "Every nation has a choice to make. In this conflict, there is no neutral ground. If any government sponsors the outlaws and killers of innocents, they have become outlaws and murderers themselves. And they will take that lonely path at their own peril."

Wait a second here.

Congress did not grant Bush the title of grand executioner of global terrorism.

As vast as the Congressional resolution authorizing the use of force was, it was limited to the culprits behind the September 11 attack.

But Bush is not content to stop there. He sees himself on a zealous mission, and he is unilaterally and illegally grabbing power to undertake it.

The most powerful man in the world, unchecked by Congress and the media, now suffers delusions of military grandeur, and innocent people will pay with their lives.

A doomed mission

It's a mission that is doomed from the start.

He cannot kill every terrorist in the world.

(And by the way, is he going to bomb Bogotá because it works with the paramilitaries, who are "outlaws and killers of innocents"? Unlikely, since Colombia is our ally in the war on drugs.)

What's more, the bombings are probably already creating more terrorists at this very moment, who will be willing to kill and die to stand up to an America they see as the aggressor.

Yes, Osama bin Laden and Al Qaeda, or whoever were the authors of the atrocity of September 11, need to be brought to justice. They should be apprehended and hauled before an international tribunal for committing a crime against humanity.

And yes, the United States needs to secure itself against future attacks.

But terrorism itself will not disappear after bin Laden and Al Qaeda are gone.

It will not disappear if Bush levels Kabul, Baghdad, Khartoum, and Damascus, all at once, as some on the far reaches of the Republican Party seem to be proposing.

Roots of terror

War is not the answer. The answer is getting at the roots of terror.

And there are many roots, some of them watered by the United States.

It watered them in Afghanistan in the 1980s by recruiting, arming, and training tens of thousands of Islamic fundamentalists and by virtually reviving the very concept of jihad.

It watered them during the Gulf War and especially afterwards, when the United States insisted that the U.N. impose economic sanctions that have killed more than 500,000 Iraqi children.

It watered them for the last thirty-four years by backing Israel even as it maintained its illegal occupation of Palestinian land and repressed Palestinians on a daily basis.

Some roots are separate, watered by one of the longest polluted rivers in the world, which is anti-Semitism, or watered by another rancid pool, which is religious fundamentalism.

Add to that the combination of Third World poverty and repressive rule (both of which the United States bears some responsibility for), and you can get a handle on the complex phenomenon that is terrorism.

These roots cannot be eradicated at gunpoint; they cannot be pulled up by bombs.

But many of them can be dried up if the United States adopted a more benign foreign policy. (And it certainly would help if Bush spoke in a secular, not a religious, voice. There he was again Sunday telling us all about his prayers.)

Bush has set the nation upon an endless course of war.

For the moment, the people are behind him.

But this might change.

The costs of war may soon be excessive: in innocent lives killed abroad; in the deaths of U.S. soldiers; in a wobbly and swooning economy; in world chaos.

Bush has rolled the bombs. Now we all may feel the fallout.

14

Bombing Afghanistan Was a Necessary Step in the War Against Terrorism

Michael Kelly

Michael Kelly is the editor of the Atlantic Monthly *and a columnist for the* Washington Post. *He is the author of* Martyrs' Day: Chronicle of a Small War, *an account of his experiences as a journalist covering the 1991 Persian Gulf War.*

The bombing of Afghanistan that began on October 7, 2001, was America's answer to the September 11 terrorist attacks. Those who still question whether it was the right answer should pay close attention to terrorist leader Osama bin Laden's taped message released that day, in which he calls for Muslims to engage in holy war against America and the West. The terrorists led by bin Laden constitute a serious threat to Americans, who should be prepared for a long, daunting, but necessary war.

Sunday [October 7, 2001] was a day of clarification on various levels. The first was the most basic. We have been under attack by Osama bin Laden and his al Qaeda network for some years now, but we did not fully admit to that until Sept. 11. On Oct. 7 we answered Sept. 11. There was a feeling to the day of something like relief. Well, that's that; war is joined, and we must win it.

What we must win was also made clear. Incredibly, in the light of 6,000 dead, some (mostly on the left) have persisted in the delusion that we are involved here in something that can be put into some sort of context of normality—a crisis that can be resolved through legal or diplomatic efforts, or handled with United Nations resolutions, or addressed by limited military "reprisals." We have been warned not to see this in too-large terms—as a holy war, or a crusade or a clash of civilizations.

Osama bin Laden himself put the lie to all that with a videotaped message that apparently had been recorded after Sept. 11 but in anticipation of Oct. 7. In this statement, released to the Al-Jazeera television network, bin Laden abandoned the shred of pretense that he was not responsible for the attacks of Sept. 11. He crowed his joy: "Here is America struck by God Almighty in one of its vital organs, so that its greatest buildings are destroyed. Grace and gratitude to God. America has been filled with horror from North to South and East to West, and thanks be to God."

He described the conflict repeatedly in the terms of holy war. "These events have divided the world into two camps, the camp of the faithful and the camp of infidels," he said. And: "Every Muslim must rise to defend his religion." He ended with a promise: "I swear to God that America will not live in peace before peace reigns in Palestine, and before all the army of infidels depart the land of Mohammed, peace be upon him."

Is that clear now?

President Bush's resolve

The way in which our government views this war was also made clear. In his address to the nation on Sunday, Bush dropped any suggestion that what we are about is merely a manhunt on a massive scale. He made plain that America is, in fact, at war not only with bin Laden's al Qaeda but also with the Taliban forces of Afghanistan. Bush used language—"sustained, comprehensive and relentless operations"—intended to signal that, while this may be an unconventional war, it will be a war in full, not a Clintonian exercise in a spot of bombing, a bit of missile-rattling. He went further even, warning in hard language that the war could spread to other nations that sponsor terror against America: "If any government sponsors the outlaws and killers of innocents, they have become outlaws and murderers themselves. And they will take that lonely path at their own peril."

So there it is, out on the table. We are in a war, and we will be in it for some time, and this war is being undertaken toward a great and daunting end. With Sunday's speech, no one can doubt that President Bush and his advisers see the war on the same scale of magnitude as bin Laden sees it. It is us against them, and "them" has been defined broadly enough to encompass any state that harbors or sponsors anti-American terrorism. The goal here is not to knock off a few of terrorism's foot soldiers. It is to put out of business terrorism's masters, its networks and its protectors—even if those protectors enjoy status as sovereign regimes.

That this is a goal worth fighting for may be judged by the extraordinary international support for the American effort. The world's leaders know, as Britain's Tony Blair said Sunday, that the atrocity of Sept. 11 was "an attack on us all," by fanatics who threaten "any nation throughout the world that does not share their fanatical views."

No one can know how what began on Sunday will proceed. It is certainly possible that it will proceed badly, at least at times. It may appear, at times, that it will end badly. But we start out with a serious and large intent, facing an enemy that is likewise serious and likewise ambitious. If we remember this, if we stay serious and remember that the enemy too is serious, we will win. And it should not be hard to remember this. We have 6,000 reasons to never forget.

15

The Attacks Revealed America's Lack of Preparedness Against Terrorism

Franklin Foer

Franklin Foer is an associate editor of the New Republic, *a weekly journal of political analysis and opinion.*

Many of the actions the U.S. government has taken following the September 11, 2001, attacks had been previously recommended by various blue-ribbon commissions on terrorism. One of the most publicized and prescient reports on terrorism was issued in 2000 by the National Commission on Terrorism (NCT). The NCT was commissioned by Congress to analyze American counter-terrorism policy. However, its recommendations on reducing U.S. vulnerabilities to terrorist attacks were not enacted, in part because of opposition of civil liberties groups and in part because of resistance by government agencies that opposed changes in their powers and operations. America's lack of preparedness may be partially responsible for the events of September 11.

Two weeks after George W. Bush's [September 2001] declaration of war against terrorism, a battle plan is taking shape. We are putting the screws to Pakistan to end its history of mentoring terrorists. We will now treat Afghanistan like the rogue state that it is. The Treasury Department will try to choke off Osama bin Laden's financing. Intelligence agencies, at long last, will share information with one another. And if the Bush administration has its way, the CIA will revert to its pre-1995 guidelines, which allowed operatives to recruit informants with sketchy human rights records.

All sensible moves. And they were just as sensible when the National Commission on Terrorism proposed them more than a year [before the attack]. Yet the NCT's proposals never made it into law, and the reasons why say a lot about how difficult it will be for George W. Bush to carry out his war on terrorism today. The commission, you see, wasn't merely undermined by civil liberties groups suspicious of a serious effort against terrorism. It was undone by the very government agencies tasked with carrying out that effort.

A prominent commission

In Washington, blue-ribbon anti-terrorism commissions aren't exactly rare. But from the beginning, the NCT stood out. For starters, there was its mandate: It was commissioned by Congress, in the wake of the 1998 African embassy bombings, to produce the definitive blueprint for legislation overhauling counterterrorism policy. Then there was the panel's prestige. Chaired by Ronald Reagan's counterterrorism czar, L. Paul Bremer III, the commission included a retired head of the Army's Special Operations Command (Wayne Downing), a former undersecretary of defense (Fred Iklé), and a cast of foreign policy heavyweights. So unlike many other commissions whose reports get a paragraph on A-23, the NCT grabbed the attention of editorialists and Sunday talk show hosts. As former CIA director R. James Woolsey, another of the NCT panelists, puts it, "This was the best shot at change."

And the report lived up to its billing. Even its cover—which includes an image of the World Trade Center towers—was prescient. The panel found that the U.S. government wasn't prepared to prevent an Al Qaeda attack on American soil and that "the threat of attacks creating massive casualties is growing." In response, the NCT called for, among other things, expanded wiretap authority, recruitment of linguists, and the revision of laws that prevent the FBI and CIA from sharing intelligence—exactly what John Ashcroft is calling for now.

Opposition to NCT recommendations

Civil liberties groups were predictably hostile. Within hours of the report's release, the American Civil Liberties Union (ACLU) called it an "ominous cloud." The Arab American Institute's James Zogby said it harked back to the "darkest days of the McCarthy era." Leftist commentators accused the commission of hyping the danger of terrorism so that the FBI and CIA could justify greater surveillance powers and more money. *Salon's* Bruce Shapiro suggested that the NCT's warnings of domestic attack "are a con job, with roughly the veracity of the latest Robert Ludlum novel." Robert Dreyfuss wrote in *Mother Jones* that "[f]or the national security establishment, adrift with few enemies since the end of the Cold War a decade ago, the terrorist threat seems made to order."

But the national security establishment objected to the commission's recommendations as well. Testifying before Congress in 1999, FBI director Louis Freeh tried to anticipate the report's complaints, noting that "[t]he frequency of terrorist incidents in the United States has decreased in number" and implying that the bureau was already effectively combating the danger. The CIA was even more hostile. When the report appeared, CIA spokesman Bill Harlow rejected its call for the agency to jettison its "overly risk averse" approach to recruiting informants. Three members of the commission told me that the CIA leaked the report's more controversial recommendations in order to put the NCT on the defensive.

In part, the CIA opposed the recommendations out of fear that they would rekindle the agency's cold war reputation for dirty tricks. Under Bill Clinton, the CIA furiously tried to scrub away the tarnish of its Latin American misadventures during the 1980s, especially its alliance with Guatemalan paramilitary squads. And the NCT seemed to be pushing in the opposite direction, explicitly pleading with the CIA to find more "unsavory" terrorist sources. "Since John Deutch headed the agency," one ex-CIA official told me, "the seventh floor of Langley has become very politically correct. And they're so worried about provoking critics."

The NCT's proposals never made it into law, and the reasons why say a lot about how difficult it will be . . . to carry out . . . [a] war on terrorism today.

But mostly, the CIA opposed the NCT's recommendations for the same reason virtually every other government department and agency did: They trespassed on its turf. On CNN's *Late Edition*, Madeleine Albright countered the NCT's finding that the administration needed to get tougher with Pakistan and Greece. "We are pressing them [already]," she told Wolf Blitzer. And she warned that "in looking at how we fight [terrorism], we have to remember what kind of a society we are"—implying that the commission wanted to trample civil liberties. Deputy Attorney General Eric Holder told reporters that the NCT recommendations siphoned too much power away from the FBI. And the administration's civil rights chief, Bill Lan Lee, implied in a speech to the American-Arab Anti-Discrimination Committee that Arab-Americans were being unfairly smeared. (Never mind that the report didn't once mention Arab-Americans.)

A missed opportunity

Still, for one brief moment, Congress looked like it might impose change. Using the NCT report as their template, in July 2000 Senators Jon Kyl and Dianne Feinstein attached the recommended reforms to an intelligence authorization bill. As one Senate staffer told me, "It could have been one of the most important overhauls of American intelligence in recent memory." But the Kyl-Feinstein legislation quickly ran aground thanks largely to one man: Vermont's Patrick Leahy. Warning of CIA mischief and "risks to important civil liberties we hold dear," Leahy threatened to hold up the entire intelligence authorization bill to sink the reforms; so Kyl and Feinstein untethered the proposals from the budgetary process. Then, in October, bin Laden blew a hole in the USS *Cole* and Kyl and Feinstein's effort gained new momentum. But this time, instead of trying to defeat the legislation outright, Leahy weakened it so much that it became essentially useless. By threatening to place a hold on the bill, he extracted countless concessions. And when the legislation finally cleared the Senate in November, it did nothing to loosen CIA recruitment guidelines or expand the FBI's wiretapping authority. "It was so watered down by the time we got the bill," says one House Republican aide, "it wasn't worth taking up." And so the legislation died.

Would the Kyl-Feinstein changes have prevented September 11? Who knows? But September 11 utterly confirmed the commission's assertion that the government agencies charged with fighting terrorism were doing a woefully inadequate job. Unfortunately, those agencies proved more skilled at protecting themselves from bureaucratic encroachment than at protecting the country from Al Qaeda. And they received critical help from civil libertarians who saw counterterrorism as merely a ruse for the expansion of government power. In Washington, denial was a river in Egypt. And barely anyone except the NCT believed that terrorists might be lurking on its banks.

16

The Terrorist Attacks Clarified the Meaning of Good and Evil

William J. Bennett

William J. Bennett, a former secretary of education, is a director of Empower America, a public policy organization, and the author of several books, including The Book of Virtues.

The terrible terrorist attacks of September 11, 2001, have brought a sense of moral clarity to the United States. For too long teachers and other influential leaders have questioned whether good and evil really exist, or whether America is truly better than its enemies. Such questioning should be a thing of the past in the wake of September 11.

I n the aftermath of the attacks on the World Trade Center and the Pentagon, America will be changed politically, militarily, culturally, psychologically. It is too close to the events to understand their full impact. But one certain result is that these events have forced us to clarify and answer again universal questions that have been muddled over the past four decades.

Speaking about World War II, C.S. Lewis put it this way: "The war creates no absolutely new situation. It simply aggravates the permanent human situation so that we can no longer ignore it. Human life has always been lived on the edge of a precipice."

A moment of moral clarity

For too long, we have ignored the hostility shown toward America and democratic principles by some Muslims who adhere to a militant and radical interpretation of the Koran. We have created a moral equivalence between Israel and the Palestinians who seek to eradicate Israel. We have ignored Islamic clarion calls for our destruction and the bombings of our embassies and the U.S. destroyer Cole. This situation has not changed,

From "Faced with Evil on a Grand Scale, Nothing Is Relative," by William J. Bennett, *Los Angeles Times*, October 1, 2001. Copyright © 2001 by the *Los Angeles Times*. Reprinted with permission.

62

but now we realize what the situation is. This is a moment of moral clarity in the United States. For almost 40 years, we have been a nation that has questioned whether good and evil, right and wrong, true and false really exist. Some—particularly those in our institutions of higher learning and even some inside our own government—have wondered whether America is really better than its enemies around the world. After the events of Sept. 11, we should no longer be unsure of these things, even in the academy. We have seen the face and felt the hand of evil. Moral clarity should bring with it moral confidence and we must be reassured of some things.

America was not punished because we are bad, but because we are good.

Good and evil have never gone away; we merely had the luxury to question their existence. At the beginning of Allan Bloom's classic *The Closing of the American Mind,* he says, "There is one thing a professor can be absolutely certain of: Almost every student entering the university believes, or says he believes, that truth is relative." Can one culture, it was asked, really presume to say what should be the case in other cultures? Are there any cross-cultural values?

Yes. The use of commercial airplanes as missiles, guided into buildings where civilians work, is evil. The goal of the hijackers was the intentional destruction of innocent life so as to strike fear into the heart of America. And what they did was wrong. Not wrong given our point of view or because we were the victims or because of our Judeo-Christian tradition but simply wrong.

It has been said that these attacks were the inevitable reaction to modern-day American imperialism. They are retribution, it is claimed, for our support of Israel, our attacks on Saddam Hussein, cruise missiles launched at Afghanistan and Sudan.

Americans are good

This is nonsense. America's support for human rights and democracy is our noblest export to the world. And when we act in accord with those principles, time after time after time, we act well and honorably. We are not hated because we support Israel; we are hated because liberal democracy is incompatible with militant Islam. Despite what Hussein and Osama bin Laden and, shamefully, some American clerics have said, America was not punished because we are bad, but because we are good.

It is, therefore, past time for what novelist Tom Wolfe has called the "great relearning." We have engaged in a frivolous dalliance with dangerous theories—relativism, historicism, values clarification. Now, when faced with evil on such a grand scale, we should see these theories for what they are: empty. We must begin to have the courage of our convictions, to believe that some actions are good and some evil and to act on those beliefs to prevent evil.

And so we must respond to these attacks and prevent future attacks.

We do this to protect our own citizens and our own way of life. We do this to protect the idea that good and evil exist and that man is capable of soaring to great heights and sinking to terrible lows. We do this, in the end, to prevent the world from becoming the prisoner of terrorists, their way of battle, their way of thinking, their way of life, their way of death.

The recognition that some things are right and some things are wrong has come at a terrible cost of thousands of lives lost. The only comparable tragedy in American history, I believe, was the Civil War. And so we must join in the hopes of our 16th president and pray "that these dead shall not have died in vain, that this nation under God shall have a new birth of freedom and that government of the people, by the people, for the people shall not perish from the Earth."

17

Evil Is Too Simplistic an Explanation for the Terrorist Attacks

Joel Bleifuss

Joel Bleifuss is editor of In These Times, *a newsmagazine that promotes political and economic democracy.*

While the killing of thousands of innocents understandably gives rise to feelings of anger and hate, defining the subsequent struggle as a "monumental struggle of good versus evil," as President George W. Bush has done, oversimplifies the tragedy and brings Americans down to the level of the terrorists. Too often in history, mass atrocities have been committed against people and groups demonized as the evil enemy. Americans should resist such thinking.

The slaughter of thousands of innocent people in the attacks on the World Trade Center and the Pentagon gives rise to sharp emotions—numbness, sorrow, horror, despair, fear, anger, revenge and hate. All these feelings are understandable. Not all are noble.

In the wake of this atrocity, President George W. Bush is talking war. He defined the enemy stalking our world as an "evil" force. He characterized this war as "a monumental struggle of good versus evil."

Rallying the nation against dark forces may accomplish the administration's political objectives—putting a white hat on Bush while priming public opinion for the counterattack, and death of more innocent people, that is sure to follow. But pandering to people's fear of evil does nothing to promote peace. Indeed, it stokes the worst in human nature.

In Chicago after the attacks, a Muslim grade school was attacked with a Molotov cocktail; "Kill the Arabs" graffiti was scrawled along a major thoroughfare; more than 300 people waving American flags marched on a mosque in suburban Bridgeview.

From "The Problem with Evil," by Joel Bleifuss, *In These Times*, October 15, 2001. Copyright © 2001 by the Institute for Public Affairs. Reprinted with permission.

A simplistic explanation

Yes, people throughout history have done immensely cruel things to their fellow human beings. In some cases, the perpetrators are innately bad seeds—evil, if you will. Yet that is all too simple.

Eighteenth-century Americans and English gave smallpox-infected blankets to the Indians. Southern plantation owners traded captive African slaves like animals. Upstanding citizens persecuted German-Americans in World War I and Japanese-Americans in World War II. Members of the U.S. military bombed the people of Vietnam back to the Stone Age. This is not to mention the ongoing imposition by some Western leaders of sanctions against Iraq that have cost perhaps a million lives.

Were these historical actors all evil? Or were they, more often than not, normal folks who employed rationalizations to deny the humanity of people who were different, who were "the enemy," or who were conveniently deemed less than human to bolster the power of the established order?

One can also play the game of comparing crimes. The day after the bombings, the *New York Times'* Clyde Haberman took the your-atrocity-is-bigger-than-mine approach. He used the attacks on New York and Washington to justify Israel's policy of targeted killings, asking "Do you get it now?" to those who "damned Israel for taking admittedly harsh measures to keep its citizens alive."

In a similar vein, other commentators, mostly on the left, have explained, in some ways excused, the attacks as the understandable reaction of people subjugated to years of persecution.

All of these relativist justifications are problematic. They deny the power of human agency and thereby excuse the inexcusable—attacks on the World Trade Center and the Pentagon by Islamic extremists or Israel's state-sponsored assassinations. An action (or reaction) may be understandable— we do get it—but that doesn't make it right.

Need for leadership

It is no help at all for Bush to simplify the situation as a battle between good and evil. Such a stance, though publicly palatable, reduces things to such a degree that all subtlety and complexity is gone.

As Gary Younge observed in the *Guardian* of London: "Right now America needs a statesman, but wants a cowboy. Bush must steel himself to lead, not allow himself to follow."

Alas, this president, apparently incapable of speaking on his own, is not up to the task. When Bush, puppet-like, repeatedly invokes the word "evil," his peaceful intentions, indeed his competence, must be questioned.

Too often in modern history the inhuman "enemy" has been deemed "evil" as a prelude to mass death. Such was the thinking, no doubt, that went through the heads of the men who plotted the carnage visited on New York and Washington. But for our elected leaders to respond with the same kind of mindset can only make this tragic situation worse.

18

The World Must Respond to the Attack on New York City

Rudolph W. Giuliani

At the time of the September 11, 2001, attacks, Rudolph W. Giuliani was finishing a second term as mayor of New York City. He addressed the United Nations General Assembly at a special session on terrorism on October 1, 2001.

New York City, the most diverse city in the world, was the victim of a vicious and unjustified attack. The terrorist attacks were directed at the ideals of the United States and the United Nations, including peace, tolerance, and political and economic freedom. While the long-term solution to terrorism is the spread of the principles of democracy and freedom, the immediate response of nations must be to band together to condemn and combat terrorist groups and to ostracize countries that support terrorism. The coming struggle is not a war between religions, but one between democracy and tyranny.

Thank you, President of the General Assembly Dr. Han Seung-Soo. Thank you, Secretary General Kofi Annan.

Thank you very much for the opportunity to speak, and for the consideration you've shown the City in putting off your General Session. As I explained to the Secretary General and the President of the General Assembly, our City is now open, and any time we can arrange it, we look forward to having your heads of state and your foreign ministers here for that session.

A vicious attack

On September 11th, 2001, New York City—the most diverse City in the world—was viciously attacked in an unprovoked act of war. More than five thousand innocent men, women, and children of every race, religion, and ethnicity are lost. Among these were people from 80 different nations. To their representatives here today, I offer my condolences to you

From Rudolph W. Giuliani's "Opening Remarks to the United Nations General Assembly Special Session on Terrorism," October 1, 2001.

as well on behalf of all New Yorkers who share this loss with you. This was the deadliest terrorist attack in history. It claimed more lives than Pearl Harbor or D-Day.

This was not just an attack on the City of New York or on the United States of America. It was an attack on the very idea of a free, inclusive, and civil society.

It was a direct assault on the founding principles of the United Nations itself. The Preamble to the UN Charter states that this organization exists "to reaffirm faith in fundamental human rights, in the dignity and worth of the human person . . . to practice tolerance and live together in peace as good neighbors . . . [and] to unite our strength to maintain international peace and security."

Indeed, this vicious attack places in jeopardy the whole purpose of the United Nations.

This massive attack was intended to break our spirit. It has not done that.

Terrorism is based on the persistent and deliberate violation of fundamental human rights. With bullets and bombs—and now with hijacked airplanes—terrorists deny the dignity of human life. Terrorism preys particularly on cultures and communities that practice openness and tolerance. Their targeting of innocent civilians mocks the efforts of those who seek to live together in peace as neighbors. It defies the very notion of being a neighbor.

This massive attack was intended to break our spirit. It has not done that. It has made us stronger, more determined and more resolved.

The bravery of our firefighters, our police officers, our emergency workers, and civilians we may never learn of, in saving over 25,000 lives that day—carrying out the most effective rescue operation in our history—inspires all of us. I am very honored to have with me, as their representative, the Fire Commissioner of New York City, Tom Von Essen, and the Police Commissioner of New York City, Bernard Kerik.

The determination, resolve, and leadership of President George W. Bush has unified America and all decent men and women around the world.

The response of many of your nations—your leaders and people—spontaneously demonstrating in the days after the attack your support for New York and America, and your understanding of what needs to be done to remove the threat of terrorism, gives us great, great hope that we will prevail.

America's response and beliefs

The strength of America's response, please understand, flows from the principles upon which we stand.

Americans are not a single ethnic group.

Americans are not of one race or one religion.

Americans emerge from all your nations.

We are defined as Americans by our beliefs—not by our ethnic origins, our race or our religion. Our beliefs in religious freedom, political freedom, and economic freedom—that's what makes an American. Our belief in democracy, the rule of law, and respect for human life—that's how you become an American. It is these very principles—and the opportunities these principles give to so many to create a better life for themselves and their families—that make America, and New York, a "shining city on a hill."

There is no nation, and no City, in the history of the world that has seen more immigrants, in less time, than America. People continue to come here in large numbers to seek freedom, opportunity, decency, and civility.

Each of your nations—I am certain—has contributed citizens to the United States and to New York. I believe I can take every one of you someplace in New York City, where you can find someone from your country, someone from your village or town, that speaks your language and practices your religion. In each of your lands there are many who are Americans in spirit, by virtue of their commitment to our shared principles.

It is tragic and perverse that it is because of these very principles—particularly our religious, political and economic freedoms—that we find ourselves under attack by terrorists.

Our freedom threatens them, because they know that if our ideas of freedom gain a foothold among their people it will destroy their power. So they strike out against us to keep those ideas from reaching their people.

The terrorists are wrong, and in fact evil, in their mass destruction of human life in the name of addressing alleged injustices.

The best long-term deterrent to terrorism—obviously—is the spread of our principles of freedom, democracy, the rule of law, and respect for human life. The more that spreads around the globe, the safer we will all be. These are very powerful ideas and once they gain a foothold, they cannot be stopped.

In fact, the rise that we have seen in terrorism and terrorist groups, I believe, is in no small measure a response to the spread of these ideas of freedom and democracy to many nations, particularly over the past 15 years.

The terrorists have no ideas or ideals with which to combat freedom and democracy. So their only defense is to strike out against innocent civilians, destroying human life in massive numbers and hoping to deter all of us from our pursuit and expansion of freedom.

Acting together to stop terrorists

But the long-term deterrent of spreading our ideals throughout the world is just not enough, and may never be realized, if we do not act—and act together—to remove the clear and present danger posed by terrorism and terrorists.

The United Nations must hold accountable any country that supports or condones terrorism, otherwise you will fail in your primary mission as peacekeeper.

It must ostracize any nation that supports terrorism.

It must isolate any nation that remains neutral in the fight against terrorism.

Now is the time, in the words of the UN Charter, "to unite our strength to maintain international peace and security." This is not a time for further study or vague directives. The evidence of terrorism's brutality and inhumanity—of its contempt for life and the concept of peace—is lying beneath the rubble of the World Trade Center less than two miles from where we meet today.

No room for neutrality

Look at that destruction, that massive, senseless, cruel loss of human life . . . and then I ask you to look in your hearts and recognize that there is no room for neutrality on the issue of terrorism. You're either with civilization or with terrorists.

On one side is democracy, the rule of law, and respect for human life; on the other is tyranny, arbitrary executions, and mass murder.

We're right and they're wrong. It's as simple as that.

And by that I mean that America and its allies are right about democracy, about religious, political, and economic freedom.

The terrorists are wrong, and in fact evil, in their mass destruction of human life in the name of addressing alleged injustices.

No excuses for terrorism

Let those who say that we must understand the reasons for terrorism come with me to the thousands of funerals we are having in New York City and explain those insane, maniacal reasons to the children who will grow up without fathers and mothers, to the parents who have had their children ripped from them for no reason at all.

Instead, I ask each of you to allow me to say at those funerals that your nation stands with America in making a solemn promise and pledge that we will achieve unconditional victory over terrorism and terrorists.

There is no excuse for mass murder, just as there is no excuse for genocide. Those who practice terrorism—murdering or victimizing innocent civilians—lose any right to have their cause understood by decent people and lawful nations.

On this issue—terrorism—the United Nations must draw a line. The era of moral relativism between those who practice or condone terrorism, and those nations who stand up against it, must end. Moral relativism does not have a place in this discussion and debate.

There is no moral way to sympathize with grossly immoral actions. And by trying to do that, unfortunately, a fertile field has been created in which terrorism has grown.

Ways to fight terrorists

The best and most practical way to promote peace is to stand up to terror and intimidation. The Security Council's unanimous passage of Resolution 1373, adopting wide ranging anti-terrorism measures in the international community is a very good first step. It's necessary to establish accountability for the subsidizing of terrorism.

As a former United States Attorney, I am particularly encouraged that the UN has answered President Bush's call to cut terrorists off from their money and their funding. It's enormously important. We've done that successfully with organized crime groups in America. By taking away their ability to mass large amounts of money, you take away their ability to have others carry on their functioning for them, even if they are removed, arrested, prosecuted, or eliminated through war or through law enforcement. It cuts off the life-blood of the organization. So I believe this is a very good first step.

But now it's up to the member states to enforce this and other aspects of the resolution, and for the United Nations to enforce these new mechanisms to take the financial base away from the terrorists. Take away their money, take away their access to money, and you reduce their ability to carry out complex missions.

Each of you is sitting in this room because of your country's commitment to being part of the family of nations. We need to unite as a family as never before—across all our differences, in recognition of the fact that the United Nations stands for the proposition that as human beings we have more in common than divides us.

If you need to be reminded of this, you don't need to look very far. Just go outside for a walk in the streets and parks of New York City. You can't walk a block in New York City without seeing somebody that looks different than you, acts different than you, talks different than you, believes different than you. If you grow up in New York City, you learn that. And if you're an intelligent or decent person, you learn that all those differences are nothing in comparison to the things that unite us.

This is not a dispute between religions or ethnic groups.

We are a City of immigrants—unlike any other City—within a nation of immigrants. Like the victims of the World Trade Center attack, we are of every race, religion, and ethnicity. Our diversity has always been our greatest source of strength. It's the thing that renews us and revives us in every generation—our openness to new people from all over the world.

So from the first day of this attack, an attack on New York and America, and I believe an attack on the basic principles that underlie this organization, I have told the people of New York that we should not allow this to divide us, because then we would really lose what this City is all about. We have very strong and vibrant Arab and Muslim communities in New York City. They are an equally important part of the life of our City. We respect their religious beliefs. We respect everybody's religious beliefs—that's what America's about, that's what New York City is about. I have urged New Yorkers not to engage in any form of group blame or group hatred. This is exactly the evil that we are confronting with these terrorists. And if we are going to prevail over terror, our ideals, principles, and values must transcend all forms of prejudice.

This is a very important part of the struggle against terrorism.

This is not a dispute between religions or ethnic groups. All religions, all decent people, are united in their desire to achieve peace, and understand that we have to eliminate terrorism. We're not divided about this.

There have been many days in New York when I was running for Mayor, and then since I've been Mayor, when I would have a weekend in which I would go to a mosque on Friday, and a synagogue on Saturday, and a church—sometimes two churches—on a Sunday. And by the time I finished, I would say to myself, 'I know that we're getting through to God.' We're talking to him in every language that He understands, we're using every liturgy that exists, and I know that we are getting through to the same God, even though we may be doing it in slightly different ways. God is known by many different names and many different traditions, but identified by one consistent feeling, love. Love for humanity, particularly love for our children. Love does eventually conquer hate, but it needs our help. Good intentions alone are not enough to conquer evil.

The only acceptable result is the complete and total eradication of terrorism.

Remember British Prime Minister Neville Chamberlain, who—armed only with good intentions—negotiated with the Nazis and emerged hopeful that he had achieved peace in his time. Hitler's wave of terror was only encouraged by these attempts at appeasement. At the cost of millions of lives, we learned that words—though important—are not enough to guarantee peace. It is action alone that counts.

For the UN, and individual nations, decisive action is needed to stop terrorism from ever orphaning another child.

The resilience of life

That's for nations. For individuals, the most effective course of action they can take to aid our recovery is to be determined to go ahead with their lives. We can't let terrorists change the way we live—otherwise they will have succeeded.

In some ways, the resilience of life in New York City is the ultimate sign of defiance to terrorism. We call ourselves the Capital of the World in large part because we are the most diverse City in the world, home to the United Nations. The spirit of unity amid all our diversity has never been stronger.

On Saturday night [September 29, 2001] I walked through Times Square, it was crowded, it was bright, it was lively. Thousands of people were visiting from all parts of the United States and all parts of the world. And many of them came up to me and shook my hand and patted me on the back and said, "We're here because we want to show our support for the City of New York." And that's why there has never been a better time to come to New York City.

I say to people across the country and around the world: if you were planning to come to New York sometime in the future, come here now.

Come to enjoy our thousands of restaurants, museums, theaters, sporting events, and shopping . . . but also come to take a stand against terrorism.

We need to heed the words of a hymn that I, and the Police Commissioner, and the Fire Commissioner, have heard at the many funerals and memorial services that we've gone to in the last two weeks. The hymn begins, "Be Not Afraid."

Freedom from Fear is a basic human right. We need to reassert our right to live free from fear with greater confidence and determination than ever before . . . here in New York City . . . across America . . . and around the World. With one clear voice, unanimously, we need to say that we will not give in to terrorism.

Surrounded by our friends of every faith, we know that this is not a clash of civilizations; it is a conflict between murderers and humanity.

This is not a question of retaliation or revenge. It is a matter of justice leading to peace. The only acceptable result is the complete and total eradication of terrorism.

New Yorkers are strong and resilient. We are unified. And we will not yield to terror. We do not let fear make our decisions for us.

We choose to live in freedom.

Thank you, and God bless you.

19

The Attacks Revealed the Importance of the Public Sector

Jeff Faux

Jeff Faux is president of the Economic Policy Institute, a nonprofit think tank that performs research and analyses on issues affecting low- and middle-income workers.

Prior to September 11, 2001, it was fashionable in many circles to denigrate the public sector and public service. Such attitudes changed when terrorists attacked the World Trade Center and the Pentagon. Americans turned to firefighters and other public workers and institutions for help following the attacks. In addition, the attacks revealed the price America has paid for making airport security a privatized matter in which low costs and wages were more important than reliable security.

There is no silver lining to the cloud of horror that descended on America on September 11, 2001. And the avalanche of pain, terror, and death we have witnessed may be just the beginning.

But life, as always, slowly picks up and moves on. Despite the nagging sense that it is unseemly to begin thinking about the economic consequences, the country is once again back in the market. Investors are selling the stocks of insurance companies and airlines, buying those of military contractors and companies that will benefit from the new security-conscious society. Economists are calculating the gains and losses and guessing about the odds of a recession.

Many are engaged in burying the dead and tending to the survivors, or facing the awesome responsibility of satisfying the national demand for action that serves justice rather than multiplying evil. Those of us who are going back to business have an obligation, as we do, to reflect on what we have seen.

The attacks of September 11 revealed some truths about the American political economy that have been obscured in recent years.

The working class

One is just how much of our economy is made up of what used to be called the "working class"—the non-supervisory, non-college-educated people who make up 70 percent of our labor force. For the last half-dozen years the media saw economic trends through the eyes of the glamorous, globe-trotting, business executive—to the point where it seemed to many that they must represent the vast majority of American workers. And one could hardly find a more fitting symbol of the new global economy than the World Trade Center—surrounded in the evening with a herd of sleek limousines waiting to serve the masters of the universe at the end of the day.

And yet, it turns out that the building was run by thousands of data clerks and secretaries, waiters and dishwashers, janitors and telecommunication repair people. The roll of trade unions mourning their dead is long: firefighters, hotel and restaurant employees, police, communication workers, service employees, teachers, federal employees, pilots and flight attendants, longshoremen, professional engineers, operating engineers, the electrical workers, federal employees, building trades, and state, county, and municipal employees.

And many were in no union, meaning job insecurity, no benefits, and certainly no limousines.

The importance of government

A second insight revealed by the awful gaping hole in the Manhattan skyline was how ill-served we have been by a politics that perpetuates the illusion that we are all on our own and, in particular, holds the institutions of public service in contempt. For two decades, politicians of both parties have celebrated the pursuit of private gain over public service. Shrinking government has become a preoccupation of political leaders through deregulation, privatization, and cuts in public services.

The attacks . . . revealed some truths about the American political economy that have been obscured in recent years.

One result is that the U.S. is the only major nation that leaves airline and airport security in the hands of private corporations, which by their very nature are motivated to spend as little as possible. So the system was tossed in the lap of lowest-bid contractors who hired people for minimum wages. Training has been inadequate and supervision extremely lax. Turnover was 126 percent a year and the average employee stayed in airline security for only six months. Getting a job at Burger King or McDonald's represented upward mobility for the average security worker. In an anti-government political climate the airline corporations were able to shrug off the government inspections that consistently revealed how easy it was to bring weapons on board. The competition for customers sacrificed safety to avoid any inconvenience. How else to explain the insane notion that a 3-1/2 inch knife blade is not a weapon?

Private provision of public services has been the dominant philosophy of government in our time. Only natural, the economists told us. People were motivated by money. It's human nature. "Greed is good," said the movie character in the send-up of Wall Street—a sentiment echoed by politicians of both parties. "Collective solutions are a thing of the past. . . . The era of big government is over. . . . You are on your own." Public service was "old" economy, just for losers. A teacher in New York City schools starts at $30,000. A brand new securities lawyer starts at $120,000. Does anyone believe that this represents sensible priorities?

When the chips are down, where do we turn? To the government's firefighters, police officers, rescue teams.

And does anyone believe that the firefighters who marched into that inferno did it for money? Does anyone think that people working for a private company hiring people for as little as possible would have had the same motivation—would have been as efficient? At the moment when efficiency really counts?

When the chips are down, where do we turn? To the government's firefighters, police officers, rescue teams. To the nonprofit sectors' blood banks and shelters. And to Big Government's army, navy, and air force. During his campaign, the president of the United States constantly complained that the people knew how to spend their money better than the government did. Overnight, we just appropriated $40 billion for the government to spend however it sees fit. Who else would we trust?

The stock market itself made one point. Despite calls for investors to exercise patriotic restraint, the market opened with an avalanche of sell orders, driving the Dow to its largest point loss in history. As one broker said, "This is how capitalism is supposed to work." Just so. The market is about prices, not values.

America's identity

Finally, perhaps we learned something about our national identity.

It is common—almost a cliché—among political philosophers and pundits to define America as an "exception." For many, America's exceptionalism means that it is the best place to get rich. For others, it is our unique set of laws—our Bill of Rights. Still others see America not in national terms at all, but as a patchwork of ethnic groups and regional interests.

There is some truth in all of these views. But those who risked and gave their lives—both the public servants and the brave civilian passengers who rushed the terrorists and forced the airliner down in Pennsylvania before it could get to Washington—are unlikely to have acted out of reverence for the deregulated market or for our court system or for some ethnic or religious loyalty.

Everything we know tells us that they acted as human beings responding to the agony of other human beings, or trying in one last desperate effort to spare their country more damage, not because it is the world's superpower but simply because it is their country. No country has a monopoly on simple patriotism.

If America is, as the politicians often remind us, the "last best hope" for humankind, then it is not because we as individuals are exceptional and different from the rest of the world, but because we are much the same—full of the normal set of human traits, which at times of stress often bring out the best in us.

It is obvious that we can no longer rely on our exceptionalism to keep us safe. In the coming weeks and months and years we are likely to be reminded of that. To get through this, we need to be disabused quickly of the illusion that we are all on our own. America's strength, like the strength of any other society, is in our ability to be there for each other.

20

The Attacks Marked the End of the Post–Cold War Era

Robert D. Kaplan

Robert D. Kaplan is a senior fellow at the New American Foundation and the author of seven books on international affairs, including The Coming Anarchy: Shattering the Dreams of the Post–Cold War.

The September 2001 terrorist attacks marked the end of an era that began in 1989 with the fall of the Berlin Wall and the end of the cold war, during which the United States tried to impose its vision of democracy on the world. The American people learned in the 2001 attacks that preservation of security at home and power abroad is the primary function of foreign policy. They will tolerate alliances with questionable regimes and restrictions on their own liberties in the coming struggle against terrorism.

President George W. Bush saw the big change needed in America's foreign policy long before the intellectuals and the media did. Bush's campaign rhetoric and subsequent foreign affairs strategy—in which he has sought to clear the decks of nonessential overseas involvements in order to concentrate on security threats for a new military and technological age—while wrong in some specifics, have been proven tragically prescient in their overall conception. It is not that Bush foresaw specifically the recent terrorist attack; but his insistence that humanitarian missions are not a signal priority in a dangerous world—where America has to look after its own—showed considerable instinct regarding what has happened.

Moreover, his conception is firmly grounded in history. It realizes that America's continued dominance—like that of Britain and Rome before it—is not certain. Thus, improving the chances of America remaining a dominant power requires the husbanding of our foreign policy resources and the continued adaptation of our military establishment to new kinds of threats. What seems absolutely ahistorical today is the vision of a permanently secure America that will have the luxury of open-ended overseas deployments in places such as Bosnia and Kosovo.

The latest spasm of triumphalist idealism—first injected into our conduct of foreign affairs by President Woodrow Wilson in the early 20th century—ended with the destruction of the World Trade Center. We can no longer afford the luxury of noblesse oblige in foreign policy now that the assumption of security at home is absent. Foreign policy must return to what it traditionally has been: the diplomatic aspect of national security rather than a branch of Holocaust studies.

End of an era

The 20th century did not, as many have claimed, end ahead of schedule in November 1989, with the fall of the Berlin Wall. The 1990s were not the beginning of a new, more enlightened era in international relations; rather, they were a coda to the Cold War in Eastern Europe and a period when the World War II Nazi slaughter of the Jews was uppermost in our minds as we tried to grapple with ethnic hatreds in the Balkans and elsewhere.

The 20th century ended behind schedule—in September 2001. The post–Cold War era will be seen in future decades as a 12-year interregnum—from the collapse of the Berlin Wall to the collapse of the World Trade Center—in which the United States, basking in its victory over communism and with a seemingly unstoppable economy, tried to impose its moral vision on the rest of the world, while neglecting its homeland defense. Security became lax at airports, and the military and intelligence establishments were neither reformed nor beefed up, even as we dispatched troops to trouble spots only marginally related to our national interests. But following the most deadly terrorist incident in history, the American people have learned that to influence the world morally requires first the preservation of their own security, as well as their reputation for power.

The need for security

The need to maintain power and security must now come first: Our values will follow in their wake. After all, democratization in places such as Eastern Europe has not been a natural and inevitable event; it is a direct consequence of our Cold War military victory. If the destruction of the World Trade Center diminishes America's reputation for power—if it seems to paralyze this nation and make it appear unduly fearful—the democratic values that we promote abroad will be similarly eclipsed.

Now we are truly in an age of new technological threats—particularly chemical and biological weapons—that will return us to an earlier epoch, at the beginning of the 19th century, when realism flourished under men like John Adams and Alexander Hamilton while we were being threatened on our own continent by the French and Spanish, as well as by the British fleet. Such realism posits that foreign affairs entails a separate, sadder morality than the kind we apply in domestic policy and in our daily lives. That is because domestically we operate under the rule of law, while the wider world is an anarchic realm where we are forced to take the law into our own hands. This is a distinction that the public will tolerate now that its security has been shaken. The public will likely have little trouble comprehending why Bush may have to perpetrate a certain amount of evil in coming months and even years in order to do a greater amount of good.

Even our vision of democracy must now undergo subtle realistic alteration. Rather than demand that countries such as Pakistan, Egypt and Tunisia democratize, we will have to increasingly tolerate benign dictatorships and various styles of hybrid regimes, provided that they help us in our new struggle. Nor will there be anything amoral or cynical about that. For, in the long term, the world will be a better place if the American people feel secure.

In the new age of warfare, speed will be the killer variable, making democratic consultation an afterthought. Striking terrorist cells before they strike us—hitting not just hijackers, but the computer command centers of our future adversaries before they can launch computer viruses on the United States, for instance—will need to be accomplished by surprise if it is to be effective. That will leave no time for the president to sound out the public or even many members of Congress.

Liberal elites vs. the American public

The public will not likely mind, provided the attacks are seen to contribute to its safety. The more prosperous a society is, the more moral compromises it will be ready to make to preserve its material well-being. One of the false beliefs of the age of globalization has been that economic power has superseded military power. In fact, the reality is the reverse. The greater the economic power, the more military power is required to protect it, especially because of the envy and resentment that such economic power generates. Blather about how financial markets are the new foundation of power—the mantra of optimists transfixed by globalization throughout the 1990s—can only be indulged in when the physical security of those markets can be taken for granted. And it no longer can be.

Unfettered idealism of the sort associated with Woodrow Wilson is feasible only so long as the United States feels itself geographically invulnerable. Whenever we have failed to implement our lofty vision abroad, we have been able to retreat back across great oceans, as we did after World War I. Today, however, because of technology, places such as the Middle East are as close to us as the Ottoman Turkish Empire was to Europe. Oceanic distance from global hot spots such as the West Bank no longer exists. The duo of idealism and isolationism will have to be replaced by realism and constant engagement: engagement consistent with our national interest.

The 20th century ended behind schedule—in September 2001.

In his novel "The Secret Agent," Joseph Conrad wrote that the greatest threat to terrorism is ordinary citizens: the throngs of working- and middle-class people who—because they just want to get on with their lives—are willing to trust the grim details of their protection to the police and other security organs. Following Sept. 11, 2001, these ordinary citizens will determine foreign policy. It has ceased to be the realm of cosmopolitan elites in the media and academia, who for the past 12 years have been more concerned with universal values of justice than with our national security. But the elites' dream of an international civilization has been stillborn. Globalization, like the Industrial Revolution before it, is merely a phase of technological development—not a system of international security. Wars will go on, because beyond the liberal elites, humanity is as divided as ever.

Organizations to Contact

The editors have compiled the following list of organizations concerned with the issues debated in this book. The descriptions are derived from materials provided by the organizations. All have publications or information available for interested readers. The list was compiled on the date of publication of the present volume; the information provided here may change. Be aware that many organizations take several weeks or longer to respond to inquiries, so allow as much time as possible.

American Civil Liberties Union (ACLU)
125 Broad St., 18th Floor, New York, NY 10004-2400
(212) 549-2500
e-mail: aclu@aclu.org • website: www.aclu.org

The American Civil Liberties Union is a national organization that works to defend Americans' civil rights guaranteed by the U.S. Constitution, arguing that measures to protect national security should not compromise fundamental civil liberties. It publishes and distributes policy statements, pamphlets, and press releases with titles such as "In Defense of Freedom in a Time of Crisis" and "National ID Cards: 5 Reasons Why They Should Be Rejected."

American Enterprise Institute (AEI)
1150 17th St. NW, Washington, DC 20036
(202) 862-5800 • fax: (202) 862-7177
website: www.aei.org

The American Enterprise Institute for Public Policy Research is a scholarly research institute that is dedicated to preserving limited government, private enterprise, and a strong foreign policy and national defense. It publishes books including *Study of Revenge: The First World Trade Center Attack* and *Saddam Hussein's War Against America*. Articles about terrorism and September 11 can be found in its magazine, *American Enterprise*, and on its website.

Anti-Defamation League (ADL)
823 United Nations Plaza, New York, NY 10017
(212) 885-7700 • fax: (212) 867-0779
website: www.adl.org

The Anti-Defamation League is a human relations organization dedicated to combating all forms of prejudice and bigotry. The league has placed a spotlight on terrorism and on the dangers posed for extremism. Its website records reactions to the September 11, 2001, terrorist incidents by both extremist and mainstream organizations, provides background information on Osama bin Laden, and furnishes other materials on terrorism and the Middle East. The ADL also maintains a bimonthly online newsletter, *Frontline*.

The Brookings Institution
1775 Massachusetts Ave. NW, Washington, DC 20036
(202) 797-6000 • fax: (202) 797-6004
e-mail: brookinfo@brook.edu • website: www.brookings.org

The institution, founded in 1927, is a think tank that conducts research and education in foreign policy, economics, government, and the social sciences. In 2001 it began America's Response to Terrorism, a project that provides briefings and analysis to the public and which is featured on the center's website. Other publications include the quarterly *Brookings Review*, periodic *Policy Briefs*, and books including *Terrorism and U.S. Foreign Policy*.

CATO Institute
1000 Massachusetts Ave. NW, Washington, DC 20001-5403
(202) 842-0200 • fax: (202) 842-3490
e-mail: cato@cato.org • website: www.cato.org

The Institute is a nonpartisan public policy research foundation dedicated to limiting the role of government and protecting individual liberties. It publishes the quarterly magazine *Regulation*, the bimonthly *Cato Policy Report*, and numerous policy papers and articles. Works on terrorism include "Does U.S. Intervention Overseas Breed Terrorism?" and "Military Tribunals No Answer."

Center for Strategic and International Studies (CSIS)
1800 K St. NW, Suite 400, Washington, DC 20006
(202) 887-0200 • fax: (202) 775-3199
website: www.csis.org

The center works to provide world leaders with strategic insights and policy options on current and emerging global issues. It publishes books including *To Prevail: An American Strategy for the Campaign Against Terrorism*, the *Washington Quarterly*, a journal on political, economic, and security issues, and other publications including reports that can be downloaded from its website.

Council on American-Islamic Relations (CAIR)
453 New Jersey Ave. SE, Washington, DC 20003
(202) 488-8787 • fax: (202) 488-0833
e-mail: cair@cair-net.org • website: www.cair-net.org

CAIR is a nonprofit membership organization that presents an Islamic perspective on public policy issues and challenges the misrepresentation of Islam and Muslims. It publishes the quarterly newsletter *Faith in Action* and other various publications on Muslims in the United States. Its website includes statements condemning both the September 11 attacks and discrimination against Muslims.

Federal Aviation Administration (FAA)
800 Independence Ave. SW, Washington, DC 20591
(800) 322-7873 • fax: (202) 267-3484
website: www.faa.gov

The Federal Aviation Administration is the component of the U.S. Department of Transportation whose primary responsibility is the safety of civil aviation. The FAA's major functions include regulating civil aviation to promote safety and fulfill the requirements of national defense. Among its publications are *Technology Against Terrorism, Air Piracy, Airport Security, and International Terrorism: Winning the War Against Hijackers*, and *Security Tips for Air Travelers*.

Institute for Policy Studies (IPS)
733 15th St. NW, Suite 1020, Washington, DC 20005
(202) 234-9382 • fax (202) 387-7915
website: www.ips-dc.org

The Institute for Policy Studies is a progressive think tank that works to develop societies built around the values of justice and nonviolence. It publishes reports including *Global Perspectives: A Media Guide to Foreign Policy Experts*. Numerous articles and interviews on September 11 and terrorism are available on its website.

International Policy Institute of Counter-Terrorism (ICT)
PO Box 167, Herzlia 46150, Israel
972-9-9527277 • fax: 972-9-9513073
e-mail: mail@ict.org.il • website: www.ict.org.il

ICT is a research institute dedicated to developing public policy solutions to international terrorism. The ICT website is a comprehensive resource on terrorism and counterterrorism, featuring an extensive database on terrorist attacks and organizations, including al-Qaida.

Islamic Supreme Council of America (ISCA)
1400 16th St. NW, Room B112, Washington, DC 20036
(202) 939-3400 • fax: (202) 939-3410
e-mail: staff@islamicsupremecouncil.org
website: www.islamicsupremecouncil.org

The ISCA is a nongovernmental religious organization that promotes Islam in America both by providing practical solutions to American Muslims in integrating Islamic teachings with American culture and by teaching non-Muslims that Islam is a religion of moderation, peace, and tolerance. It strongly condemns Islamic extremists and all forms of terrorism. Its website includes statements, commentaries, and reports on terrorism, including *Usama bin Laden: A Legend Gone Wrong* and *Jihad: A Misunderstood Concept from Islam*.

Middle East Media Research Institute (MEMRI)
PO Box 27837, Washington, DC 20038-7837
(202) 955-9070 • fax: (202) 955-9077
e-mail: memri@erols.com • website: www.memri.org

MEMRI translates and disseminates articles and commentaries from Middle East media sources and provides original research and analysis on the region. Its Jihad and Terrorism Studies Project monitors radical Islamist groups and individuals and their reactions to acts of terrorism around the world.

U.S. Department of State, Counterterrorism Office
Office of Public Affairs, Room 2507
U.S. Department of State
2201 C St. NW, Washington, DC 20520
(202) 647-4000
e-mail: secretary@state.gov • website: www.state.gov/s/ct

The office works to develop and implement American counterterrorism strategy and to improve cooperation with foreign governments. Articles and speeches by government officials are available at its website.

War Resisters League (WRL)
339 Lafayette St., New York, NY 10012
(212) 228-0450 • fax: (212) 228-6193
e-mail: wrl@warresisters.org • website: www.warresisters.org

The WRL, founded in 1923, believes that all war is a crime against humanity, and advocates nonviolent methods to create a just and democratic society. It publishes the magazine *The Nonviolent Activist*. Articles from that magazine, as well as other commentary and resources about September 11 and America's war against terrorism, are available on its website.

Bibliography

Books

Yonah Alexander and *Usama bin Laden's al-Qaida: Profile of a Terrorist*
Michael S. Swetman   *Network.* Ardsley, NY: Transnational Publishers, 2001.

Peter L. Bergen   *Holy War Inc.: Inside the Secret World of Osama bin Laden.*
New York: Free Press, 2001.

Noam Chomsky   *9-11.* New York: Seven Stories Press, 2001.

Martha Crenshaw   *Encyclopedia of World Terrorism.* Armonk, NY: Sharpe
and John Pimlott, eds.   Reference, 1997.

Laura K. Egendorf, ed.   *Terrorism: Opposing Viewpoints.* San Diego: Greenhaven
Press, 2000.

Philip B. Heymann   *Terrorism and America: A Commonsense Strategy for a Democratic Society.* Cambridge, MA: MIT Press, 1998.

James F. Hoge Jr. and   *How Did This Happen? Terrorism and the New War.* New
Gideon Rose, eds.   York: Public Affairs, 2001.

Jessica Kornbluth and   *Because We Are Americans: What We Discovered on
Jessica Papin, eds.   September 11, 2001.* New York: Warner Books, 2001.

Bernard Lewis   *What Went Wrong? Western Impact and Middle Eastern Response.* New York: Oxford University Press, 2001.

Jon Ronson   *Adventures with Extremists.* New York: Simon and Schus-
ter, 2002.

Barbara Shangle, ed.   *Day of Terror, September 11, 2001.* Beaverton, OR: American Products, 2001.

Strobe Talbott and   *The Age of Terror: America and the World After September
Nayan Chanda, eds.   11.* New York: Basic Books, 2002.

Periodicals

David Aaron   "The New Twilight Struggle," *American Prospect,* October
22, 2001.

Michael Albert and   "September 11 and Its Aftermath," *Z Magazine,* October
Stephen R. Shalom   2001.

Jonathan Alter   "Blame America at Your Peril," *Newsweek,* October 15,
2001.

Benjamin R. Barber   "Beyond Jihad vs. McWorld," *Nation,* January 21, 2002.

Max Boot — "The Case for American Empire," *Weekly Standard*, October 15, 2001.

Business Week — "Keeping America's Gates Open. Just Watch Them Better," November 19, 2001.

David Carr — "The Futility of Homeland Defense," *Atlantic Monthly*, January 2002.

Congressional Digest — "War on Terrorism," November 2001.

Economist — "The Day the World Changed," September 13, 2001.

Richard Falk — "Defining a Just War," *Nation*, October 29, 2001.

John Lewis Gaddis — "Setting Right a Dangerous World," *Chronicle of Higher Education*, January 11, 2002.

Adolfo Gilly — "The Faceless Enemy," *NACLA Report on the Americas*, November/December 2001.

Lee Griffith — "Terror and the Hope Within," *The Other Side*, January/February 2002.

Michael Howard — "What's in a Name?: How to Fight Terrorism," *Foreign Affairs*, January/February 2002.

David E. Kaplan and Kevin Whitelaw — "The CEO of Terror, Inc." *U.S. News & World Report*, October 1, 2001.

James Kitfield — "Ending State Terror," *National Journal,* October 2, 2001.

Charles Krauthammer — "The Real New World Order," *Weekly Standard*, November 12, 2001.

Lewis H. Lapham — "Drums Along the Potomac," *Harper's Magazine*, November 2001.

Michael Lerner — "The Case for Peace," *Time*, October 1, 2001.

Brink Lindsey — "Poor Choice—Why Globalization Didn't Create 9/11," *New Republic*, November 12, 2001.

Richard Lowry — "Profiles in Cowardice," *National Review*, January 28, 2002.

Wayne Madsen — "Why Wasn't Bush Warned?" *In These Times*, October 15, 2001.

W.J.T. Mitchell — "911: Criticism and Crisis," *Critical Inquiry*, Winter 2002.

Chris Mooney — "Holy War," *American Prospect*, December 17, 2001.

Sabeel Rahman — "Another New World Order? Multilateralism in the Aftermath of September 11," *Harvard International Review*, Winter 2002.

Richard Rhodes et al.   "What Terror Keeps Teaching Us," *New York Times Magazine*, September 23, 2001.

Matthew Rothschild   "The New McCarthyism," *Progressive*, January 2002.

Arundhati Roy   "New World Disorder," *In These Times*, November 26, 2001.

Nelson D. Schwartz   "Learning from Israel," *Fortune*, January 21, 2002.

Benjamin Schwartz and Christopher Layne   "A New Grand Strategy," *Atlantic Monthly*, January 2002.

Jay Tolson   "Early Drafts of History," *U.S. News & World Report*, January 14, 2002.

Index